INTERNATIONAL
Children's
Bible
Handbook

INTERNATIONAL
Children's
Bible
Handbook

LAWRENCE RICHARDS

Editors: Byron Williamson, Carol Bartley
Assistant Editor: Stephanie Terry
Consulting Editor: Dr. Neale Pryor
Educational Editor: Barbara Bolton
Graphic Design: Koechel/Peterson Design

Sweet Publishing
Ft. Worth, TX 76137

INTERNATIONAL
Children's
Bible
Handbook

Library of Congress Cataloging in Publication Data

Richards, Larry, 1931-
International Children's Bible Handbook.

    Includes index.
    Summary: A handbook of informative data about the Bible containing illustrations, photographs, maps, charts, and diagrams of biblical articles, places, and concepts.
    1. Bible — Handbooks, manuals, etc.   2. Bible — Juvenile literature. [1. Bible —Handbooks, manuals, etc.
    2. Bible]   I. Williamson, Byron, 1946-   . II. Pryor, Neale, 1935-   . III. Bolton, Barbara J. IV. Title.
BS539.R53   1986   220.6'1   86-5995
ISBN 0-8344-0133-9

Illustrations: Chris Garborg, Jim Padgett

Photographs: American Bible Society; Ed Arness; The Bettmann Archive; DRK Photo; Ewing Galloway; Eye-O-Graphic Holy Land Exhibit; Genesis Project; Israel Museum, Jerusalem; Koechel/Peterson Design; KSTP Weather Services; Dick Lederhaus; Larry Lundstrom; John McRay; Terry White; Wide World Photos. Photographs from the *New Media Bible* were used by permission of the Genesis Project, 630 Fifth Avenue, New York, NY 10020.

Maps: Myron Netterlund

Printed in the United States of America

10 9 8 7 6 5 4 3 2 1

A special book for children

*T*he Bible is an exciting book. It is filled with familiar stories that children and adults love to read. But the Bible is far more than a book of stories. It is a history of what God has done in our world. It is a message from God about his Son, Jesus. The Bible is a book about God's love for people, and about how people need to love and obey God.

We believe that boys and girls want to understand the Bible. That's why this handbook uses the *International Children's Bible, New Century Version*, a warm and accurate translation at a unique, third-grade reading level. How exciting to have a version of the Word of God available that even the youngest students can read and understand for themselves.

That same concern for boys and girls led to this *International Children's Bible Handbook*. There are literally hundreds of children's storybooks and reference books. But there have been no books written in the simple third-grade style of the *International Children's Bible, New Century Version*, that answer the questions boys and girls ask about the Bible. And it's so easy for you to use.

What are the other features in this children's handbook that make it a very special aid? Here are some of the things children will like.

▪ Questions and statements that interest children introduce each brief section. The format helps the reading of this handbook to be an adventure in discovery for boys and girls.

▪ The handbook does not just retell familiar stories. It adds extra information that is fresh and new to children.

▪ Colorful maps, photographs and illustrations keep each page bright and interesting. Boys and girls see, as well as read about, biblical themes, so familiar events come alive.

▪ Charts tell children where to find the Bible stories they already know — and where to read exciting stories that are new.

▪ A unique *Good News* feature at the beginning of each chapter alerts children to Bible truths that enrich the lives of boys and girls.

▪ Special *To Think about and Do* activities at the end of each chapter lead children into the Bible itself — and help them apply God's word to their own lives.

▪ A clear Dictionary and Index explains difficult terms and tells where each topic is discussed in the handbook.

But this *International Children's Bible Handbook* isn't just for children! It's for parents, Sunday schools and for Christian schools.

Moms and dads will appreciate the way it helps them answer questions boys and girls have about the Bible. Its index, maps and charts help them locate, and then read about, Bible places and people. The handbook helps parents explain, in words and concepts children understand, difficult biblical subjects. Its activities suggest fun things families can do together for enjoyable family devotions.

And the *International Children's Bible Handbook* is a "must" resource for Sunday schools and Christian day schools. Coverage is weighted to emphasize portions of scripture children are most likely to study. Learning activities suggested at the end of each chapter can enrich any curriculum. The handbook provides vital background for teachers, while research projects can be assigned to children to match the "questions" asked throughout the book. If you teach children, or have children of your own, this handbook belongs in your classroom and home.

Contents

Page

New Testament

1

What you should know about the Bible

*T*he Bible is the best selling book in the world. People have printed millions more copies of the Bible than of any other book. And the Bible has been translated into over 2,000 different languages!

Why is this book so special? How was it written? And why is the Bible so important to you and me?

How was the Bible written?

The Bible is very old. It is really a collection of 66 different books. And they were written by about 40 different people. The first books of the Bible were written about 1,500 years before the last book was written. And the first books of the Bible are nearly 3,500 years old!

The Bible was written in different languages. The Old Testament was written mostly in Hebrew. A few parts are in Aramaic. The New Testament was written in Greek.

These languages are very different from English. The Hebrew language does not even have letters for the vowels, A, E, I, O or U. If we use English letters but write the way the Hebrews did, "The Lord is my Shepherd" would be "th lrd s my shphrd." But Hebrew is read from left to right, so it would really be: "drhphs ym s drl ht." It was hundreds of years after Jesus lived that Jewish scholars added dots and dashes above and below the Hebrew letters for vowel sounds.

How was the Bible kept safe?

Today English translations of the Bible are made from Hebrew and Greek manuscripts. These manuscripts were copied hundreds or

---

What Bible alphabets look like

English: ABCDEFGHIJKLMNOPQRSTUVWXYZ

Hebrew: אבגדהוזחטיכךלמםנןסעפףצץקרששת

Greek: ΑΒΓΔΕΖΗΘΙΚΛΜΝΞΟΠΡΣΤΥΦΧΨΩ

This portion of the book of Isaiah is one of the scrolls that were found in 1947 in the caves by the Dead Sea.

even thousands of years after the Bible was first written. But we know those copies are accurate.

When the Dead Sea Scrolls were found, Bible students compared these ancient copies of the Old Testament with the newer copies they had. In a thousand years of copying and recopying, there were almost no differences! How could this be?

The Jewish people were sure their Old Testament was special. Every time a scribe (a person who copied the Bible) sat down to write, he was very careful. When the scribe started he would say, "I am writing the Torah [Law] in the name of its holiness and the name of God in its holiness." He would read the sentence he was about to copy, read it again out loud and then write the sentence. Each time the scribe copied the name of God, he would say, "I am writing the name of God for the holiness of his name." When the scribe finished copying an Old Testament book, he would count all the words and letters in the original and in his copy. He would find the middle word and the middle letter in each to make sure they were the same. These

careful checks helped the scribe avoid copying errors.

So the Bible was kept safe and was passed on from century to century. God's people have always believed the Bible is so special that no one should ever change it.

Two of the jars that contained the Dead Sea Scrolls.

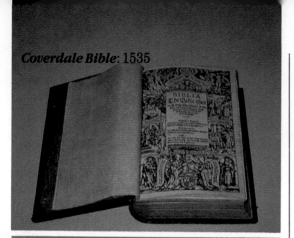

Coverdale Bible: 1535

In our troubles and adversity, we have found that God is our refuge, our strength and our help (Psalm 46:1).

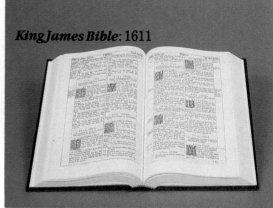

King James Bible: 1611

God is our refuge and strength, a very present help in trouble (Psalm 46:1).

What about Bible versions?

Every message from God is important and should be studied by everyone. That's why the Bible has been translated into over 2,000 different languages! And that is why we have many different English versions of the Bible. Each version tries to make God's message a little clearer to readers.

The different versions of the Bible are not different Bibles. There is only one Bible. Versions are just ways to help people read the Bible in their own language in the simplest, clearest words possible.

Here is how different versions translate Psalm 46:1. Each version gives the same message. Are some of the versions easier for you to understand?

What makes the Bible special?

Some religious books are written to tell what people think about God. The Bible is different. The Bible is a message from God.

Over 2,600 times the writers of our Bible claim to speak or write God's words, not their own! Again and again the Bible tells us "this is what the Lord says." Again and again the writers of the Bible report things like "this is the word the Lord spoke to Jeremiah."

The writers of the Bible were sure what they said and wrote was not something they thought up or imagined. The writers were sure that what they said and wrote was God's message to people.

What is inspiration?

The Bible says, "all Scripture is given by God" (2 Timothy 3:16) and that "men led by the Holy Spirit spoke words from God" (2 Peter 1:21).

God did not speak the exact words to be written down by Bible writers. But God was able to work in the writers so that what they wrote was the exact message God intended to share. Because of inspiration we can trust our Bible completely. What the Bible says is true, for our Bible really is a message from God.

What is revelation?

One way to say the Bible is a message from God is to call it revelation. What does revelation mean?

Well, there are some things a person can find out for himself. For example, when you wonder if a friend is home, you can telephone. Or you can go over to his house and look. It doesn't take revelation to find out what you can discover for yourself.

But suppose you want to know what your mom and dad are thinking? You can guess. But you can't be sure what they think unless they tell you. A person has to "reveal" his thoughts

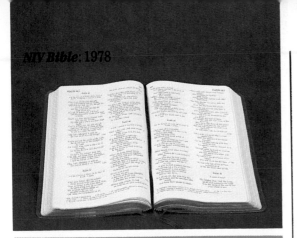

NIV Bible: 1978

God is our refuge and strength, an ever present help in trouble (Psalm 46:1).

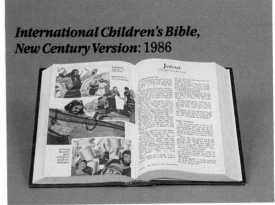

International Children's Bible, New Century Version: 1986

God is our protection and our strength. He always helps in times of trouble (Psalm 46:1).

for you to know what is happening inside him.

God is so great and wonderful that there is no way for people to guess what God thinks or knows. But we don't have to guess! We can be sure about what God thinks and wants, about what he feels and plans. God has revealed these things to us in the Bible.

The Bible is special because only the Bible has God's message to people. Only the Bible reveals things we would not be able to know without it.

What is prophecy?

How do we know we can trust the Bible as God's own Word? Prophecy gives us one kind of proof. God told Isaiah, "From the beginning I told you what would happen in the end. A long time ago I told you things that have not yet happened" (Isaiah 46:10). God has told us about things that have not happened yet.

The Bible talks about many things that were to happen in the future. The prophet Micah named the town where Jesus would be born 700 years later (Micah 5:2). And Jesus was born in that place—Bethlehem! The prophet Isaiah described many details about Jesus' death (Isaiah 53) hundreds of years before he died on a cross. Daniel described powerful nations that would rise and fall during the 500 years after his own death (Daniel 4, 7, 8). And everything happened just as the Bible predicted!

Only God knows the future. The Bible can reveal what God alone knows only if it really is God's Word.

There is more proof that the Bible is God's Word. The Bible puts together writings of 40 different people who lived hundreds of years apart. Their writings are in a single book and have the same wonderful message. This is called the of Scripture.

So we really can trust the Bible. What the Bible says is true. And what the Bible says is important. The Bible really is a message to us from God.

Telling the future

How did God's Old Testament people know when a person who claimed to speak God's words was really telling the truth? Deuteronomy 18:22 gives this test. "What a prophet says in the name of the Lord might not come true. If it doesn't, then it is not the Lord's message." Telling the future was always a way to test those who claimed to speak God's Words.

Jesus and the Bible

Jesus trusted the Bible as God's Word. Talking about the Old Testament Jesus said, "Surely you have read *what God said to you*" (Matthew 22:31; italics mine). Jesus also said, "You should believe everything the prophets said" (Luke 24:25).

11

The International Children's Bible, New Century Version, is the same Bible that adults use. But this version helps children hear God's message by using words that young people can understand better.

Why is the Bible important?

The Bible is the only book inspired by God. The Bible is the only book of revelation from God. That alone makes it important.

But the Bible is also important because of what it tells us. Here are some of the questions the Bible answers.

- Where did the world come from?
- What is God like?
- What is right and what is wrong for a person to do?
- How can you make friends and keep them?
- Why did Jesus have to die on the cross?
- How can you be forgiven when you do something wrong?

- What can you do when you are afraid?
- How do you talk to God?
- How can you make the choices that please God?
- What is heaven and how do you go there when you die?
- How can you be happy and thankful?

In fact, you can learn the answers to just about any important question you have!

But the Bible isn't just a book for learning things. The Bible is a guide. The Bible shows us how to live. The Bible points us away from choices that hurt us and make us unhappy. It guides us toward the choices that help us and bring us joy.

Most important of all, the Bible tells you how you can know God and become his friend. You find out in the Bible just how much God loves you, and you learn how to love him in return.

To Think about and Do

1. What does the Bible teach about itself? To find out (a) Look up 1 Corinthians 2:9-13 and 2 Timothy 3:15,16. (b) Read Jeremiah 6 and write down phrases that tell you Jeremiah is speaking God's words instead of just his own.

2. Match the Old Testament prophecies with their New Testament fulfillments. Then look in a Bible dictionary. See if you can find out how many hundred years each prophecy was fulfilled after it was written.
   Prophecies: Psalm 22:15,18; 34:20; Micah 5:2; Hosea 11:1; Zechariah 9:9; 12:10; 13:7.
   Fulfilled: Matthew 2:6,15; 8:17; 21:5; Mark 14:27; John 19:24,28,36,37.

3. Pretend to be a scribe making a copy of John 3:16 by hand. Make your copy just the way the scribes did, as described on page 9.

4. Why do you think there are so many English versions of the Bible? Look up the two verses below in the King James version of the Bible. See if you can say in your own words what they mean. Then look up the verses in a newer version, like the International Children's Bible, New Century Version. Look up Ephesians 4:31 and 1 Thessalonians 4:15.

5. Near the end of this chapter is a list of things we can learn from the Bible. Look up at least five of these Bible passages and match them with one of the items on the list.
   Passages: Genesis 1:1; Exodus 20:1-17; Proverb 17:17; Matthew 6:9-13; Matthew 6:25-34; John 1:3; John 3:16; Romans 5:8-10; Philippians 4:4-7; Hebrews 13:5,6; 1 John 1:9.

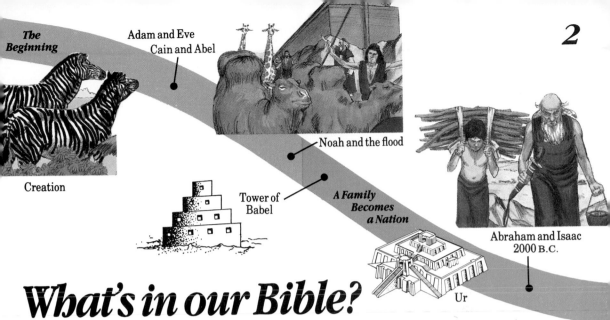

2

The Beginning

Adam and Eve
Cain and Abel

Noah and the flood

Creation

Tower of
Babel

A Family
Becomes
a Nation

Abraham and Isaac
2000 B.C.

Ur

What's in our Bible?

*T*he Bible tells the exciting story of how God has revealed himself to people. This did not happen all at once. The Bible is the history of what God did and said over hundreds of years.

Imagine that the Bible takes us on a journey, and that years are the mile markers along a sort of history highway. Follow that highway on the next few pages, and you will get a good idea of what is in the Bible. As you follow it you'll see some of the people of the Bible and some of the exciting events the Bible describes.

Where does the Bible History Highway begin and end? The highway really began when God created the world. The Bible History Highway leads from creation to the most important person ever born, Jesus the Christ, and to his church.

The beginning

Genesis 1-11 takes us back before any history books were written. God reveals things no one could have witnessed—how he created the universe we live in, and how he created the first people.

In this book of beginnings, we read about the first sin and about the first family. We learn about a great flood God sent to punish the world when people chose to do evil all the time. But God saved Noah, the one man who obeyed him. God waited until Noah built a great floating ark for his family and the animals. After many more years the world was again full of people. Then God spoke to Abram and the Bible History Highway continued.

A family becomes a nation 2100 B.C.

Abraham lived in the very old city of Ur when God spoke to him. God made a special agreement, called a covenant, with Abraham. Abraham was to go to a land that God promised to give to him and his descendants. God also promised to be with Abraham's family and to bless the whole world through them. It was through this family that God gave us the Old Testament. It was from this family that Jesus, the Savior, came!

Genesis tells us the story of Abraham, his son Isaac, his grandson Jacob, and his great-grandson Joseph. The family lived for a time in the promised land of Canaan. But then Jacob's children moved to Egypt after his son Joseph became a ruler of that great land.

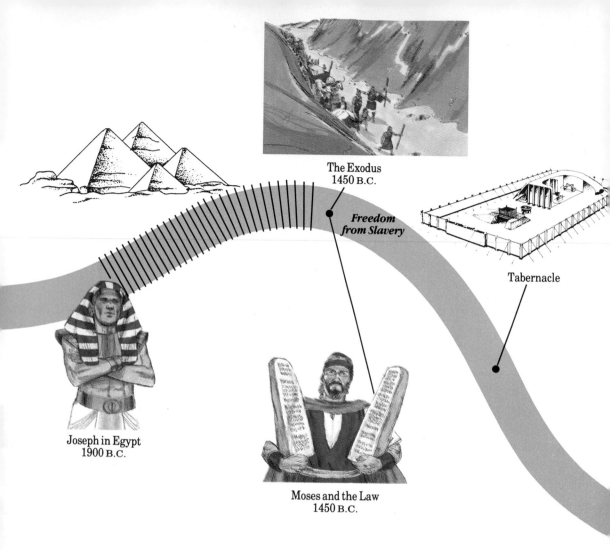

The Exodus
1450 B.C.

Freedom from Slavery

Tabernacle

Joseph in Egypt
1900 B.C.

Moses and the Law
1450 B.C.

Freedom from slavery 1450 B.C.

Jacob's family lived in Egypt for about 400 years and grew to about two million people. During that time the Pharaoh (King) of Egypt made them slaves. God chose Moses to deliver his people from slavery and lead them to the promised land, Canaan.

Egypt's king didn't want to let his slaves go. So God sent ten terrible disasters. The Egyptians became afraid of the Lord and let his people go. Exodus tells about these ten disasters. It also tells how God made a pathway through the sea to help his people escape from the Egyptian army!

Abraham's family is now called the people of Israel or Israelites. They had many adventures on the way to Canaan. God spoke to them in a thundering voice at Mount Sinai. He gave them his law to keep. Exodus, Leviticus and Deuteronomy are Bible books that explain that law. They tell how God's Old Testament people were to worship him.

On the way to Canaan the Israelites often disobeyed God and were punished. Finally, after many years, the people were ready to enter the promised land.

Mount Ararat?

• Haran

Mediterranean Sea

River Tigris

CANAAN

River Euphrates

• Jerusalem

EGYPT

LANDS OF THE BIBLE

Red Sea

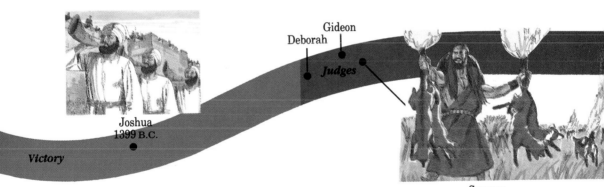

Gideon

Deborah

Judges

Joshua
1399 B.C.

Victory

Samson
1070 B.C.

Victory 1399 B.C.

Moses died before the people of Israel entered Canaan. Joshua, an army general, became the leader of the Israelites. The book of Joshua tells about the battles God's people fought to take the promised land. God helped his people. He made the walls of Jericho fall down when his people obeyed him. But God's people had to fight hard for victory. Finally, after a seven year war, the Israelites took the promised land, and Canaan became the land of Israel.

Judges 1380-1058 B.C.

For 400 years the people of Israel lived in their land, but they had many troubles. They often forgot God. They worshiped idols and chose to sin instead of keeping God's law. Again and again God let other peoples invade Israel and punish the Israelites. When the people of Israel turned back to God, the Lord sent leaders like Deborah, Gideon and Samson to help them defeat their enemies. These judges were both military leaders and rulers. They led God's people to trust and to obey him.

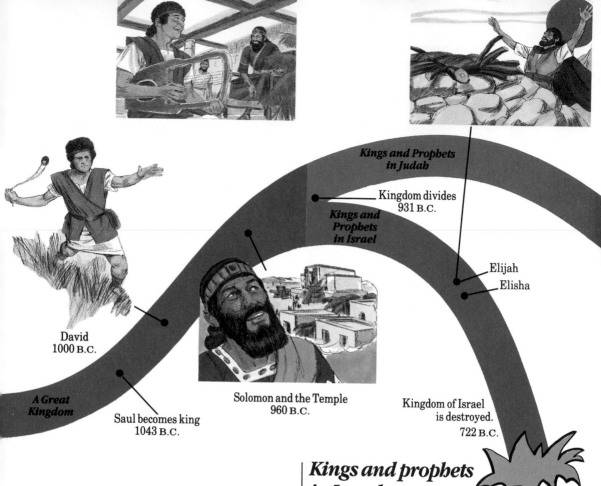

Kings and Prophets
in Judah

Kingdom divides
931 B.C.

Kings and
Prophets
in Israel

Elijah
Elisha

David
1000 B.C.

A Great
Kingdom

Solomon and the Temple
960 B.C.

Saul becomes king
1043 B.C.

Kingdom of Israel
is destroyed.
722 B.C.

A great kingdom 1043-931 B.C.

About a thousand years before Jesus was
born, the people of Israel wanted a king. The
first king, Saul, won many battles but did not
obey God. Then God chose David, who loved the
Lord and tried to obey him, to become Israel's
king. The Bible tells many stories about David.
He killed the giant Goliath when he was just a
teenager. With David as leader, Israel became a
powerful nation and captured nearly all the
land God had promised his people.

David's son Solomon was a great king, too.
He made Israel rich as well as powerful. Solomon built a beautiful temple in Jerusalem
where God's people were to worship. During the
time David and Solomon lived many of the
Bible's great poems (in Psalms) and wise sayings
(in Proverbs) were written.

Kings and prophets
in Israel 931-722 B.C.

When Solomon died in 931 B.C., the land
was divided into two countries. In the North the
new country kept the name Israel. This Israel
was led by a series of evil kings. They refused to
honor God or let their people worship God at the
Temple in Jerusalem. God sent special messengers called prophets to warn the kings and the
people of Israel. The prophets reminded everyone of God's law. They warned that God would
punish the nation if the people would not return
to the Lord. There are many stories about the
brave prophets Elijah and Elisha in our Bible.
We also have Bible books written by the
prophets Amos, Joel and others.

The kings and people of Israel refused to
return to God. So in 722 B.C. the armies of
Assyria destroyed that evil kingdom and took
its people away as captives.

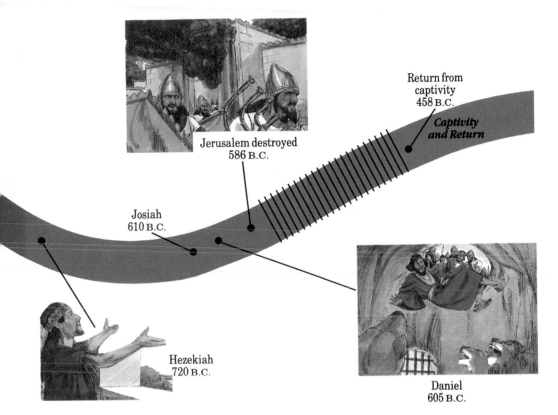

Return from
captivity
458 B.C.

*Captivity
and Return*

Jerusalem destroyed
586 B.C.

Josiah
610 B.C.

Hezekiah
720 B.C.

Daniel
605 B.C.

Kings and prophets in Judah 931-586 B.C.

When Solomon's kingdom was divided, the nation in the South was called Judah. The kings of Judah were all from King David's family. Some of them, like Josiah and Hezekiah, were good kings who trusted God and tried to follow his law. But there were many evil kings too. God's people often turned against his law and worshiped false gods.

God also sent prophets like Isaiah, Jeremiah and Habakkuk to Judah. But the kings and people of Judah did not listen to them.

Finally, in 586 B.C., the Babylonians under their great king Nebuchadnezzar burned Jerusalem and Solomon's wonderful Temple. And they took the people of Judah to Babylon as captives.

God's people sinned. So their nation had been destroyed. And the people were taken away from the promised land.

Captivity and return 458 B.C.

In Babylon many of God's people turned back to him. They began to study his teachings, and they stopped worshiping idols. The books of Daniel and Esther tell how God protected his people when they were captives.

After 70 years in Babylon, some of the people of Judah returned to the promised land. They were led by Ezra and Nehemiah, and urged on by prophets like Haggai and Zechariah. And they rebuilt the Temple and the walls of Jerusalem.

Then God's people settled down for a long, long wait. It would be four hundred years before another prophet came to speak to them. When that prophet came, he would have exciting news for God's people. He would tell them that the promised Savior, Jesus, was about to appear!

17

Jesus

Death of Jesus
A.D. 30

The Church
of Jesus

Letters to Christians
A.D. 45-90

Birth of Jesus
5 B.C.

The Church begins
A.D. 30

Jesus 5 B.C.-A.D. 30

The Bible History Highway leads from creation directly to Jesus.

Jesus is from Abraham's family. Jesus is the one God promised Abraham would bless all the people of the world.

The Gospels (Matthew, Mark, Luke and John) tell us about Jesus. They tell us about his special birth, without a human father. Jesus is the Son of God. The Gospels tell about Jesus' miracles and his teaching. The Gospels tell us how Jesus died on the cross and returned to life after he had been buried.

When we read the Gospels we come to know Jesus and God better. When we study what Jesus did and think about what he said, we learn about God. This is because Jesus is the Son of God.

Some of the New Testament books are letters. These letters tell us more about Jesus. They explain that Jesus had to die for our sins so we could be forgiven. The New Testament letters teach us how Jesus gives us the strength we need to obey God today.

The church of Jesus A.D. 30–

Jesus died on a cross. Then he was raised to life again. Today Jesus is in heaven, and God has promised that one day Jesus will come to earth again.

Ever since Jesus returned to heaven, people who believe in Jesus have gathered to worship him and to love each other. The people of Jesus are called Christians. They are his church.

The Bible book of Acts tells how the church began and how it grew. The followers of Jesus began to tell everyone about him. Peter led Jesus' followers in Israel. Paul was a missionary who traveled all over the world to tell people about the Lord. Peter and Paul and other leaders wrote letters to teach Christians how to follow Jesus and worship him. These special letters are now books in our New Testament.

Yes, the Bible really is the story of Jesus. The Old Testament tells how God prepared people to understand why he must send his Son to earth. The Gospels tell how Jesus came, how he lived and how he died for our sins. And the rest of the New Testament tells how people who believe in Jesus and love him can live to please God.

Books of the Bible

THE OLD TESTAMENT

Books of Law
- ☐ Genesis
- ☐ Exodus
- ☐ Leviticus
- ☐ Numbers
- ☐ Deuteronomy

Books of History
- ☐ Joshua
- ☐ Judges
- ☐ Ruth
- ☐ 1 Samuel
- ☐ 2 Samuel
- ☐ 1 Kings
- ☐ 2 Kings
- ☐ 1 Chronicles
- ☐ 2 Chronicles
- ☐ Ezra
- ☐ Nehemiah
- ☐ Esther

Books of Poetry
- ☐ Job
- ☐ Psalms
- ☐ Proverbs
- ☐ Ecclesiastes
- ☐ Song of Solomon

Books of the Prophets
- ☐ Isaiah
- ☐ Jeremiah
- ☐ Lamentations
- ☐ Ezekiel
- ☐ Daniel
- ☐ Hosea
- ☐ Joel
- ☐ Amos
- ☐ Obadiah
- ☐ Jonah
- ☐ Micah
- ☐ Nahum
- ☐ Habakkuk
- ☐ Zephaniah
- ☐ Haggai
- ☐ Zechariah
- ☐ Malachi

THE NEW TESTAMENT

The Gospels
- ☐ Matthew
- ☐ Mark
- ☐ Luke
- ☐ John

Church History
- ☐ Acts

Letters to Christians
- ☐ Romans
- ☐ 1 Corinthians
- ☐ 2 Corinthians
- ☐ Galatians
- ☐ Ephesians
- ☐ Philippians
- ☐ Colossians
- ☐ 1 Thessalonians
- ☐ 2 Thessalonians
- ☐ 1 Timothy
- ☐ 2 Timothy
- ☐ Titus
- ☐ Philemon
- ☐ Hebrews
- ☐ James
- ☐ 1 Peter
- ☐ 2 Peter
- ☐ 1 John
- ☐ 2 John
- ☐ 3 John
- ☐ Jude

Book of Prophecy
- ☐ Revelation

To Think about and Do

1. How many Bible stories do you know? Make a list. Then decide which stories in your list are from the Old Testament. Which stories are from the New Testament?

   You can also form teams in your classroom. Guess where along the History Highway each story you wrote down belongs. Give 2 points for each right answer.

2. Look through the different chapters in this Bible Handbook. Can you find the bar of color at the beginning of each chapter that matches a color along the History Highway? The color bar will help you know how each part of the Bible fits with other parts.

3. Make a list of the sections of the Bible History Highway. Memorize the sections, and memorize the color.

4. Work with other Sunday school classes to make a Bible History Highway map for the hallways or basement of your church. Each class can take one section of the highway. On a long piece of paper draw the people and events that took place in your section of the highway. Put the pieces together in order. Then you and your parents can walk along the highway and remember the wonderful story told in our Bible.

5. Look at the map on page 15. Make dotted lines that show where the journey through history took God's Old Testament people up to the time of Jesus. (Hint: Before you try, check other maps in this handbook.)

In the beginning

Where did our world come from? Why is it a friendly place to live? The other planets around our sun are dusty and chilly like Mars, or hot and empty like Mercury. But when God made the universe, he made Earth a special place. God made Earth a world to be lived in.

The good news

• Genesis 1 tells that there really is a God who created Earth as a special and wonderful place for people to live. Even creation is good news. From the things God has made we know about his power, wisdom and trustworthiness. And we know about his love for you and me.

• We can respond to God by praising him for creating. And we can thank him for his wonderful gifts to us.

• The Genesis story of creation answers many important questions. But the Genesis story raises questions too.

• Some of the important questions that Genesis answers are "Where did the universe come from?" "Why did God make our world?" "What is God the creator like?"

• Some of the questions Genesis 1 raises are "How old is Earth?" and "How do dinosaurs fit into creation?"

God created the skies and the earth as a place for his creations to live.

• When we read Genesis 1 we want to understand the important questions. And we want to think about possible answers to the hard questions too.

Where did the universe come from?

No one knows when the universe began. Some scientists talk about a *Big Bang* that they think happened about four and a half billion years ago. They think the universe began with a great explosion and everything that exists came from that Big Bang. Scientists agree that once nothing existed. But what caused the explosion? Scientists do not know.

The Bible also tells us that once there was nothing—nothing but God. Then God spoke, and the universe began (Genesis 1:1; John 1:1-3). The Bible does not tell us when God created the universe. But the Bible does tell us that the power that made everything was God, not a Big Bang.

How did God create?

Genesis 1 tells us that "God said"—and creation happened (Genesis 1:3,6,7,14)! God did not have to use tools. God simply spoke a word of command.

> *"They should praise the name of the Lord, because they were created by his command."*
> Psalm 148:5

Creation teaches us that everything comes from God, including our life itself. How great God is! He only needed to speak a word, and the universe began. Our great God is surely able to help you and me as we live in this world he made.

Why did God create?

Genesis shows us God's purpose in creating the universe. It was to make a place for people. How do we know this? We know from the description of the six days of creation. In the first three days of creation, God carefully shaped our world. In the next three he beautified it.

When all was ready, God made people and gave the world to us to rule and enjoy (see Genesis 1:29). Earth was made as a wonderful gift: a place for us to live, to enjoy, and to be thankful for.

What does creation tell about God?

Did you know that the things God made tell us many things about him?

The great size of the universe tells us that God must be very powerful.

The design and planning revealed in our world tell us God must be very wise. For instance, birds are designed to fly in the air. Their bones are hollow so they weigh less, and it's easier for them to fly. Fish are designed to live in water. Yet fish are different enough so some can live in salt water and others in fresh water.

The dependability of the world tells us that God is trustworthy. God shaped the world to help us feel safe and secure. When we go to bed, we know the sun will rise in the morning. Every day lasts just 24 hours. Someone who jumps up always comes back down. Dependability in our world helps us know we can trust God. He does not change suddenly but keeps on loving us.

Genesis 1 says that as God shaped and beautified our world he called his work good. God must love us very much to care about making the world a good place for us to live. Everything that is good in our world tells us that God is good too, and that he loves us.

Responding to God

When we realize that God planned and made this wonderful world for us to enjoy, we want to praise and thank him. The Bible contains many poems written to praise God for creation. Look at the picture of just one of the great galaxies in our universe, and join in the praise.

Psalm 148:1-6

Praise the Lord!
Praise the Lord from the heavens.
    Praise him in the high places.
²Praise him, all you angels.
    Praise him, all you armies of heaven.
³Praise him, sun and moon.
    Praise him, all you bright stars.
⁴Praise him, highest heavens
    and the waters above the sky.
⁵They should praise the name of the Lord,
    because they were created by his command.
⁶He set them in place forever and ever.
    He made a law that will never end.

What does "rule over" mean?

God made people to "rule over" the living things in his creation (Genesis 1:26,28). "Ruling" is a special word that means being responsible for. People have been put in charge of this world. We are to take care of God's world and living creatures.

Taking good care of pets is a way young people can have a part in this special work. Sometimes a state or nation sets aside land for animals and birds. These lands are called national parks or wildlife refuges. This is one way governments do what God intended. He gave people rule over our beautiful world.

What happened during creation?

The first three days of creation were days of preparation. God flooded the universe with light, made Earth's waters and sky. And he formed its dry land and made the plants.

The next three days God decorated what he had made. He filled space with stars and with our sun and moon on the fourth day. He filled the waters of Earth with fish and the sky with birds on the fifth day. And on the sixth day, he made the animals that live on the land.

God made the world beautiful to be a home for you and me.

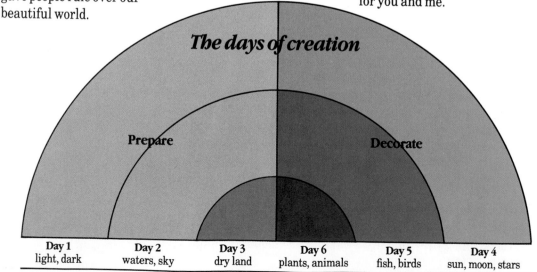

The days of creation

Prepare | Decorate

| Day 1 light, dark | Day 2 waters, sky | Day 3 dry land | Day 6 plants, animals | Day 5 fish, birds | Day 4 sun, moon, stars |

What about dinosaurs?

Many bones of these great animals that scientists believe lived ages ago have been found preserved in the earth. Where do dinosaurs fit in the Genesis account?

Some think that each day in Genesis 1 was followed by an age of hundreds of thousands or millions of years (2 Peter 3:8). The "morning" of each day marks a new creation by God. The "evening" marks the end of a very long age. During each long, long day, or age, much growth and change took place. So they believe the dinosaurs existed in one of the early ages and were gone before God created people near the end of the sixth day.

Others believe God created the universe in seven 24-hour days. The earth God made already had the Grand Canyon, tall trees that seemed to be 200 years old, full-grown animals, etc. Fossils that seem to be remains of ancient dinosaurs and plants were built into the world. They now provide the gas and oil we need in our day.

We don't know for sure how old the earth is or where dinosaurs fit in. But we do know from the Bible and from creation itself that God did create everything. He made the world for us to live in.

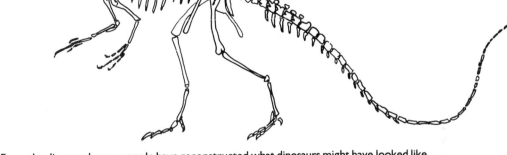

From the dinosaur bones, people have reconstructed what dinosaurs might have looked like.

To Think about and Do

1. What are some of the things you like (ice cream?) or like to do (watch TV?). What did God have to make so you could enjoy the things you like?

2. Make a list of what God did each day of creation. Memorize the list.

3. Do an experiment. Put all kinds of things in a bag or box. Use nuts and bolts, parts from old radios, etc. Shake them all together as many times as you want. Does just shaking things together make anything you can use?
   What do you think the careful design of everything in our world shows?

4. Read Romans 1:20 and Psalm 19:1-8. What is one way God tells people about himself? What can everyone know about God from the things God has made?

5. Here are some Bible passages that tell about God as Creator: Psalm 104; Job 36,37. Read them, and then write a praise poem of your own to thank God for making our world.

God creates man and woman

When you look in a mirror, you see an image of your face. That image isn't you. But it is like you in many ways. When God made Adam and Eve, he made them in his image. So people are like God in many ways. But something terrible happened, and in some important ways people are no longer like God.

The good news

▪ We are all special, for only people have been created in God's image.

▪ Adam and Eve sinned, but God continued to love them. And he keeps on loving us when we sin.

▪ God must punish people who keep on sinning and will not respond to him. But Noah reminds us that God will always help those who trust in him and do good.

Why are people special?

Genesis 1,2

When God finished shaping Earth, he created people. What makes people so special is that only they were made "in the image of God" (Genesis 1:27).

The Genesis description of the Garden of Eden helps us understand how people are in God's image. God planted trees in Eden that "were very beautiful" (Genesis 2:9). God enjoys

God created all the animals, fish and birds, but only people were made to be like God himself.

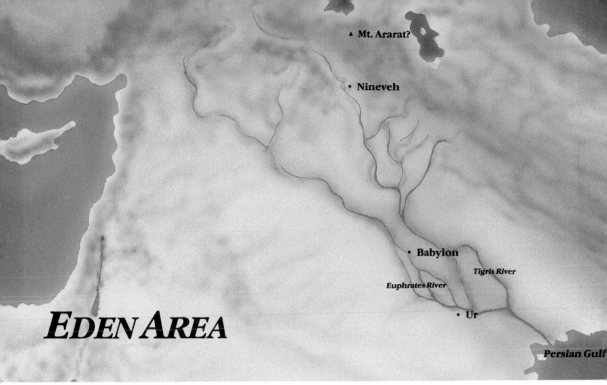

EDEN AREA

Mt. Ararat?

Nineveh

Babylon

Tigris River

Euphrates River

Ur

Persian Gulf

beauty and made us able to enjoy beauty too. God had Adam "work and care for" the garden (Genesis 2:15). God found pleasure in his work of creation (Genesis 1:12,18,21,25,31). He made us able to find satisfaction in our work. God even permitted Adam to name the animals (Genesis 2:19,20). Like God, people have minds to use and to invent new things, like the names of animals.

God is holy, too. He always chooses to do what is right. And this is another way that people were made like God. God made it possible for people to make choices between right and wrong. That may be why God planted one tree in Eden whose fruit Adam was commanded not to eat (Genesis 2:16,17). Adam had to have the chance to make choices between right and wrong.

How special people are! In all God's creation only people were made "in the image of God"!

Where was Eden?

Where was Eden? Genesis 2 says it was located at the source of four rivers. We know two of those rivers: the Euphrates and Tigris. If you look at the map on this page you'll be able to find the general area where most believe Eden was.

How are men and women alike?

God made Adam first and then made Eve from Adam's rib (Genesis 2:20-24). Have you ever wondered why? Many Bible teachers think God had important reasons. (1) Adam lived alone in Eden for a long time. He felt more and more lonely. His time alone taught Adam that people need other people to love and to love them. (2) When God made Eve he took a rib from Adam. When Adam saw her he said that she is "someone whose bones came from my bones. Her body came from my body" (Genesis 2:23). Adam recognized that the woman was actually like him, even though she was different in some ways. Men and women equally share the image of God, and neither is more or less important than the other.

What was the first sin?

Genesis 3

To be truly like God, Adam and Eve would always have to choose to do what is right. Adam and Eve did not keep on choosing right, and sin came into the world.

25

We don't know how long Adam and Eve lived happily in the Garden of Eden. We don't know how many times they looked at the tree and chose not to eat. But we know that one day Satan tempted Eve, and she and Adam made the wrong choice. They disobeyed God and ate the fruit that God had told them not to eat.

That first sin had terrible results.

What happened when man sinned?

In many ways people still bear the image of God (see Genesis 9:6; James 3:9). But that image has been twisted and broken. God always chooses what is right and good. Adam and Eve had done wrong. They were no longer truly good as God is good.

One result of sin is seen in what Adam and Eve did when God visited Eden to talk with them. Adam and Eve felt guilty and ashamed. So they ran from God and tried to hide. When we do wrong we feel guilty and ashamed, too. And we try to hide what we have done from others.

Why did God make clothes?

Adam and Eve tried to cover themselves with leaves (Genesis 3:7). Later God made them clothing of animal skins (Genesis 3:21). Why? Some believe that this was the very first sacrifice. It showed Adam that sin must be punished by death. But God was willing to accept the death of a substitute instead of taking Adam's life. Jesus' death on the cross was a sacrifice. Jesus died for our sins so we can be forgiven.

Animal sacrifices in the Old Testament taught that sin brings death. It is only when sin is punished that God can accept a sinner.

How did Adam and Eve die?

God warned Adam he would die if he ate the forbidden fruit (Genesis 2:17). The moment Adam and Eve ate, their bodies began to die. But in the Bible "death" is spiritual as well as physical. A spiritually dead person does not respond to God. Like Adam and Eve, he tries to avoid him. Ephesians 2:1-3 describes how a spiritually dead person acts. And Genesis 4 shows us the great tragedies that sin and spiritual death cause.

What else did sin cause?

God came where Adam and Eve were hiding. He told them what their wrong choice meant for them (Genesis 3:16-19). Because of sin the earth would be filled with weeds that choke out good crops. Adam's work would become hard labor instead of play. Having children would be painful for Eve. Even though Adam and Eve still loved each other, their relationship would not be as close as it had been.

Worst of all, though Adam and Eve did not know it yet, their children would be more like them than like God. Sin had come into the world, and everyone yet to be born would sin. All too often they would choose to do wrong instead of right.

How terrible is sin?

Genesis 4 shows us. Cain, one of Adam's sons, killed his brother Abel because he was jealous and angry. Many years later Lamech disobeyed God's will for marriage by taking two wives. And he excused himself for murdering an enemy. Sin is in everyone. Our newspapers today are filled with terrible stories of people who do wrong and hurt others.

How long did people live?

Genesis 5

Genesis 5 names persons who lived for 782 years, 805 years, even 969 years. How can we explain such long lives?

People who study old things have found ancient Mesopotamian lists of kings before the flood and after the flood. Some of the kings before the flood were said to have ruled as long as 42,000 years! So it is not just the Bible that speaks of long life before a great flood.

But how could people live hundreds of years? Many believe the world was quite different before the flood in Genesis. It did not rain (Genesis 2:5), and much water vapor was held in thick clouds in the sky (Genesis 1:7). Even the animals during this period did not eat meat (compare Genesis 1:29,30 with Genesis 9:3). In this time before the flood, the water vapors in the air may have kept out certain rays of the sun. Scientists have shown these rays help cause aging.

Is this the reason for long lives before the flood? We do not know for sure. But the Bible does say that people then lived a very long time.

Will God punish sin?

Genesis 6-9

What does God think about sin? And what will he do if people keep on choosing wrong?

Many hundreds of years after Adam and Eve, perhaps millions of people lived on earth. Even though these people must have heard about God, they did "only evil all the time" (Genesis 6:5). Even though God's "heart was filled with pain" he knew he must punish this

Cain was a farmer, and Abel cared for animals. God was pleased with Abel's offering, but he was not pleased with Cain's offering. This made Cain angry, and he killed his brother Abel.

world of sinners (Genesis 6:6). So God decided to send a great flood that would destroy all living things.

Why was Noah special?

Noah was one man who did good instead of evil (Genesis 6:8,9). God takes care of those who love and obey him. God warned Noah of the coming flood. He told him to build a great boat called an ark. It was 450 feet long, 75 feet wide, and 45 feet high. It had to be large enough to hold Noah, his wife, his three sons, their wives and many animals.

Was the flood world-wide?

Some Bible students believe the flood of Genesis was local. They think that only a low-lying area in Mesopotamia where Adam's descendants had settled was flooded. If men had remained in that area and not moved across the world, a local flood would have done what God wanted. It would have destroyed all of mankind and animals (Genesis 6:7).

Others point out that the Bible says "that even the highest mountains under the sky" were covered to a depth of more than 22 feet (Genesis 7:19,20). But today there isn't enough water in all the oceans and in the air to cover earth that deep. Is there an answer? Some scientists who are Christian suggest that before the flood the

mountains weren't as high. They believe the weight of the flood waters pushed the ocean bottoms down and thrust the mountains up higher.

What did God promise Noah?

Nearly a year after the rains began, Noah, his family and the animals left the ark. It had settled on the side of Mount Ararat. Noah built an altar and sacrificed some of the animals to God. And the Lord made Noah a promise: "I will never again destroy every living thing" (Genesis 8:21).

The rainbow is a reminder of this promise. Whenever clouds gather and the rains come, we can see the rainbow in the sky. Then we remember God's promise. Never again will a flood cover our earth (Genesis 9:12-16).

God's image

God did make people like him in some ways. All the good and wonderful things about people are there because God made us to be like him.

But in some ways we are no longer like the Lord. People sometimes choose to do what is wrong and evil. God always chooses to do what is right and good.

Adam and Eve and the flood show us that God will punish those who keep on doing wrong. It is right to punish sin. And even though God loves all, he will do what is right.

God sent two of every kind of animal and bird to Noah so that he could save them on the ark from the flood. He sent seven pairs of some animals and birds. After the flood was over, these creatures filled the earth again.

When the flood waters finally began to go down, Noah's ark settled on top of Mount Ararat. Explorers are still searching for the ark there today in the country of Turkey.

To Think about and Do

1. Read Genesis 2,3 and 6. What do these chapters teach us about God?

2. Satan tricked Eve into doing wrong. Look at Genesis 3:1-6. How did Satan try to make Eve doubt God's Word? To doubt God's love? What was it that made Eve want to eat the forbidden fruit?
   What can you learn from this that will help you choose right when you feel like doing something you know is wrong?

3. Look at the front page of a newspaper. What on that page shows that people are still like God in some ways? What tells you people are not like God in other, important ways? What on that page shows you how terrible sin really is?

4. How big really was Noah's ark? Go to a football field (300 feet long). How long does it take the fastest person in your class to run the length of a football field? The ark was 450 feet long: 1½ football fields!
   Go to a five-story building. How hard is it to run up five flights of stairs? Look down from the roof. The ark was about as high as this building.

5. Talk with a friend about Noah and the ark. Tell him why it took so long to build the ark, why God gave Noah directions for building the ark and what happened during the flood.

Father Abraham

*T*hree world religions look back and call Abraham the "father" of their faith. Each of them—Islam, Judaism and Christianity—believes that God spoke to Abraham. Each is sure that God had a special purpose in speaking to Abraham in his pagan homeland, Ur. What did God say to Abraham? What was his purpose? And how did Abraham win the title of "father" of our faith?

The good news

• God gives wonderful promises to those he loves. Like Abraham, we can claim God's promises by trusting him and doing what he says.

• God kept his promise to Abraham. His son Isaac was born when Abraham was about a hundred years old. God keeps his promises to us, too, even when what he says he will do may seem impossible.

4,000 years ago

Abraham's world was wealthy, busy and exciting. Traveling groups carried fine goods— gold, metal tools, pottery, lumber, grain and clothing. Trade routes went between cities and kingdoms. All these lay in a half-circle of well watered lands called the fertile crescent. It is shown by the dark area on the map.

The world was civilized long before Abraham. One city, Ebla, (see map) had a library of

One way to measure a man's wealth in the days of Abraham was by the number of camels, tents and other possessions he had. Abraham had thousands of animals and a great many tents.

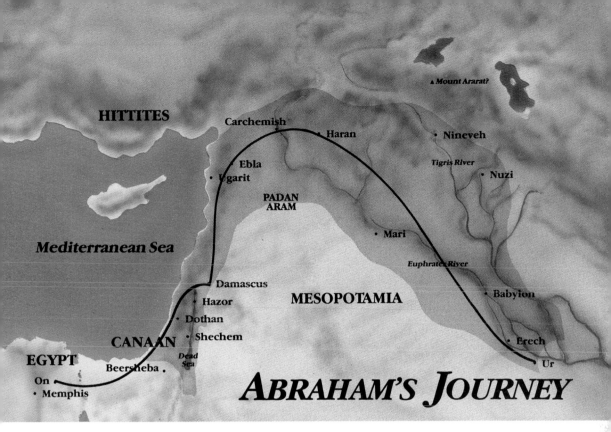

ABRAHAM'S JOURNEY

Map labels: HITTITES, Mount Ararat?, Carchemish, Haran, Nineveh, Ebla, Tigris River, Ugarit, Nuzi, PADAN ARAM, Mari, Mediterranean Sea, Euphrates River, Damascus, Babylon, Hazor, MESOPOTAMIA, Dothan, Shechem, Erech, CANAAN, EGYPT, Dead Sea, Ur, Beersheba, On, Memphis

thousands of clay tablets and a population of 260,000 people. It was destroyed in war some 500 years before Abraham lived! Long before Abraham, Egypt had pyramids. Astronomers studied the stars and doctors wrote medical textbooks. Well-written laws protected citizens and travelers.

How do we know so much about laws and customs in Abraham's time? Some 20,000 clay tablets written in the Babylonian language have been found at Nuzi (*Nu' ze*). These tell us about many customs of early times.

The ancient world was different from our world, of course. Travel was slower. There were no telephones, no radio or TV. But in many ways Abraham's world was like our own.

Where was Ur?

Abraham lived in the prosperous city of Ur, beside the Euphrates River (see map). People who study old things have discovered many things about this very old city. It had sewer drains, wide streets and two-story houses. Care-

ful city records were kept of contracts and other business activity. Golden dishes found in the royal tombs show the wonderful skill of Ur's artists.

Abraham was probably a wealthy merchant in Ur, enjoying the best this great city could offer. But Abraham did not know God. But when God did speak to Abraham, he listened.

Promises God made to Abraham
Genesis 12

God spoke to Abraham. He told Abraham to leave Ur and go to a new land. God gave him wonderful promises. Here are some of the promises God made to Abraham.

God promised to make Abraham a great nation. The Jewish people, and the Arabs, come from Abraham.

God promised to bless Abraham, and God took care of him his whole life.

God promised to make Abraham's name great. Today Muslims, Jews and Christians think of Abraham as a great man.

God promised to make Abraham a blessing to everyone. Jesus, our Savior, was born in Abraham's family.

God promised to give Abraham's family a land God would show him. Today the Jewish people have a nation in Palestine, the ancient promised land.

Are the promises God made to Abraham important?

We know the promises to Abraham are very important. This is because God made a special agreement with him, called a covenant. In Abraham's day the agreement (covenant) was like a contract. By making this kind of agreement, God made sure Abraham knew the Lord would never break or go back on his promises.

God's promises to Abraham help us understand God's plan for his people as it unfolds in the Bible. God is always faithful. He keeps his promises to us today just as he kept his promises in Bible times. Knowing how God always keeps his promises encourages us to trust him. We can count on God to do what he says he will do.

Why does Abraham have two names?

Genesis calls the same man Abram and Abraham. Why? Names in Bible times had special meaning. "Abram" means "father." "Abraham" means "honored father." God changed Abram's name to Abraham as a sign of God's promise to make Abraham the father of many nations.

What was Abraham like?

Although Abraham was a special person, he was not perfect. What was Abraham like? He was sometimes fearful, but fair, courageous, law-abiding and caring. And Abraham was a man of real faith.

Genesis 12: Fearful. Abraham bravely left Ur when God told him to. But he was still a fearful person. When Abraham traveled to Egypt, he was afraid the Egyptians would want his

A ziggurat is similar to the Mayan temples in Yucatan, Central America today. The ruins of Ur discovered in 1922 contained a ziggurat. Some scholars believe the Tower of Babel was a ziggurat.

beautiful wife and would kill him. He asked Sarah to lie and say she was only his sister. Later, Abraham did the same thing again (Genesis 20). Fear can sometimes make us forget that God will take care of us when we choose to do what is right.

Genesis 13: Fair. Abraham traveled with his nephew Lot. Both were rich with large herds of sheep and cattle. The herds became too big for them to travel together. So Abraham gave Lot the first choice of the land. Abraham was older and could have insisted on having first choice. God was pleased with Abraham's fairness. He promised that Abraham's family would one day have the whole land forever.

Genesis 14: Courageous. Lot had moved to Sodom. He was taken away when an army sent by four kings captured that city. Abraham armed his 318 trained fighters. He surprised the enemy army and was able to release his nephew and the other captives.

Genesis 16: Law-abiding. Abraham's wife had no children. So she wanted Abraham to have a child with her maid Hagar. In Abraham's day laws permitted a childless woman to do this. She could raise her servant's child as her own. Later, Sarah insisted Abraham send the boy, named Ishmael, away (Genesis 21). Abraham didn't want to because he loved his son. And it was against the laws of that day to send him away. But God told Abraham to send away Ishmael and promised to take care of him.

Genesis 18,19: Caring. God told Abraham that he was going to destroy the wicked cities of Sodom and Gomorrah. Abraham pleaded with God not to do it if even ten good people lived there. There was really only one. It was Abraham's nephew Lot. God waited until Lot could escape before destroying the cities by fire. Abraham was a caring person. But God cared even more and would not harm even one good person when he punished the wicked.

Where are Sodom and Gomorrah?

Today many believe the ruins of Sodom and Gomorrah lie under the salty waters at the south end of the Dead Sea (see map). God destroyed Sodom and Gomorrah by fire falling from heaven. Some think he caused an earthquake and explosion of petroleum gases mixed with sulphur and asphalt of the area. In 1953, Israel's first oil well was drilled in this area.

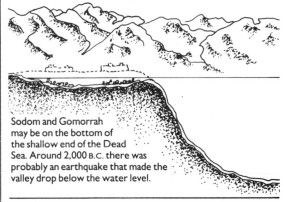

Sodom and Gomorrah may be on the bottom of the shallow end of the Dead Sea. Around 2,000 B.C. there was probably an earthquake that made the valley drop below the water level.

Because of the great amount of salt in the Dead Sea, animals and fish cannot live in and around it, but swimmers find its salty waters great for floating.

How did Abraham show his faith?

Abraham's faith was tested three times. First, God told Abraham to leave Ur. Abraham trusted God enough to go (Genesis 12).

Second, God promised Abraham that he and Sarah would have a son. Abraham believed God even though both of them were much too old to be able to have children (Genesis 15).

The Dome of the Rock is on Mount Moriah where Abraham prepared to sacrifice his son Isaac.

Third, God told Abraham to kill his son Isaac as a sacrifice. Abraham began to obey (Genesis 22). He was sure that even if God had to bring his boy back from the dead, God would do it (see Genesis 22:5; Hebrews 11:17-19).

Abraham showed that he had a real trust in God by obeying God's commands. He obeyed even when it was hard to do. People who have a real faith in God today will also be willing to obey the Lord.

What happened to Abraham's sons?

Ishmael was protected by God after Abraham sent him away (Genesis 21:1-21). The Arab people came from the family of Ishmael (Genesis 25:12-18).

Isaac stayed with his parents until they died. God's wonderful promises to Abraham were passed on to Isaac. After him they were passed on to Isaac's son Jacob.

To Think about and Do

1. Read these verses to discover some of the promises God has made. Tell someone about one of these promises you are glad God makes to you. Psalm 32:8; Isaiah 41:10; 41:13, 49:15; 54:10; John 14:13; 1 John 1:9.

2. Find on the map on page 31 the places mentioned in this chapter. Use a Bible encyclopedia to find out more about these places.

3. Pretend you are a newspaper reporter sent to interview Abraham. Make a list of questions you want to ask. Read parts of Genesis 12-25 and Hebrews 11:8-19. Write down the answers you think Abraham would give.

4. Abraham was a person like you and me. He knew fear. He was fair, courageous and caring. And he trusted God. How are you like Abraham? Tell about something you said or did that shows you are like him.

5. Tell what each of these stories teaches you about God. Abraham prays for Sodom (Genesis 18). Abraham is tested (Genesis 22). Abraham's servant finds a bride for Isaac (Genesis 24).

Safe in Egypt

*A*braham's grandson Jacob was the next person to inherit God's covenant promise. Jacob lived a life of adventure. He ran from home when his brother wanted to kill him. But God was faithful to his agreement and brought Jacob back to the promised land. One of Jacob's sons, Joseph, was sold as a slave into Egypt. God was with Joseph and helped him to become a ruler in that great land. As a ruler Joseph was able to feed his family when there was a terrible time of hunger. And he brought them to Egypt where they would be safe.

The good news

• Jacob was slow in learning to do right. But God did not give up on him. God does not give up on you and me, either.

• Joseph had a hard life and many painful experiences. But God brought good out of Joseph's sufferings. God can bring good out of our hard times, too.

What was Esau's birthright?

Genesis 25

Isaac had two sons. Esau was the older, and Jacob was the younger. According to custom, the older son, Esau, would inherit most of Isaac's property and also God's promise. Esau's "birthright"—something he had a right to because he was born first—was that special relationship

The family of Israel moved to Egypt where Joseph was a powerful ruler.

with God which the Lord promised to Abraham's family.

But one day Esau was very hungry. He traded his special relationship with God to his brother Jacob for a bowl of vegetable soup! Esau didn't think the relationship with God was worth very much at all!

Later Jacob and his mother tricked Isaac into giving the blessings of God to Jacob instead of to Esau (Genesis 27). It was wrong for Jacob to lie and trick his father. But at least Jacob thought God's promises were important to have.

Does God speak in dreams?
Genesis 28

Esau was so angry he planned to kill his brother Jacob. So Jacob fled to stay with relatives in Padan Aram (see map on page 31).

When Jacob was on the way, God spoke to him in a dream. God gave him the same promises he had given Abraham. God said, "I will not leave you until I have done what I have promised you" (Genesis 28:15).

In Jacob's time God sometimes did talk to people in dreams. The Bible had not been written yet, so when God wanted to give a message to people he sometimes used dreams.

Why Jacob had four wives
Genesis 29,30

While Jacob was with his relatives he fell in love with their daughter Rachel. Jacob promised to work for her father Laban for seven years if Laban would let Jacob marry Rachel. Jacob worked hard. But Laban tricked Jacob and married him to Rachel's sister Leah. Jacob still loved Rachel, and he worked another seven years for her. Later Leah and Rachel asked Jacob to take their servants Bilhah and Zilpah as wives, too.

Today the Moslem religion teaches that a man can have four wives because Jacob did. God's plan is for each husband to have just one wife and each wife one husband. But Jacob followed the customs of his land. He did not understand what God wants marriage to be (see Matthew 19:3-9).

How is the name Israel used?

After twenty years Jacob returned to his homeland with his wives, his children, and with large flocks and herds. On the way Jacob received a blessing, and his name was changed to "Israel" (Genesis 32).

The name Israel is used in many different ways in the Bible. When we read "Israel" in the Bible we need to know which use is meant. Here are some of the meanings.

▪ Israel is the new name of the man Jacob.

▪ Israel is the name given to Jacob's descendants, who are also called "Israelites" and "the children of Israel."

▪ Israel is the name given to the land God promised to Abraham.

▪ Israel is the name of one of the Jewish countries that formed later when the kingdom David and Solomon ruled was divided in two. The name of the other country was Judah.

The wonderful covenant God gave to Abraham, then to Isaac and then to Jacob, was passed on to the whole family of Israelites (see chart).

Each of these sons became the father of large families. The Bible calls them "tribes" or "clans." Later Joseph's two sons, Ephraim and Manasseh, took his place as "children of Israel." About 400 years after Jacob/Israel died, God brought the children of Israel back from Egypt to the land he had promised Abraham. Then each tribe was given its own area to live in (see map on page 71).

Why Joseph's brothers hated him
Genesis 37

Joseph was the son of Jacob's favorite wife Rachel. Joseph's brothers were jealous of Joseph because their father liked Joseph best. Joseph also told his brothers about a dream he had. Joseph dreamed that one day he would be greater than his brothers and even greater than his father and mother. This made the brothers very angry.

The brothers hated Joseph so much that they planned to kill him. Instead, when Joseph was only 17, his brothers sold him to be a slave.

The Children of Israel	Jacob's [Israel's] Sons		
With wife Leah	**With wife Rachel**	**With wife Bilhah**	**With wife Zilpah**
Reuben Simeon Levi Judah Issachar Zebulun	Joseph Benjamin	Dan Naphtali	Gad Asher

Joseph was taken to Egypt. But his brothers let their father think Joseph was killed by a wild animal.

What was Egypt like?

Egypt is a long land, surrounded by desert and sea. Only the ground close to the Nile River and watered by it would grow crops. So most of the people lived near the river.

Egypt became one nation about 3100 B.C. Hundreds of years before Abraham, wonderful buildings were constructed. Great artists worked, and books were written. By Joseph's time there were short stories and adventure books, even a book on the *Pleasures of Fishing and Fowling*!

▪ Egyptian women used cosmetics much like our own, with lipstick, eye shadow and rouge.

▪ Egyptian scientists studied mathematics, and astronomers mapped the stars.

▪ Egyptian traders traveled on land and sea to bring riches to Egypt's cities.

▪ Egyptian armies were very powerful. Often Egypt was the strongest nation in the ancient world.

The Egyptians had many gods who were often in the form of animals. The most important gods were Ra, the sun god, and Osiris (*O si'ris*). The Egyptians believed in life after death, and Osiris was thought to rule the afterlife.

Wealthy people and royalty had their dead bodies dried and wrapped as mummies. The Egyptians believed the soul was part of the body. So the body had to be preserved after death. The poor who could not afford the expen-

Ra

Osiris

The writing of the Egyptians was called *hieroglyphics* and was often carved into stone tablets.

EGYPT

Mediterranean Sea

• Damascus

Jordan
River

• Jerusalem

• Memphis

Nile River

• Thebes

Red Sea

sive funeral had no hope. In fact, ordinary people were not even allowed in the great temples that the kings, called Pharaohs, built.

Egypt had a great and powerful civilization when Joseph was taken there as a slave. In 13 years Joseph would rise to be a ruler.

What was Joseph like?

Genesis 39

Joseph may not have been wise to tell his dreams to his brothers. But Joseph trusted God and always did the best he could.

Joseph worked hard for his Egyptian owner, Potiphar. And he was soon put in charge of everything this high officer owned. Joseph refused to sin with Potiphar's wife. She lied about Joseph and had him thrown into prison. Even there Joseph tried hard. Soon the warden put him in charge of running the jail.

It must have hurt Joseph to be accused when he was innocent, just as it hurt to be sold as a slave by his own brothers. But Joseph kept on trusting God and trying to do what is right. The Bible says that "the Lord was with Joseph. The Lord made Joseph successful in everything he did" (Genesis 39:23).

Who can explain dreams?

Genesis 40,41

Jacob had a dream in which the Lord talked with him. Most dreams are different from Jacob's. Most dreams are full of symbols, not words.

In Egypt, dreams were thought to be very important. The Egyptian Pharaoh (king) had magicians and wise men who were paid to explain the meaning of his dreams!

Two of Pharaoh's officers had dreams when they were in prison with Joseph. The man who served wine dreamed about a vine. The baker dreamed about baskets of bread. God helped Joseph explain the meaning of the dreams: the man who served wine was to be freed, and the baker was to be killed! Two years later Pharaoh had a dream that none of his magicians could explain. Then the man who served wine remembered Joseph. Pharaoh sent for Joseph and asked him to explain his dream.

Pharaoh's dream was a warning sent by God. Joseph explained what God wanted Pharaoh to know. Egypt would have seven years of full harvests. Then they would have seven

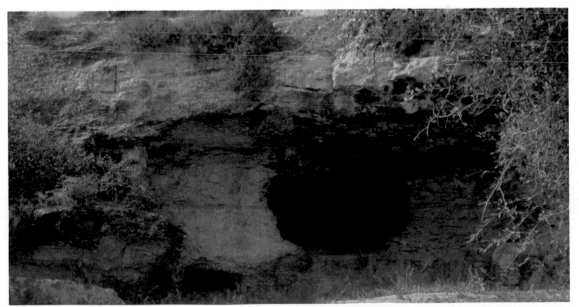

Abraham bought the cave of Machpelah from the Hittites as a burial place for his wife Sarah. Later, both Abraham and Jacob were also buried in the cave.

years of famine. Joseph then gave Pharaoh a plan to save Egypt during the seven years of hunger. Pharaoh was so impressed that he made Joseph the ruler of Egypt, second only to Pharaoh himself. Joseph was just 30 years old at the time!

When was Joseph in Egypt?

People who doubt the Bible once argued that the story of Joseph was made up many years after Joseph was supposed to have lived. Today people who study old things know this story was not just made up. Too many details in Genesis have been shown to be correct.

The titles of Egyptian officers named in Genesis are accurate. The Bible tells how Pharaoh honored Joseph (Genesis 41:42,43). Pictures and inscriptions have been discovered that show this was really Egyptian custom.

Very old records tell of years of hunger when the Nile River failed to flood Egypt. The land was not watered, so crops could not grow.

While no written records yet found mention Joseph, a letter has been found showing that at least one other foreigner (by the name of Dudu, or David) held a position like Joseph's in Egypt.

Scholars do not agree about the date Joseph became ruler in Egypt. But it was probably about 1885 B.C. All scholars do agree that every detail of Joseph's story fits what people have learned about Egyptian customs those many centuries before Christ.

Why did God want Israel in Egypt?

When the time of hunger Joseph predicted happened, Joseph's brothers came to Egypt to buy food. On their second trip Joseph told them who he was!

Joseph forgave his terrified brothers and moved the whole family to Egypt. Pharaoh let them live in a rich farm area called Goshen (see map). The children of Israel would stay in Egypt for 400 years!

Why did God lead the Israelites to a land where they would become slaves? To protect them! Many wars were fought in Canaan during the years Israel was in Egypt. In Egypt the 70 people who settled there were safe. They grew to some three million men, women and children! When God finally brought the Israelites back to their land, there were enough of them to become a nation.

To Think about and Do

1. Many stories in Genesis 25-50 are about families. Read three, and answer these questions. Is the family happy? What might each person do to make the family happier? How can I make my family happier?

2. Read about Jacob and Esau (Genesis 27), Joseph and his brothers (Genesis 37) and Joseph forgiving his brothers (Genesis 45).

3. Many books have pictures and stories about ancient Egypt. Find some books on Egypt in a library. What interests you most about Egypt?

4. Play "good news, bad news." Pick a story in Genesis 25-50 and retell it as "good news, bad news." (For example: "Good news, Joseph, you found your brothers! Bad news, they want to kill you. Good news, Joseph, they decided not to kill you. Bad news, they're going to sell you as a slave!") How do the stories you retell end? With good news or bad news? Or you might want to make a cassette recording of a "good news, bad news" news broadcast from ancient Egypt.

5. Joseph kept on doing good even when others were unfair to him. When are others unfair to you? Make a chart showing unfair things done to you and then show how you will act to be like Joseph.

Freedom from slavery

Safe inside the powerful country of Egypt, the Israelites multiplied. But a Pharaoh who did not remember Joseph made them slaves! Then, about 400 years after the family had entered Egypt, God chose Moses to free his people and lead them back to the land he had promised Abraham.

The good news

- God cared about the suffering of his people in Egypt. He cares when we suffer, too.
- God kept his promises to Moses and the Israelites and freed them from slavery. God keeps his promises to us, too.
- Seeing God's power helped the Israelites and the Egyptians realize that God is real.

Who made Israel slaves?

About a hundred and fifty years after Joseph brought his father and brothers to Egypt, a people called the Hyksos (*Húk sos*) began to rule in Egypt (about 1730 B.C.). These

But why make Israel slaves? There were probably more Israelites than Hyksos in Egypt! The Egyptians may have made the Israelites slaves because they were afraid. Israel might help the Hyksos foreigners and fight against the Egyptians.

Why put straw in bricks?
Exodus 5

For years people wondered why the Egyptians used straw in making bricks. Later chemists explained. There are chemicals in the chopped straw that was mixed with river mud and sand. They helped the bricks dry more quickly and made them stronger.

This illustration of a panel from Thebes shows the workers making bricks.

people came from the same part of the world as the Israelites.

Later the native Egyptians were able to drive the Hyksos foreigners out of Egypt (by 1570 B.C.).

The "new king, who did not know who Joseph was" (Exodus 1:8) may have been Ahmose (1584-1560). He finally drove out the Hyksos.

Why did God deliver Israel?

God explained to Moses why he wanted to help Israel. God said "I have seen the troubles my people have suffered in Egypt...and I am concerned about their pain" (Exodus 3:7). God knows when we have troubles, too, and cares about our pain.

God also explained he was going to bring

The Israelites made bricks by hand, using chopped straw mixed with river mud and sand.

the Israelites to the land he had promised Abraham (Exodus 3:8). God always keeps his promises.

What is God's name?

Exodus 3

God is called many things in the Bible. He is the Holy One, the Almighty, the God of Abraham, the Lord God. These and other words describe God, but they are not his name. It's like saying someone is a schoolteacher and church elder. The words describe him but don't name him.

God told Moses that his name is I AM. The Hebrew word was probably pronounced *Yahweh*. The Jewish people viewed this word as so holy they usually just said "the Name." What does Yahweh mean? Most Bible scholars agree that it means "The One Who Is always Present."

Is the name Yahweh in our Bible? Yes. In some Bibles the English word LORD is written in the Old Testament in capital letters. The Hebrew word it translates is Yahweh!

When God told Moses his name, God said "this will always be my name" (Exodus 3:15). This is the name God wants us to remember.

Why? Because God wants us to know that he is present with you and me, too. We are never alone because God is always present with us.

God, or the gods of Egypt?

People everywhere have worshiped gods. But are the gods people worship real? Could the gods of Egypt protect the Egyptians?

When Moses went to Pharaoh, the proud king of Egypt laughed at him. "Who is the LORD?" Pharaoh joked. He did not believe the God of slaves could hurt him.

God sent plagues that the Egyptian gods could not prevent. Each plague was worse than the one before. With the last one all the firstborn children in every Egyptian family died the same

MEET MOSES

If Moses were interviewed on TV today, here is what he might say about his life. Each Bible reference about Moses is one that you can look up and read.

TV: Moses, tell us about some important events in your life.

Moses: Well, I was found by a princess when I was a baby. Then I was raised to be an Egyptian prince (Exodus 2:1-10). When I was forty, I planned to rescue my people from slavery. But I had to flee when I killed an Egyptian who was beating an Israelite (Exodus 2:11-25).

I was eighty, and just an ordinary shepherd, when God spoke to me from a burning bush (Exodus 3:1-6). He told me to go to Egypt and deliver Israel.

TV: You must have been excited! Your old dreams were coming true.

Moses: No, I was afraid and worried. I even argued with God. But finally I went back to Egypt (Exodus 3:11-4:17).

TV: You were successful, though. You did lead the Israelites out of Egypt.

Moses: It was really God's work. At first Pharaoh wouldn't let us go. So God brought terrible plagues. These were to convince the Egyptians that our God is real and to make Pharaoh let us go (Exodus 7-11).

TV: Pharaoh must have been glad to get rid of you after that!

Moses: No, when we left Pharaoh sent an army to make us come back and be slaves again. But God opened up the sea for us to pass through. When the Egyptian army tried to follow, the waters flooded back and every soldier was killed (Exodus 14).

TV: And then you marched right to the promised land?

Moses: No, then my troubles began! You see, the Israelites didn't know how to trust God or obey him. They grumbled and complained. Why, sometimes they were even ready to kill me and go back to Egypt to be slaves again (Exodus 17:1-7)!

So God led us to Mount Sinai and gave us his law (Exodus 19). The Law tells us what is good and right. It shows us how to love God and other people.

TV: Was everything all right after God gave the Israelites his law?

Moses: No, I'm afraid not. They kept on rebelling, even though God had to punish them when they broke his law (Numbers 11). God led us right to the edge of the promised land. But the Israelites were afraid and wouldn't obey when God said to go up and conquer the land (Numbers 14).

TV: So what happened?

Moses: God led us out into the desert. He fed us and took care of us for 40 years in all. This was until all the adults who refused to trust him had died.

TV: All of them!

Moses: All but three of us—myself, Joshua and Caleb. We were adults who wanted to obey God when he told us to conquer the promised land.

TV: What happened then?

Moses: Well, all the children who grew up during those years did trust God and obey him. Joshua led this new generation to victory and captured the land God promised to us.

TV: What about you?

Moses: I'm afraid I had disobeyed God, too (Numbers 20:1-13). God let me see the land, but I couldn't enter it.

TV: Moses, your 120-year long life was exciting. Thanks for being with us.

Moses: Thank you, too. And if you want to read some adventures I haven't mentioned, here are five really exciting stories you can read in the Bible. Look them up in Exodus 32; Exodus 33; Numbers 12; Numbers 16; Numbers 21.

PTAH

SETH

OSIRIS

ISIS

HORUS

HATHOR

night! Finally Pharaoh realized that Egypt's gods were not real and that our God is. Only then would Pharaoh let Israel go.

The Bible gives three reasons God had for sending the terrible plagues that struck Egypt. (1) Israel would always remember how powerful their God is, and what God did to rescue them from slavery (Exodus 6:7). (2) Pharaoh and the

Locusts can eat and destroy plant life.

Egyptians would learn that the LORD is the only real God (Exodus 7:5). And (3) the false gods of Egypt were powerless, unable to help the Egyptians (Exodus 12:12).

Did God make Pharaoh stubborn?

Sometimes the Bible says that Pharaoh "became stubborn" and refused to obey God (Exodus 8:15; 8:32). At other times the Bible says that God is the one who "made Pharaoh stubborn" (Exodus 7:3; 9:12). Did God really make Pharaoh unwilling to obey him? Would it be fair then to punish Pharaoh and Egypt for

doing something God made them do?

This has bothered many people. But the question should be *what* did God do that caused Pharaoh not to obey? Really, all God did was show Pharaoh more and more of his power. The more Pharaoh learned about God, the more he refused to obey.

Were the ten plagues miracles?

Things like the plagues that struck Egypt had also happened at other times. There had been too many frogs (the second) and lice (the third). Cattle had gotten sick before (the fourth), and hail storms had killed a few animals (the seventh). Great clouds of grasshopper-like locusts had eaten Egypt's crops (the ninth). These were disasters when they happened but not really miracles.

If these were natural disasters, how could they be miracles?

What is a *miracle*, anyway? In the Old Testament a miracle is a special sign from God, something difficult or wonderful that God himself does to accomplish his purpose. We know the plagues on Egypt were miracles because (1) each plague was announced ahead of time, (2) each plague came and went at Moses' command, (3) each plague was much worse than usual and (4) most of the plagues struck the Egyptians but did not strike the places where the Israelite slaves lived.

Even the Egyptians were finally convinced that the plagues were really miracles, caused by the one true God.

When did the exodus happen?

When Pharaoh finally surrendered to God and released his slaves, the Israelites went out

44

The many gods of Egypt

MIN

ANUBIS

MAAT

THOTH

AMUN-RE

of Egypt. This is called "the exodus," because "exodus" means "going out."

Bible students do not agree just when the people of Israel went out of Egypt and started back to Canaan, the promised land. Some think it happened about 1300 years before Christ. For many reasons, most think it happened about 1450 years before Jesus was born.

What is Passover?

Exodus 12

Passover is the first and most important of the special religious holidays God set apart for Israel. On the night of the tenth plague on Egypt, each Israelite family killed a lamb. They put its blood on their doorframes. Inside, they ate the roasted lamb. The Israelites did this fully dressed and ready to leave Egypt. The blood on the doorframes protected the Israelites when God killed the Egyptians' firstborn children. God "passed over" the Israelites' homes!

The Israelites were told to have a Passover supper every year on the 14th day of the Hebrew month of Abib (which falls in our March or April). The Jewish people still keep Passover every year. This is to honor God who saved their ancestors from slavery in Egypt.

Joseph's family settled in the area of Goshen.

The Red Sea is about 1,450 miles long and up to 225 miles wide.
It is between northeast Africa and the Arabian Peninsula.

Dates from Abraham through Joshua

- Abraham born about 2166 B.C.
  - enters Canaan about 2091 B.C.
- Isaac born • about 2066 B.C.
- Jacob born • about 2006 B.C.
- Joseph born • about 1915 B.C.
- sold to Egypt • about 1898 B.C.
- made ruler • about 1885 B.C.
- moved family to Egypt • about 1859 B.C.
- Hyksos rule • 1730 B.C.
- Israelites made slaves by Ahmose • about 1570 B.C.
- Moses born / Thutmose I • about 1526 B.C.
- Moses moved to Midian / Thutmose III • about 1486 B.C.
- The Exodus / Amenhotep II • about 1446 B.C.
- Conquest of Canaan about 1390 B.C.•

| 2200 | 2100 | 2000 | 1900 | 1800 | 1700 | 1600 | 1500 | 1400 | 1300 |

How many people left Egypt?

The Bible says there were about 600,000 men, with women and children (Exodus 12:37). All together there were probably about 2,500,000 Israelites for Moses to lead out of Egypt!

Were the Israelites poor?

You would think that slaves were poor, wouldn't you? They had been. But Moses told the Israelites to ask the Egyptians for gold, silver and clothing when they left that country. God made the Egyptians so frightened and glad to be rid of the Israelites that they gave their former slaves whatever they asked for (Exodus 12:35-36). God's people were actually rich when they left Egypt!

What sea opened for Israel?

English Bibles call it the "Red Sea." The Hebrew words are *yam suph*, which mean "Sea of Reeds" (Exodus 13:18). Many believe the Sea of Reeds was a deep ancient lake north of the Bitter Lakes (see map, Desert Wanderings, page 55).

Opening the waters surely was a wonderful miracle. The Israelites passed through "on dry land, with a wall of water on both sides" (Exodus 14:22). When the Egyptians followed, the waters flowed back over the army. Every soldier Pharaoh had sent to recapture his Israelite slaves was drowned.

To Think about and Do

1. Pretend you're an Israelite slave in Egypt. How did you feel about God when you were a slave? Then you see God's plagues strike your Egyptian masters (you can read about them in Exodus 7-11). Now what do you think and feel about God? Draw pictures showing how big or great you thought God was before and after.

2. Read one or more of the stories about Moses mentioned in his TV interview. Which do you like best? Why?

3. Read Psalm 23. How does knowing that the name of the LORD means "The One Who Is always Present" make this psalm even more special?

4. Read about the Passover service in Exodus 12:24-28. Or you can write to the American Board of Missions to the Jews, P.O. Box 2000, Orangeburg, New York 10962 (phone 914-359-8535), and get a paper explaining how the whole ceremony is conducted today.

5. List what you can learn about God from Exodus 1-15. Then make up a praise song like the song of Moses (Exodus 15).

Law and the Holy Tent

Moses led the freed Israelites to Mount Sinai. There God gave the people his law to teach them how to live. The law also taught the Israelites how to worship God.

God gave Moses ten commandments for the Israelites to follow. The first four told them how to live close to God. The last six told them how to live with other people.

The good news

▪ God's law reveals his goodness and teaches us how to be good, too.

▪ God does care how we live. He will reward us for doing good and punish people who do wrong.

Did Israel need God's law?
Exodus 15:22–18

Laws tell us what is right and what is wrong. They tell us how to behave to get along with other people. God had rescued the Israelites from Egypt. But the way the Israelites were acting showed they did not understand how to get along with God! Instead of being thankful and trusting the Lord, they complained and grumbled. To see why Israel needed the law read these stories:

(1) Water in the desert (Exodus 15:22-27).
(2) Food in the desert (Exodus 16:1-36).
(3) Water from a rock (Exodus 17:1-7).

What was manna?
Exodus 16

There were no food supplies in the desert. What would the Israelites eat? God had the answer: manna. Flakes of this bread-like food appeared on the ground each morning for the forty years that the children of Israel traveled in the desert.

Manna had to be eaten the day it was gathered. It spoiled if it was kept overnight. But on the Sabbath day (Saturday) it did not rain manna. The Sabbath was God's day of rest. No Israelite was to work on the Sabbath. So what did the Israelites eat on the Sabbath? Manna!

One possible location of Mount Sinai is in northeast Egypt between the Gulf of Suez, the Gulf of Aqaba and the Strait of Tiran. This mountain is over 8,500 feet high. God gave Moses the Ten Commandments on Mount Sinai.

Where is Mount Sinai?

Exodus 19

After the Israelites left Egypt, Moses led them through a dry desert to Mount Sinai. The map on page 55 shows the path the Israelites took to Mount Sinai, also called Mount Horeb.

Mount Sinai is important because it is the place where God gave Moses the Ten Commandments and his law.

The Israelites and God made an agreement at Mount Sinai. The Israelites promised to obey God's law. And God promised that he would bless his people when they obeyed. But God also warned Israel. When the people disobeyed the law, God promised to punish them.

The Israelites camped at Mount Sinai for almost a year. The law was written there, and a special place for worship was built. Moses' brother Aaron and his sons were given to the Lord's service there as priests to lead in Israel's worship.

What are the Ten Commandments?

Exodus 20

Everyone knows about the Ten Commandments. But not everyone knows what they mean. The first four commandments told Israel how to live close to God. The next six told them how to live with other people. Here are the commandments and what each means.

The manna gathered Friday did not spoil at night! This miraculous food showed the Israelites every day that God was with them and was taking care of them.

How to treat God	
1. Put no gods before me.	Trust God only.
2. Have no idols.	Worship God only.
3. Do not take God's name in vain.	Use God's name in ways that honor him.
4. Keep the Sabbath holy.	Rest and think about God.

How to treat people	
5. Honor father, mother.	Respect and obey parents.
6. Do not murder.	Protect human life.
7. Do not commit adultery.	Be true to your husband or wife.
8. Do not steal.	Don't take what belongs to others.
9. Do not give false testimony.	Don't lie about others.
10. Do not covet.	Be satisfied with what you have.

Jesus once said that the whole law could be put in two commands. "Love the Lord your God. You must love him with all your heart, all your soul, and all your mind." And, "Love your neighbor as you love yourself." If we love others, we will do nothing that might hurt them (see Matthew 22:34-39).

Why were there so many laws?

God gave Israel many rules for living, not just the Ten Commandments. Why are there so many laws in the Old Testament?

Many of the laws are "case laws." They are examples, or cases, that show how to put the Ten Commandments into practice. Here are some of the "case laws" that helped explain to Israel how to obey the Ten Commandments. Which commandment do you think each "case" here helps to explain?

"Do not lie to each other.

You must not make a false promise using my name. If you do that, you will show that you don't respect your God. I am the Lord.

You must not cheat your neighbor. You must not rob him.

You must not keep a hired worker's salary all night until morning.

You must not curse a deaf man. And you must not put something in front of a blind person to make him fall. But you must respect your God. I am the Lord.

Be fair in your judging. You must not show special favor to poor people or great people. You must be fair when you judge your neighbor.

You must not spread false stories against other people.

You must not do anything that would put your neighbor's life in danger. I am the Lord.

You must not hate your brother in your heart.

If your neighbor does something wrong, tell him about it. If you do not, you will be partly to blame.

Forget the wrong things people do to you. You must not try to get even. Love your neighbor as you love yourself. I am the Lord."

Leviticus 19:11-18

What else is in God's law?

Exodus 21-23

Old Testament law contains much more than the Ten Commandments. The Israelites were soon to become a nation. God's law covered many of the same things our country's laws

In Bible times law codes, such as the Ur Nammu Law Code shown above, were often written on stone or clay tablets.

cover. But God's law also contains many religious rules.

Here are some difficult legal questions covered in God's Old Testament law. How would you answer these questions? You can discover how God's law answers each question by looking up the verse with it.

What should be done if someone kills a person on purpose (Exodus 21:12-14)?

What should be done if someone injures another person in a fight (Exodus 21:19)?

What should be done if a man steals a bull and sells it (Exodus 22:1)?

What should be done if a man borrows an animal and the animal is killed while he has it (Exodus 22:14,15)?

How much should a man charge a poor person who wants to borrow money (Exodus 22:25)?

Should a person take the side of a poor man in court (Exodus 23:3)?

There are many other laws in the Old Testament. Most are recorded in the books of Leviticus and Deuteronomy.

Where did Israelites worship?

God gave Moses careful instructions for building a Holy Tent called a Tabernacle. This special worship tent could be carried wherever the Israelites traveled. The tent was 45 feet long, 15 feet wide and 15 feet high. Surrounding it was a wall 150 feet long on two sides and 75 feet on the others.

God also told Moses just what to put outside and inside the tent. Each item was important, for the Tabernacle is also called the Meeting Tent. It was the place where God's Old Testament people came to meet with the Lord.

What was in the Holy Tent?

Exodus 25-30; 35-40

Each object associated with the Holy Tent had spiritual meaning. The New Testament says each was like a shadow, showing us truths we can understand now that Jesus has come. What were some of the objects, and what do they mean?

▪ Just inside the doorway was an altar. Every day sheep and other animals were killed and burned on the altar as *sacrifices*. This teaches us that a blood sacrifice is required by anyone who comes to God. Jesus died on Calvary to be our sacrifice (Hebrews 9:28; 10:11-18).

▪ Inside the Most Holy Place there was a wooden box or ark, covered with gold, called the Box of the Agreement. Two gold creatures with wings spread their wings over its top. Once a

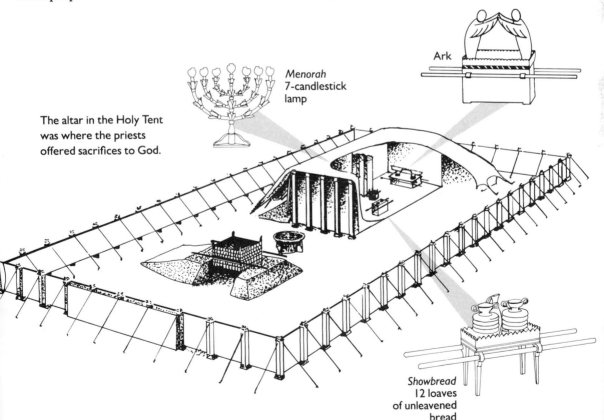

Menorah
7-candlestick
lamp

Ark

The altar in the Holy Tent was where the priests offered sacrifices to God.

Showbread
12 loaves
of unleavened
bread

• There was only one doorway through the outer wall that surrounded the Holy Tent. This part of the plan may show us that there is only one way to God, as Jesus said (John 14:6). year the high priest of Israel carried the blood of a sacrifice into the Most Holy Place. He sprinkled the blood on the top of the Holy Box. God promised he would forgive the sins of his people when the high priest brought this blood to him (Leviticus 16). The blood of the sacrifice was a picture of the blood Jesus would shed on Calvary to pay for human sins.

• There were other objects in the Holy Tent. Each one has spiritual meaning. That is why such careful directions are given for making the Holy Tent and its furnishings.

• The Holy Tent was divided into two rooms. The first room was 30 feet long, and the second was 15 feet long. The second room was called the Most Holy Place because God's presence was there in a special way.

What did priests do?

The family of Aaron, Moses' brother, was given for service by God as priests for Israel.

Only the priests could offer sacrifices to God. The priests were also to teach God's law to the Israelites (Deuteronomy 33:8-10). The priests checked to make sure people were free of disease (Leviticus 13-15). And they served as judges in difficult cases (Deuteronomy 17:8-9).

Today when Christians pray for others, or teach them about God, we are being priests to them. But we do not offer animal sacrifices as the Old Testament priests did. When Jesus died for us, his sacrifice of himself won us complete forgiveness for our sins. We will never need another sacrifice besides the one sacrifice of Jesus.

What is in Leviticus?

The book of Leviticus is a book of laws, not a book of stories. Here is what you can find in Leviticus.

Rules for worship	Chapters 11-15
The Day of Cleansing	Chapters 16-17
Rules for holy living	Chapters 18-22
Rules for special holidays	Chapters 23-25
More rules and promises	Chapters 26-27

To Think about and Do

1. What did God do at Mount Sinai to show the Israelites his law was very important? Read Exodus 19, and make a list.

2. The Israelites promised to obey God's law (Exodus 24:3). But did having the law make Israel good? Read about the Gold Calf (Exodus 32:1 – 33:6) and try to answer this question.

3. What do the Ten Commandments tell you about the kind of person God is? (Hint: What kind of person would tell people "do not murder" and "do not steal"?)

4. Make a diarama of the Holy Tent. Trace and color pictures of the Holy Tent furniture. Stand the pictures up inside a shoebox where the furniture would have stood in the Holy Tent. Use cloth to make the inside curtain and the outside tent cover.

5. Often the way church buildings are built has special meaning, too. Find out what things about your church building and its furnishings have special meaning.

Living in the wilderness

God led the Israelites away from Sinai to the land of Canaan. This was the land he had promised to give Abraham's family. But the Israelites had made a promise, too. They promised to keep God's law. The first generation did not obey the Lord and was punished. The next generation did obey and entered the promised land.

The good news

▪ God provided food and water for his people in the wilderness. God gives us what we need, too.

▪ No enemies were able to curse Israel or defeat God's people when they obeyed the Lord.

▪ People who trust and love God obey him and are blessed.

Days of rebellion
Numbers

God's fiery cloud
Numbers 9

When Israel set up the Meeting Tent (the Tabernacle), a pillar of cloud hovered over it. When God wanted the Israelites to move, the cloud lifted into the air to lead them. If the cloud stayed over the Holy Tent, the Israelites did not move. So God showed Israel the path they should travel. And the pillar of cloud reminded the people daily that God was there, with them.

What was Canaan like?
Numbers 13

Moses sent some men out to explore Canaan. These men discovered Canaan was a beautiful land, with fertile fields and rich crops.

People once doubted the Bible's description of Canaan, because today the land is dry and dusty, without trees or rich crops. What has happened to the land? Over hundreds of years of terrible wars, the ancient trees have been cut down. This let the rich soil wash away. People who study old things tell us the land once was very rich.

The grapes and sycamore trees of Canaan.

53

The land of Israel today is becoming rich and beautiful again.

Today in Israel the land is becoming rich and beautiful again. The modern Israelis are watering the land. Trees and rich crops are growing again in the promised land.

How did Israel rebel?
Numbers 11-14

Even though the pillar of cloud was there to remind Israel of God, this first generation rebelled (turned against) against him.

When the people left Sinai they complained again (Numbers 11). When God gave his law at Sinai, he had warned Israel that he would punish disobedience. So when the people complained, God sent fire and sickness (Numbers 11).

Even Moses' brother Aaron and sister Miriam turned against God (Numbers 12). When they did this, Miriam was given a harmful skin disease. Aaron and Miriam realized they had sinned. They begged Moses to pray to God for her. Miriam had to wait outside the camp for seven days, and then God healed her.

Then the Israelites did a worse thing. Israel came to the border of Canaan. God told the people to go up and fight for the land. But the people refused (Numbers 14). This made God very angry. So God led them into the wilderness. He made Israel wait in the desert for 40 years until all those adults died and a new nation of adults had grown up.

God is holy. He is to be respected, and his word is to be obeyed.

Where did Israel wander?
Numbers 15-19

Numbers 33 lists the places Israel camped after leaving Egypt. We do not know today where many of these places are. The map on page 55 shows the places we have identified.

The Israelites had refused to fight for Canaan as God commanded. So they spent the next 40 years either at Kadesh or traveling in the wilderness of Paran. They wandered back and forth between Paran and Ezion-geber, a distance of only 85 miles.

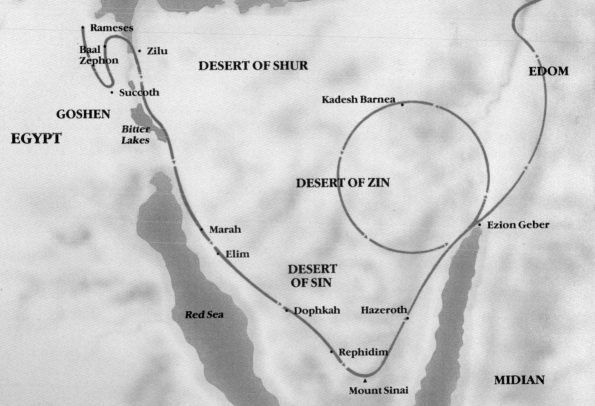

THE DESERT WANDERINGS

Jordan River

Mediterranean Sea

Jericho

Heshbon

Dead Sea

Rameses

Baal Zephon

Zilu

DESERT OF SHUR

EDOM

Succoth

GOSHEN

EGYPT

Bitter Lakes

Kadesh Barnea

DESERT OF ZIN

Marah

Elim

Ezion Geber

DESERT OF SIN

Red Sea

Dophkah

Hazeroth

Rephidim

MIDIAN

Mount Sinai

Possible route of the desert wanderings.

During this time everyone who was over 20 years old when the people disobeyed God died, except Joshua and Caleb. They were the two men who trusted God. They wanted to attack Canaan as God told his people to do.

A count was taken at the end of that time. There were 601,730 fighting men in Israel in place of the 603,550 men who would not fight 40 years earlier! The group who disobeyed God had died, and their children had grown up. They were ready to obey the Lord!

Do donkeys talk?
Numbers 22

Balak was king of the Moabites. He was afraid of Israel. So he sent for Balaam, a man believed to have magical powers. God told Balaam not to go to Balak. But Balaam wanted the money Balak promised him. Finally God allowed Balaam to go, but on the way his donkey stopped. Even when Balaam beat the donkey, she would not move.

Then God made the donkey speak, and let Balaam see an angel standing there ready to kill him. Balaam realized he had sinned and offered to go back home. The angel let Balaam go on, but warned him to speak only what God would tell him.

What is a curse?
Numbers 23, 24

Balak asked Balaam to curse Israel. What did he really want? In those days almost everyone thought some people could do magic. A person with magical powers could curse someone, and the cursed person would no longer be strong or healthy. Balak wanted Balaam to do magic and weaken Israel's army.

But each time Balaam tried to curse Israel, God told Balaam to bless them instead. Balaam had to tell Balak "No magic works against Israel" (Numbers 23:23). God is with his people today, too. There is no evil magic to work against us, either.

Does *curse* always mean magic in the Bible? No. The Bible talks about God cursing someone or something. But *curse* means punishments that God has announced.

Donkeys were important animals in the Bible. Jesus even made his entry into Jerusalem as king of kings riding on a donkey.

What are Balaam's sins?

The New Testament warns against three sins that Balaam's story illustrates.

• The "way of Balaam" (2 Peter 2:15) is using religion to make money.

• The "error of Balaam" (Jude 11) is to want money so badly that a person is willing to disobey God.

• The "teaching of Balaam" (Revelation 2:14) is to cause people to sin.

When Balaam could not curse Israel, he told Balak to try to get the Israelites to sin (Numbers 31:16). He knew God is holy. And he hoped God would desert the Israelites if they sinned. God punished the Israelites who did sin (Numbers 25). But God did not leave his people. God will punish us if we sin. But God will not leave those who love and trust him.

What happened to Balaam? When the Israelite army defeated the Midianites, Balaam was killed (Joshua 13:22).

What is in Deuteronomy?

Deuteronomy means "second law." The book has three sermons given by Moses at Kadesh Barnea to the generation about to enter Canaan. Here are his three sermons.

• Remember what God has done for us (Deuteronomy 1:1–4:43).

• Understand the law we live by (Deuteronomy 4:44–27:28).

• Obedience is very important (Deuteronomy 28:1-30).

These sermons were given to the new generation who "continued to follow the Lord your God" and so were "still alive today" (Deuteronomy 4:4). How different these people were from the rebellious adults who left Egypt.

How can we have success?
Deuteronomy 4:39-40

Moses told God's people how to be successful in life. His advice is worth memorizing, for it is the key to our success, too. Like the Israelites, we can "know and believe today that the Lord is God. He is God in heaven above and on the earth below. Obey his laws and commands, . . . so it will go well for you and your children."

Was this the first law?

Once some people thought Moses could not have given Israel the law. They thought laws were invented after Moses' time. Today people who study old things know that many ancient people had law codes. The best known is the Code of Hammurabi (*Ham u ráb i*), from 1700 B.C. The Code of Lipit-Ishtar (1875 B.C.) and the Code of Ur-Nammu (2050 B.C.) are even earlier! The law God gave Israel through Moses covers many of the same things included in earlier codes. But only God's people are called to keep a law because God has chosen them to be good and holy.

How did God show his love?
Deuteronomy 6-8

God's law is a law of love. God gave it because he loved the Israelites and wanted the best for them. How else did God show he loved Israel? He made promises to Abraham. He kept the promises by freeing the Israelites from slavery. He fed the Israelites in the wilderness, and met all their needs. Their sandals and clothes did not even wear out in 40 years! God would keep on showing his love. He forced nations stronger than Israel out of Canaan.

Could Israel love God?
Deuteronomy 9-11

Israel could show love for God by praising him for their victories. Moses told the new generation how to love God in these words. "Now, Israel, here is what the Lord wants you to do: Respect the Lord your God; do what he has told you to do; love him; serve the Lord your God with all your heart and soul; and obey the Lord's commands and laws. I am giving them to you today for your own good" (Deuteronomy 10:12-13).

Should we fear God?

People who *fear* God respect him so much that they choose to obey him and live a good life. Fearing God does not mean to obey just because we're afraid of being punished. Fearing God means believing that God is real and that he loves us. We love God, too. And we want to do what is right to show him our love.

Did Moses tell the future?
Deuteronomy 28

Moses told the people of Israel the good things that would happen if they obeyed God. He also warned them of punishments if they disobeyed God.

Obedience would bring rich crops and herds. The people would be healthy and able to defeat their enemies. The nation would be rich and important.

Disobedience would bring curses (punishments). Crops would fail, and animals would become weak. The people would suffer with diseases and be defeated by their enemies. The rains would not come, and the people would become poorer. Finally, enemy armies would come and take the Israelites from the promised land.

Moses' words came true! The rest of the Bible tells about Israel. It shows that when the people of Israel feared and obeyed God, they were blessed. But when the people disobeyed, all the terrible things Moses warned them about really did happen.

To Think about and Do

1. Trace Israel's journey on the map (page 55), and find out:
   - Where did Israel cross the Red Sea?
   - Where did God give Israel his law?
   - Where did Israel turn against God when he told them to go into Canaan?
   - Where did the people who left Egypt die?
   - Where were the Deuteronomy sermons given?

2. What story answers each of the following questions? Match the Bible passage to the story, and answer the questions.

   Passages
   Numbers 12 • Numbers 14 • Numbers 16 • Numbers 17 • Numbers 20 • Numbers 23 Numbers 27 • Deuteronomy 21 • Deuteronomy 26

   Questions
   Why give to the Lord? • How did Moses sin? • Is it right to be jealous? • Should women own land? • What people who turned against God were killed in a "new way"? • What happened to the two spies who trusted God? • What should be done about an unsolved murder? • How did Israel know Aaron was God's choice to be high priest? • Why couldn't Balaam curse Israel?

3. What verses did Jesus quote from Deuteronomy? Read Luke 4:1-12, and then find the verses in Deuteronomy.

4. Read Deuteronomy 28, and list the curses for disobedience. Then check the *Bible History Highway* (pages 13-18). When did Israel obey God? When did Israel disobey?

5. Why do you think the people turned against God when he said to go up and take the promised land? Read Numbers 14. Then read Hebrews 3:7-18. Tell someone why Israel disobeyed God. Tell what we can learn from their example.

Victory

Moses was dead. The new generation of Israelites under Joshua crossed the Jordan River. They entered the land God had promised to Abraham. There were years of fighting ahead. But God was with Israel, and his presence meant sure victory!

The good news

- God kept his promise to fight for the Israelites when they obeyed him.

- God gave the obedient generation homes and lands in the territory he had promised to Abraham's children.

- God blesses those who promise to worship and obey him.

Who was Joshua?

Joshua 1

Joshua was Israel's general who led them in all their battles (Exodus 17:10). Many believe Joshua was an officer in Pharaoh's army before Moses came to lead the Israelites to freedom. People who study old things have found Egyptian army records that list officers with Israelite-sounding names.

The trumpets that the people used were made from rams' horns.

Joshua was also a man of great faith. Joshua was one of the spies Moses sent into the promised land. The other spies were afraid of the power of the people of Canaan. But Joshua and Caleb urged the Israelites to obey God. They were sure God was with Israel. And they were willing to fight the powerful enemy forces.

When Moses died, God chose Joshua to lead his people. God had only one thing to say to Joshua as he became leader. "Be strong and brave. Be sure to obey all the teachings" (Joshua 1:7). Joshua was courageous and did obey the Lord. It was Joshua who led Israel to victory in Canaan.

What are memorials?
Joshua 4

The Israelites had to cross the Jordan River to enter Canaan. God made the river stop flowing, and the people marched over on dry ground! When the people had crossed, Joshua told twelve men to take large rocks from the river bed and pile them up on the shore. They were to be a *memorial*.

In Israel a memorial was something that served as a symbol of how God helped his people. Joshua told the Israelites that one day their children would see the pile of rocks and say, "What do these rocks mean?" (Joshua 4:6). Then

their parents would tell how God made the Jordan River stop flowing so Israel could enter the promised land.

When the Israelites saw what God did, they were sure that the Lord was with Joshua. And they followed him gladly.

What was Jericho like?
Joshua 6

The Israelites crossed the Jordan River near the city of Jericho. This strong, walled city guarded the mountain passes that led into Canaan. The people of Israel would have to take Jericho before they could go up into the promised land (see map on page 55).

The site of Jericho was settled about 8000 B.C. In Joshua's time Jericho was a walled city enclosing about eight acres of land.

The walls of Jericho were very strong. There was a base 11 feet high. Then the walls sloped upward at a sharp angle for 35 feet. Then the main wall rose up even higher! Protected by their great wall, the people of Jericho felt safe. No enemy army could attack their walls and hope to win.

We know how God planned for Israel to take Jericho. The Israelites marched silently around the city for seven days. Then they blew their trumpets and gave a great shout. And the massive walls of Jericho simply fell down!

A *memorial* is often set up to help people remember an event or person. In the Bible a memorial was often a pile of stones or a large stone set up on its end.

Jericho was an ancient city of Palestine in the Jordan Valley north of the Dead Sea. Its ruins show it to be possibly the oldest known settlement in the world today.

Can we see Jericho's walls today?

People who study old things have dug up the high mound of earth where the old city of Jericho stood. Today you can go to Jericho. You can see some great blocks of stone. They may have been in the city's walls.

Achan and his family

Joshua 7

God told the Israelites to destroy everything in Jericho but to keep the silver and gold for the Lord's house. One soldier, Achan, kept some of the silver and gold for himself.

Joshua sent soldiers to take the nearby town of Ai. The Israelites were defeated, and 36 Israelite soldiers were killed! Joshua prayed, and God explained that the Israelites had disobeyed his command.

God showed Joshua who had sinned. Achan had buried the stolen wealth in his tent. His whole family would have known about it. Achan's disobedience caused the disastrous defeat and the death of 36 Israelites at Ai. So Achan and his family were put to death.

Then Joshua attacked Ai again and destroyed the enemy completely.

The city of Jericho was known as a city of palm trees.

What did God teach Israel?

Joshua 6, 7

God had told the Israelites to do what must have seemed a foolish thing. He just told them to march around Jericho for six days. On the seventh day they were to shout. Joshua and the Israelites obeyed God, and God himself destroyed Jericho's walls. Obedience to God had brought victory to Israel.

At Ai Israel had been defeated because one soldier had disobeyed God's command.

What an important lesson for the Israelites, and for us today. Obedience brings victory. Disobedience brings defeat.

Should Israel have destroyed everyone?

God ordered Joshua to have every person in the Canaanite cities killed—even the women and children (Joshua 6:21; 9:24). Many have thought this was cruel. Why would a God who loves people have given such a command? The Bible and a study of old things give us answers.

1) Death was a punishment for sin. God told Abraham he would not drive the Amorite and Canaanite people out of their land for 400 years. This was because "they are not yet evil enough to punish" (Genesis 15:16). People who study old things have found out much about this people's evil religion and sinfulness. Some people of

Canaan even burned their own children as a sacrifice to their gods! God used the Israelites to punish these evil people for their sins.

2) Destruction was protection for God's people. God may have left the Amorites and Canaanites alive. But the Israelites would be attracted to their religion and their sins. By ordering the sinful nations completely destroyed, God was protecting the Israelites.

Israel did capture the promised land. But not all of the evil people who lived there were killed. For hundreds of years the Israelites were drawn away from God. This was by the evil religions and sinful ways of neighbors they allowed to live.

Was Joshua a good general?

Joshua 9-12

Even today military academies and the Israeli War College study Joshua's battle plans against Canaan.

A number of enemy cities joined to attack Gibeon. This was a city that had surrendered to Israel. Joshua led his army in an all night march and caught the enemy by surprise. He destroyed the enemy armies. Now Joshua controlled the central part of Canaan.

Joshua had divided his enemies in two. He then turned south and destroyed the powerful enemy cities there.

Finally Joshua turned north to fight a number of kings. They had assembled their armies to try to defeat Israel. Joshua's smaller force crushed the combined enemy armies. And they destroyed the major city of Hazor (see map, page 71).

Joshua had followed God's advice. He had been strong and very courageous to attack powerful enemies. And Joshua had been careful to obey the law of the Lord.

Some of the enemy still lived in Canaan. But their power had been broken. The Israelites could have been as courageous as Joshua. Then each tribe could drive out the people who were left in their own territory.

How powerful were Israel's enemies?

Hazor was a leading city in Canaan. It had a population of about 40,000 people. The 175 acre city was surrounded by a 50 foot wall.

Hazor and other cities used chariots in warfare. The wheels of these chariots were often equipped with great knife-blades that whirled. And they would cut down foot soldiers. Israel had no chariots when they fought the Canaanites!

Canaanite cities were well built and planned. Many buildings had paved or plastered floors, with drainage systems to remove waste.

This illustrates what the city of Hazor might have looked like.

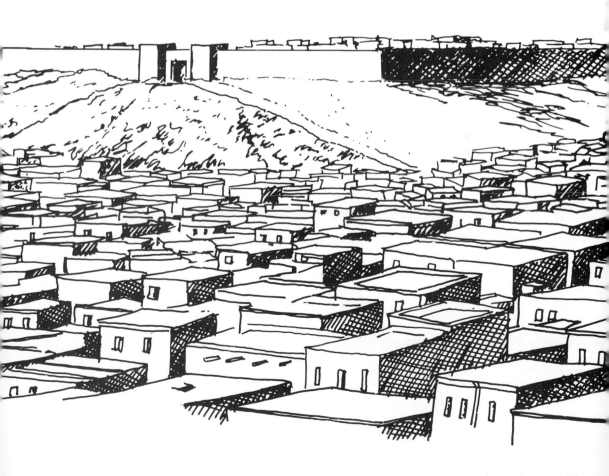

Some of the finest pottery in the world was made in Canaan. Its people were skilled metal workers. Canaanites carried on trade with many foreign countries. The land was rich, and all sorts of crops grew well.

The Canaanites were a powerful, civilized people. But their power and wealth could not help them against the Israelites and their great God.

How was the land divided?

Joshua 13-19

Joshua divided the promised land among the tribes of Israel. The map on page 71 shows the area each tribe received. Then each family was given land in the area of its own tribe.

The property given to each family in Canaan was not to be sold to anyone else. A person could sell the crops his land would grow. But the land itself was to remain in his family forever (Leviticus 25).

Israel would have to obey God and worship the Lord. Then the Israelites would be able to live in their new homes and enjoy the rich land God gave them.

The priests and Levites' land

The tribe of Levi was given for service to God. While the Israelites traveled in the wilderness, the Levites carried the Tabernacle, Israel's Meeting Tent (Numbers 3,4). When Israel settled in Canaan, the Levites were only given towns in the area of their brother tribes. The priests, who were also from the tribe of Levi, were not given land, either.

Instead, the priests and Levites were supported by gifts (tithes) given to God by the other tribes.

The priests offered sacrifices to God and taught the people God's law. What did the Levites do once Israel entered the promised land? The Levites helped the priests, took care of the Meeting Tent and later the Temple. And they were in charge of worship music (1 Chronicles 23,26; Ezra 8; Nehemiah 8).

Why serve the Lord?

Joshua 23,24

Near the end of his life, Joshua called all the Israelites together. God had been good to Israel. And the people lived in the land they had won in battle.

Now Joshua asked everyone to make a new promise to serve the Lord. Joshua reminded his people, "every good promise that the Lord your God made has come true" (Joshua 23:15).

We, too, want to serve God. We know that if we do, he will keep every promise he has made to us as well.

To Think about and Do

1. Discover the memorial in these passages—and tell what acts of God each was to help Israel remember.

Exodus 12:14; Exodus 28:12; Exodus 30:16; Joshua 4:7; Joshua 23:26,27.

2. Talk with your parents about setting up your own family memorials. How has God helped you? What might be reminders of things that God has done for you?

3. Make your own battle map. Use different colors to stand for the central, southern and northern cities that Joshua and Israel's armies defeated. Use the map on page 71 to help you.

4. How many miracles can you find in Joshua? Find at least four, and give each miracle a name.

5. How many reasons for you to serve the Lord can you find in Joshua 23 and 24? What do you think is the best reason of all?

When judges ruled

*T*he Israelites settled down in the land God promised them. But the next centuries were full of suffering. Israel was not faithful to God. As a result the Lord permitted Israel's enemies to persecute his people.

The good news

• Punishment for disobedience led Israel to return to God. We can come back to God when we do wrong, too.

• God blessed the people who returned to him.

• God gave ordinary people strength and wisdom to be leaders and help the Israelites.

What is a judge?

The judges of the Bible were not like judges in our law courts. The word translated "judge" means "ruler." Many of the Bible judges were military leaders who ruled after they led their people to victory over enemies.

Probably none of the Old Testament judges ruled over all Israel. The Israelite tribes did not become a unified nation until the time of Saul and David. Between 1350 B.C. and 1050 B.C. the twelve tribes shared a common language and the worship of God. But they had no central government. Usually each town or village ruled itself!

Why did Israel need judges?
Judges 1-3

Joshua had destroyed the strongest Canaanite cities. He gave each tribe its own area. He told the tribes to drive out the enemies that remained.

Deborah was one of the judges of Israel. She held court under the Palm of Deborah. The people went to her there to have their arguments settled.

The tribe of Judah drove out the people who lived in the hill country. But they were afraid of those on the flat plains because they had iron chariots (Judges 1:19). Other tribes could have driven out the Canaanites. But instead they made the Canaanites work for them (Judges 1:27-35).

God was angry at this disobedience. The Lord knew that the Israelites would turn away from him. He knew they would worship the false gods and goddesses of the people they let remain in Canaan.

This is just what happened! The Israelites began to marry men and women who worshiped idols. And they began to serve idols.

God punished the Israelites for their disobedience by helping their enemies defeat them. Sometimes the Israelites had to creep along hidden paths. They didn't even dare use their own roads (Judges 5:6)! Finally, when the people were suffering terribly, they returned to God. It was then God sent judges. These people led the Israelites to victory and ruled afterward. While one of the judges was living, the people he or she ruled usually remained faithful to the Lord.

This happened over and over again. The Israelites left the Lord and worshiped false gods. Then they were defeated by enemies. Finally they were driven by suffering to ask God for help. God did help his people then. He sent them the judges we read about in the Bible.

Who were Baal and Ashtoreth?

Baal (*Bal*) was the Canaanite name for "god." The Canaanites worshiped many baals. The Canaanites thought the baals owned their lands and made crops grow.

Ashtoreth (*Ásh to reth*) was the Canaanite goddess who was supposed to be the wife of Baal.

The Canaanites worshiped their gods and goddesses in groves of trees and on the tops of hills. Often the worship involved sexual sins the law of God forbids (Judges 2:17; Amos 2:7). At times the worship involved child sacrifice (Jeremiah 19:5).

How different Israel's God was from the false gods of the Canaanites! And the good life God

Baal was the most important Canaanite god.

wanted his people to live was different from the evil ways of the Canaanite religion.

No wonder God had to punish the Israelites. He had to when they turned away from him to worship the gods of Canaan.

Israel's important judges

Twelve people are named in the book of Judges. Longer stories are told about Deborah, Gideon, Jephthah, and Samson. The map and chart (pages 70,71) show how little area the Israelites held in the days of the judges. It also shows the location of enemies. Each judge probably ruled only a few of the tribes that lived near his or her own area.

Can women be leaders?
Judges 4,5

In Bible times leaders were usually men. Deborah (*Déb ō rah*) was one woman the Israelites recognized as a leader. Deborah settled arguments and gave Israel God's messages (Judges 4:5-7). Even Barak (*Bár ak*), who led Israel's troops, was willing to have Deborah lead. He knew she was close to God (Joshua 4:8-16). It is important for anyone who wants to lead God's people to be very close to the Lord.

Deborah's Song (Judges 5) is a poem. It celebrates Israel's victory over the Canaanites and their iron chariots. This poem has been called one of the most beautiful poems ever written in any language of the world.

Who won the judges' victories?
Judges 6-8

The judges are Bible heroes. But it was God who won the battles they fought. The name Gideon (*Gíd e on*) means "great warrior." But Gideon was so frightened he was hiding food when God spoke to him (Judges 6:11). This was so the Midianite enemy would not take it.

What made Gideon a hero? He was willing to obey God even when he was afraid. Gideon's family and his town worshiped Baal instead of God. But Gideon destroyed the place where idols were worshiped when God told him to.

Gideon wanted to be sure that God was with him before he fought the enemy (Judges 7:36-40). When he was sure, Gideon was willing to fight. He was willing even though God reduced his army to just 300 soldiers (Judges 7). These

300 men did not even have to fight. Gideon's soldiers sneaked up on the huge Midianite army at night. They had trumpets and hidden torches. They blew the trumpets and waved their torches at midnight. This confused the Midianites so they fought and killed each other. Then they just ran away. Other Israelites caught and killed the enemy.

Gideon ruled as a judge for 40 years. But everyone knew that God had won the great victory for his people. Gideon trusted God and obeyed him. And God fought Israel's enemies.

Did Jephthah really sacrifice his daughter?
Judges 10-12

Jephthah went to command Israel's army in a battle against the Ammonites. At that time he made a vow. A vow is a promise to God. Jephthah promised that when the victory was won, he would sacrifice to God whatever met him when he came home.

When Jephthah came home, he was met by his daughter! she was his only child. Jephthah said then that he could not break his vow (Judges 11:35). That is why the daughter asked for two months to cry with her friends about the

A threshing floor was where good grain was separated from the chaff by throwing it up in the air. Gideon was at the threshing floor when God called him.

fact that she could never marry. She did not cry about dying. But she was sad that she could never have a husband or children.

What made Samson strong?

Judges 13-16

Samson was the strongest man who ever lived. He could tear a lion apart with his bare hands (Judges 14:6). Once he killed a thousand Philistines all alone (Judges 15:14,15). Another time Samson tore down some great gates. They were in the wall of the city of Gaza. He carried them to the top of a hill. Those gates would have weighed thousands of pounds!

The Philistine enemy paid Delilah to find the secret of Samson's strength. Samson loved her. So he finally told her.

God's Spirit was the one who gave Samson his great strength (Judges 14:6; 15:14; 16:17). His parents had made a special vow (promise) to God that Samson would be a Nazirite (someone set apart to serve God). As a sign of this special promise to God, Samson's hair could never be cut (Judges 13:5). When Samson's hair was cut, the vow was broken and Samson lost his strength.

When Samson was weak, the Philistines captured him and tore out his eyes. But the Philistines didn't think about Samson's hair growing back! One day the Philistines wanted to laugh at the blind Samson and his God. So they brought him to the temple of one of their gods. It was an idol they called Dagon. Samson prayed to God for strength. And God's Spirit gave him power. He pushed down the pillars that supported the idol's temple. Samson died, but so did thousands of the Philistine enemy.

Who were the Philistines?

A great many Philistines settled on the Mediterranean coast. This was about 100 years after the time of Deborah. They built five major cities. From them they attacked the Israelites and also the Canaanites. These cities were Gaza, Ashkelon, Ashdod, Gath and Ekron. The Philistines were Israel's major enemy for about 200 years—from about 1200 to 1000 B.C. Only in the days of King David was Philistine power broken.

Why were the Philistines so strong? The main reason is that only the Philistines knew

Samson destroyed thousands of Philistines by pushing down the great stone pillars that held up their temple of the false god Dagon.

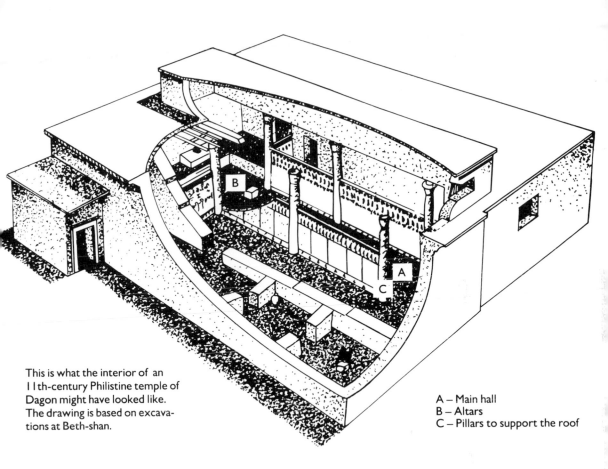

This is what the interior of an 11th-century Philistine temple of Dagon might have looked like. The drawing is based on excavations at Beth-shan.

A – Main hall
B – Altars
C – Pillars to support the roof

how to work with iron (1 Samuel 13:19-22). Their iron swords, spears and war chariots made them too powerful for their enemies.

Who was Ruth?

Ruth 1

Ruth was a woman who lived in the days of the judges. But she was not an Israelite. She married an Israelite who left his land. He moved to her country of Moab where idols were worshiped.

When Ruth's husband died her mother-in-law, Naomi, decided to return to Israel. Then Ruth made an important choice. "Your people will be my people," Ruth said, "and your God will be my God" (Ruth 1:16). Even people who were not born Israelites in Old Testament times could choose to worship the true God.

Why is Ruth in the Bible?

Ruth shows us that even in the worst of times some people are faithful to God. She and Boaz, the man she later married, were like that. Ruth is important for two other reasons. First, Ruth became the great-grandmother of David, Israel's greatest king. Second, Ruth's story is about a relative-redeemer.

Under Old Testament law if a person lost his property a near relative could buy it back for him. Boaz married Ruth so the land of her first husband could be hers again.

Jesus is our relative-redeemer. He was born as a human being (our relative). Then he could save (redeem) us from our sin and bring us back to God.

69

The Twelve Judges

Name	Passage	Enemy	Years of suffering	Years of rule
1. Othniel	3:7-11		8	40
2. Ehud	3:12-30	Moabites	18	80
3. Shamgar	3:31			
4. Deborah	4,5	Canaanites	20	40
5. Gideon	6–8	Midianites	7	40
6. Tola	10:1,2			23
7. Jair	10:3,5			22
8. Jephthah	10:6–12:7	Ammonites	18	6
9. Ibzan	12:8-10			7
10. Elon	12:11-12			10
11. Abdon	12:13-15			8
12. Samson	13–16	Philistines	40	20

To Think about and Do

1. Choose one of the major judges or Ruth. Pretend you are a friend, visiting him or her. Read the Bible passage about this person (see chart). Then tell everything you learned about him or her. Tell what this person helps you understand about our relationship to God.

2. There are other women leaders in the Bible. Here are some you can read about:
   Abigail (1 Samuel 25)   Priscilla (Acts 18, Romans 16:3)
   Esther (Esther)   Phoebe (Romans 16:1,2)

3. Judges 1:1–3:5 tells ways the people of Israel disobeyed God. Read some of the verses and begin a list of the disobedient acts. Read some more and add to your list.

4. The Philistines were one of Israel's early enemies. What can you find out from a Bible dictionary or encyclopedia about the other enemies:
   Moabites   Ammonites
   Midianites   Canaanites?

5. How strong are you? Have a weight lifting contest in your class or neighborhood. Then to see how strong Samson was, try together to lift a car. (The gates of Gaza were at least as heavy as a large van! If Samson carried them to a hill outside of Hebron, he carried them uphill for 37 miles!)

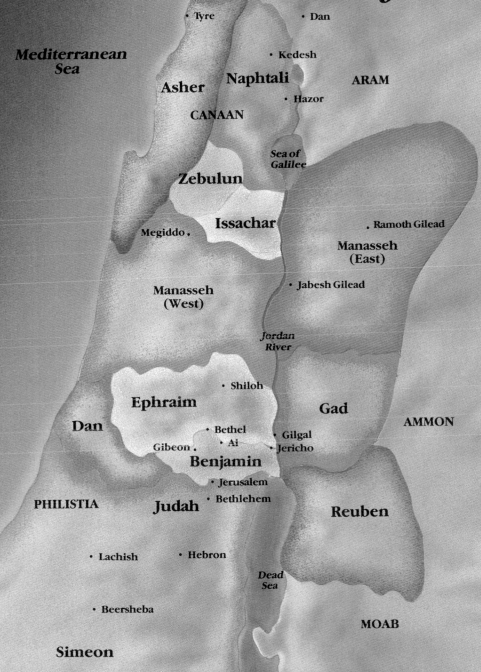

THE TRIBES OF ISRAEL DURING THE JUDGES

• Tyre

• Dan

Mediterranean
Sea

• Kedesh

Asher   Naphtali   ARAM

CANAAN

• Hazor

Sea of
Galilee

Zebulun

Issachar

• Ramoth Gilead

Megiddo •

Manasseh
(East)

Manasseh
(West)

• Jabesh Gilead

Jordan
River

• Shiloh

Ephraim

Gad

Dan

AMMON

• Bethel

• Gilgal

Gibeon •   • Ai

• Jericho

Benjamin

• Jerusalem

• Bethlehem

PHILISTIA   Judah

Reuben

• Lachish   • Hebron

Dead
Sea

• Beersheba

MOAB

Simeon

EDOM

71

Israel's first king

S amuel was Israel's last judge. When Samuel became old, the Israelites wanted to have a king to lead them. Their first king, Saul, failed. So God began to prepare someone else — someone who would be the kind of king Israel needed. God began to prepare David to lead Israel.

The good news

• David cared for his father's sheep. David teaches us that God is our Shepherd and takes care of us.

• When David felt worried and afraid he told God his feelings. God cares how we feel, too.

• David found great success because he trusted and obeyed God's Word. We have the Word of God to guide us, too.

An answer to prayer

1 Samuel 1, 2

When Hannah came to Shiloh (*Shí lo*) to the Tabernacle, Israel's Meeting Tent, she cried and prayed. Hannah had no child. And she wanted children so much. Hannah promised to give her first child to God. If God gave her a boy, he could live at Shiloh and serve God. God answered Hannah's prayer and gave her a son. Hannah named her son Samuel. The name Samuel means "asked of God." Samuel grew up at Shiloh, in the family of Eli, the high priest.

Many Christian parents today pray for their children before they are born. Many Christian parents dedicate (set aside for a special purpose) their boys and girls to the Lord, too. You may have been an answer to prayer, as Samuel was. You may have been dedicated to the Lord by your mother and father.

In the days of King Saul, Israel's tent of worship was at Shiloh.

King Saul's fortress at Gibeah.

Was God's ark magical?

1 Samuel 4,5

When Samuel was still young, the Philistines attacked Israel. The Israelites took the ark of God (Box of the Agreement) out of the Tabernacle and carried it to battle. They thought the ark was magic. They thought they would defeat the Philistines if they carried the ark with them.

But the Philistines defeated Israel. They killed the two sons of Eli. They were wicked men even though they were priests.

The Philistines thought they had defeated God, not just Israel. They took the ark to the city of Ashdod. They put it by an idol they worshiped, called Dagon. But the Philistines had not defeated God. In the morning their idol had fallen down on its face before God's ark. And the Philistines in that city began to suffer strange and terrible sicknesses. Finally the frightened Philistines sent the ark back to Israel.

The ark was not magic. But the ark was holy. It was set apart especially for the worship of God.

Israel wanted a king

1 Samuel 7-9

When Samuel was grown he led his people to victory. This was over the Philistines at Mizpah (*Miz' pah*). He drove them from Israel's territory. All his life Samuel judged Israel in peace.

But when Samuel was old the Israelites wanted a king. He would lead them and fight for them. Instead of being different, as God's special people, they wanted to "be the same as all the other nations" and have a king to "fight our battles" (1 Samuel 8:19).

It was not wrong to have a king. But it was wrong for the Israelites to want a king to fight their battles. God had promised to fight for Israel when they were faithful to him. When Israel asked for a king they turned away from God.

Saul failed as king

1 Samuel 10-15

Israel's first king was Saul. He began well, defeating an enemy army and giving God the credit (1 Samuel 11). But later Saul failed to trust God (1 Samuel 13). Then Saul disobeyed a command that God had Samuel give him (1 Samuel 15).

Saul ruled for 40 years. He built a fortress/castle that people who study old things have found at Gibeah.

David helped his father by taking care of the sheep.

As the years passed, Saul became a moody and angry man. He was king, but he had deserted God. And he lived an unhappy life.

David was the next king
1 Samuel 16

God sent Samuel to appoint David as Israel's next king. He did this by pouring sweet olive oil on David's head. In Bible times this was a sign that God had chosen that person for a special position.

Samuel was surprised when God chose David as Israel's next king. David was young and not very tall when compared to Saul. God told Samuel that people may care about how others look. But God cares about a person's heart (1 Samuel 16:7).

Saul was very tall and looked impressive. But Saul had failed to obey God. David loved the Lord and trusted him completely. This is what is important to God. And this is what would make David a great king.

David trusted in God
1 Samuel 17-26

Only David in all Israel was willing to fight the Philistine giant, Goliath. Goliath was 9'9" tall. The metal coat he wore weighed 125 pounds. And Goliath's long spear had a 15 pound iron tip! But young David was not afraid. He bravely shouted at the giant, "the battle belongs to the Lord. And he will help us defeat all of you" (1 Samuel 17:47).

Afterward David became an officer in Saul's

army. And he won many victories. He married Saul's daughter, Michal. But Saul was very jealous of David and tried to kill him.

David escaped and hid from Saul in some of Israel's desert country. Saul brought his army and tried to catch David. Two times David had the chance to kill Saul but would not (1 Samuel 24,26). God had made Saul king of Israel. And David was willing to wait until God was ready to make him king.

What kind of person was David?

Psalms

The Bible tells much about David. The book of Psalms has many poems and songs that David himself wrote. These psalms (songs) tell us many things about David.

David had been a shepherd and cared for his father's sheep. So he thought of God as a shepherd who takes care of his people (Psalm 23). David saw beauty in God's world and praised the Lord for it (Psalm 8). David felt worried and afraid at times. And he told God his feelings (Psalm 31). David trusted God's Word, and he tried to obey it (Psalm 19). Most of all David loved God. He praised God for being so good (Psalm 103).

David wrote openly about what he thought and felt. So, we can know David better than most other Bible people.

Did Jonathan help David?

1 Samuel 19,20

Jonathan was Saul's oldest son and might have been Israel's next king. But Jonathan knew that God had chosen David to be the king after his father. Instead of being jealous, Jonathan became David's best friend. He even tried to protect David when Saul wanted to kill him.

Are there witches?

1 Samuel 28

Are witches just pretend, or are they real? The Bible tells about people who talked with evil spirits. Sometimes they are called fortune-tellers. God told the Israelites not to have anything to do with such people (Deuteronomy 18:9-13).

But after Samuel died, the Philistines were ready to attack Israel again. King Saul went to a witch for help.

He asked the witch to let him talk with Samuel. When Samuel really appeared, the witch screamed in surprise. She knew only God could have brought the real Samuel back to talk with Saul.

These caves are near the town of En-gedi. David hid in these caves to escape Saul.

There are evil, supernatural beings. But their power is limited. The witch could not really have talked with the dead Samuel. And she knew it. God is far greater than witches or other evil spirits. If we love God, we don't need to be afraid of such things.

Samuel told the disobedient Saul that he and Jonathan would die in battle the next day. Israel would be defeated. After Saul's death, David would become king. David would obey the Lord, as Saul had not.

David played a lyre, which is a musical instrument like a small harp. Some of the psalms were written to be accompanied by musical instruments.

David in 1 Samuel

1. David appointed king (16:1-13)
2. David plays his harp for Saul (16:14-23)
3. David kills the giant Goliath (17)
4. David makes a good friend (18:1-9)

5. Saul becomes David's enemy (18:10-19)
6. David marries Saul's daughter (18:20-30)
7. David escapes from Saul (19)
8. David helped by Jonathan (20)

9. David takes Goliath's sword (21:1-9)
10. David pretends to be mad (21:10-15)
11. David saves a city (23:1-6)
12. David pursued by Saul (23:7-29)

13. David saves Saul's life (24)
14. David marries Abigail (25)
15. David saves Saul again (26)
16. David hides among the Philistines (27)
17. David fights Israel's enemies (29,30)

To Think about and Do

1. Talk with your parents. Did they pray for you before you were born? Did they dedicate you to the Lord? Ask them what kind of person they want you to be when you grow up.

2. Goliath seemed too big to defeat. He made everyone afraid to try. What makes you afraid or seems too hard for you? Draw a giant, and give him the name of something that is very hard for you. Pick a Bible verse from 1 Samuel 17 to write under it that will help you trust God and try.

3. What made Saul fail? Look up these verses. Then tell someone about Saul's failure.

   1 Samuel 13:7-15   1 Samuel 18:28-29
   1 Samuel 15:1-25   1 Samuel 22:6-17
   1 Samuel 18:12-15   1 Samuel 28:3-20

4. Here are some more psalms David wrote. How do you think he felt when he wrote each?
   Psalm 8:3-9   Psalm 25:16-21
   Psalm 13:1-2   Psalm 28:6,7
   Psalm 18:1-3   Psalm 55:4-8
                    Psalm 56:3,4

Write a poem telling God how you feel sometimes.

5. Choose one of the 17 stories about David in 1 Samuel and draw a comic strip that tells the story.

Israel's greatest kings

David became king of Israel after Saul died. David defeated Israel's enemies. And he enlarged the borders of his country. During the lifetime of David and his son Solomon, Israel was a rich and powerful nation.

The good news

■ King David sinned. But God forgave David when the king confessed his sin. God will forgive our sins, too.

■ Solomon, David's wise son, was successful as long as he loved and obeyed God. We are truly wise when we love and obey God, too.

David was a great king

At first David was king only of the small tribe of Judah (see map, page 81). Later he was recognized as king of all the Israelites. David was a great and successful king. He did many things for his country.

David defeated the Philistines. He destroyed the power of these people. They had been enemies of Israel for nearly 200 years. David took back land the Philistines had taken from Israel (2 Samuel 5). David captured the city of Jerusalem and made it the capital of his nation (2 Samuel 5). David brought God's ark (Box of the Agreement) to Jerusalem, too. Then the Israelites would come to Jerusalem to worship the Lord (2 Samuel 6). David built a strong army, with special warriors as commanders (2 Samuel 23; 1 Chronicles 11). He had

Arch of David's citadel (fortress) at Jerusalem. Under the reign of King David, Israel captured Jerusalem from the Philistines.

Swords from Bible times.

288,000 trained men in his army. Each month 24,000 soldiers were on duty to protect the Israelites.

David fought wars with enemy nations like Moab and Edom. David won all his wars. He soon ruled most of the land that God had originally promised to Abraham. This was ten times the area Israel held in the time of the Judges (see map, page 71)!

David also led his people in worship. David loved God and was always ready to praise him. He made sure that priests and Levites were always on duty to praise God. And David himself wrote many psalms (songs) that were used in worship services (1 Chronicles 25:1-8).

Why did Uzzah die?

2 Samuel 6

David wanted to bring God's ark to Jerusalem. So it was put on a cart pulled by oxen. When an ox stumbled, a man named Uzzah grabbed the ark — and God struck him dead.

David was very upset and angry. Why would God do such a thing? Later David learned from God's law that God's ark was to be covered up. It was to be carried by Levites, not pulled by oxen. And it must never be touched (Numbers 4:1-20).

The ark was especially holy. No one but the priests of God were even to see what it looked like.

Uzzah's death reminded David and all Israel that God is holy as well as loving. It is important to obey God and to show respect for him.

God's promise to David

2 Samuel 7

David's enemies were finally defeated, and Israel was at peace. Then David wanted to build a temple for the Lord. God did not let David build the Temple. Instead God gave David a special promise. One of David's descendants (family) would rule a kingdom forever (2 Samuel 7:12,13; 16).

Descendants of David did rule in Jerusalem as long as the Israelites had kings. But God's promise to David was about one special descendant. That special descendant is Jesus! Mary, Jesus' mother, was a descendant of David (Luke 3:1-31). The Bible says Jesus came from the family of David (Matthew 1:1), meaning that Jesus is David's descendant.

Can good people sin?

2 Samuel 11-12; Psalm 51

David was a good person who loved God. But even good people can sin. David sinned. He fell in love with another man's wife. Then he arranged for the husband to be killed in battle.

God's prophet, Nathan, was sent to accuse David of this sin. David had disobeyed the word of the Lord and done an evil thing.

But then David did the right thing. David immediately confessed his sin. He did not pretend he had done nothing wrong. David even wrote a psalm, to be read by all his people. He admitted that he had sinned and asked for God's forgiveness! Here are the words David wrote.

God, be merciful to me
    because you are loving.
Because you are merciful,
    wipe out all my wrongs.
Wash away all my guilt
    and make me clean again.

Sometimes you and I will sin, too. When we do, we can remember David and his prayer of confession. We can pray this same prayer to God. We thank God that he forgives us as he forgave David.

Did everyone like King David?
2 Samuel 13-19

David had been a good and godly king. But not everyone loved David. When David was old, Absalom, one of his own sons, turned against him. Many of the people David had ruled so well joined the secret plan.

How miserable David must have been. He hurriedly left Jerusalem with just a few faithful friends. David's son and David's own people wanted to kill their king!

In a terrible civil war Absalom was killed and David's enemies were defeated. But David was very sad for his son and for all the people who had turned against him.

When David was running from Absalom he wrote a psalm (song) telling about his trust in God. "But Lord, you are my shield," David wrote. "You are my wonderful God who gives me courage" (Psalm 3:3). People did disappoint David, but he remembered that God was with

King David built a fortress for protection, which was called the City of David. Eventually the entire city of Jerusalem came to be called the City of David because it surrounded the fortress.

him. David was right. God did help David. And God gave David the strength he needed to overcome his disappointments.

Was Solomon a great king?
1 Kings 1-14

David's son Solomon was Israel's next king. Solomon did not fight wars like his father David. Instead Solomon built powerful, strong, walled cities. Solomon had such a strong army that no one dared to attack Israel.

Solomon had copper mines at Ezion Geber and made the ore into bright metal. He built fleets of ships that set out on three-year trading trips. They returned with gold, silver, jewels, ivory and animals (1 Kings 10:14-22). Solomon's businesses earned him about 65,000 pounds of gold a year! If gold sells for $350 an ounce, that's $280,000,000 a year!

But Solomon's building plans were very expensive. So, in spite of his wealth, Solomon taxed his people heavily. And Solomon made thousands of his people work for his government without pay.

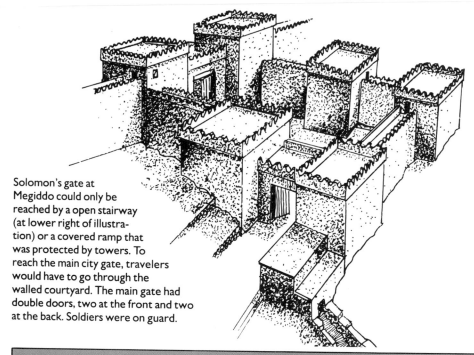

Solomon's gate at Megiddo could only be reached by a open stairway (at lower right of illustration) or a covered ramp that was protected by towers. To reach the main city gate, travelers would have to go through the walled courtyard. The main gate had double doors, two at the front and two at the back. Soldiers were on guard.

David in 2 Samuel

1. David is very sad for Saul (1:1-12)
2. David is made king of Judah (2:1-7)
3. David battles Ish-bosheth (3:6-21)
4. David kills two murderers (4:5-12)
5. David is made king of all Israel (5:1-5)
6. David conquers Jerusalem (5:6-12)
7. David defeats the Philistines (5:17-25)
8. David brings the ark to Jerusalem (6)
9. David is promised the kingdom forever (7)
10. David defeats other enemies (8:1-14)
11. David is kind to Jonathan's son (9)
12. David defeats the Ammonites (10:1-19)
13. David sins with Bathsheba (11:1-17)
14. David is warned by a prophet (12:1-14)
15. David's son Absalom turns against him (15:1-12)
16. David's army kills Absalom (18:1-18)
17. David lets Gibeonites have revenge (21)
18. David counts his army (24:1-17)
19. David makes Solomon king (1 Kings 1)

CYPRUS

Posssible extent of
Solomon's kingdom

SIDON   ARAMEANS
· Sidon
                    Damascus
    · Tyre   · Dan

Mediterranean Sea

                Jordan
                River
    · Megiddo   Ramoth Gilead
Plain of   ·
Sharon   ISRAEL
    Shechem ·   Jabbok River

PHILISTIA
        Jerusalem ·
    · Ashdod   AMMON
Ashkelon ·
        · Lachish
                Dead
    · Gaza Hebron Sea
        · Beersheba   MOAB
    JUDAH

    · Kadesh Barnea
        EDOM

DAVID AND
SOLOMON'S
KINGDOM

Solomon's greatest building

1 Kings 7

David had wanted to build God a beautiful temple at Jerusalem. But God did not let him. So Solomon spent seven and a half years building the beautiful Temple David had dreamed of. And he furnished it with gold and silver.

Solomon brought the ark of God into the Temple. Then he called all Israel together to give the beautiful building to the service of the Lord. You can read Solomon's prayer for this in 1 Kings 8.

When Solomon completed his building plans, God spoke to him. God said Solomon should love him as David had done. If he would, God would continue to help Solomon and his people.

Was Solomon wise or foolish?

1 Kings 4, 11

Solomon was very wise in some things. He wrote 3,000 proverbs (wise sayings) and 1,005 songs. He studied plants and animals. People came from all over the world to learn from Solomon. The Queen of Sheba traveled over 1,000 miles from what is now Yemen.

But Solomon was not wise enough to obey God's word all his life. He married foreign women who worshiped idols. In time Solomon even worshiped these false gods and goddesses himself !

Because of Solomon's sin God let Israel's enemies grow stronger. When Solomon died, most of his kingdom was ruled by someone other than his son.

To Think about and Do

1.   David often wrote psalms (songs) about his experiences. Read these stories about David and then read the psalms David wrote about them.

- Running from Absalom (2 Samuel 15, Psalm 3).
- Sinning with Bathsheba (2 Samuel 11, Psalm 51).
- Fighting the Arameans (2 Samuel 10; Psalm 60).

Can you find other psalms of David and read what they are about? Hint: Read the description at the beginning of a psalm. If it is about an experience of David, look in a concordance to find the story.

2.   Proverbs chapter 10 records some of the wise sayings of Solomon. Which of the proverbs in this chapter do you think is wisest? Why is it wise?

3.   Work with your dad or a friend to make a model of the Temple at Jerusalem. The description is given in 1 Kings 6.

4.   Tell who you think is wiser: a person who knows many things, or a person who does the right thing. Why do you think this?

5.   Look up Megiddo in a Bible dictionary or book about old things. What can you find out about the strong, walled cities Solomon built?

Worship and be wise

Five books of the Bible contain what is called "wisdom literature." Much in them was written during the wonderful days of King David and King Solomon. The wisdom literature of the Bible teaches us how to serve God by doing what is good. And the worship literature, Psalms, teaches us how to pray and worship the Lord.

The good news

- Psalms shows us how to praise God when we remember his power and goodness.
- Proverbs helps us be wise and make good choices.
- Job shows us that even though people suffer, God will bless them in the end.

What is praise?

Praise is a very special way to show love to God. In praise we talk directly to God. We thank him for who he is and what he has done. And we tell God how wonderful and good we know he is. Praise is very special to God. Praising God gives us joy and happiness, too.

These are the ruins of an ancient Israelite home. The home was the center of family life, the place where children learned from their parents how to live in a way that was pleasing to God. The book of Proverbs, written by King Solomon, contains the practical information that a father would share with his sons and daughters. According to tradition, King Solomon collected proverbs that he had heard and he wrote others from his own experience.

Musical instruments from Bible times.

We find praise passages in both the Old Testament and in the New Testament. But one book of the Bible, Psalms, is filled with praise.

Psalms show us how we can tell God all our troubles and our feelings. We can share sorrow or fear with the Lord. Then we will remember how great and good God is. We can praise God and be sure he will help us with our troubles.

A praise psalm of David

My soul, praise the Lord.
  All my being, praise his holy name.
My soul, praise the Lord.
  Do not forget all his kindnesses.
The Lord forgives me all my sins.
  He heals all my diseases.
He saves my life from the grave.
  He loads me with love and mercy.
He satisfies me with good things.
  He makes me young again like the eagle.
You who are his angels, praise the Lord,
  you mighty warriors who do what he says.
  Listen to what he says.
You, his armies, praise the Lord,
  you are his servants who do what he wants.
Everything the Lord has made
  wherever he rules should praise him.
My soul, praise the Lord.

Psalm 103:1-5,20-22

Is Psalms poetry?

The Psalms do not rhyme, as much of our poetry does. But psalms are poems.

The Hebrew people wrote a special kind of poetry. It does not use rhyming words. This poetry puts thoughts together rather than sounds.

How does this kind of poetry work? At times a verse of Hebrew poetry repeats the thought in the first line, like Psalm 126:2:

"Then our mouths were filled with laughing,
  and our tongues sang happy songs."

Sometimes a verse of Hebrew poetry stresses the first line of a verse with an opposite, as in Proverb 11:17:

"A kind person will be rewarded,
  but a cruel man brings trouble on himself."

Sometimes Hebrew poetry uses the second line of a verse to add to the thought of the first line, as in Psalm 4:8:

"I go to bed and sleep in peace.
  Lord, only you keep me safe."

So when we read Psalms and even Proverbs, we are reading Bible poetry. It is poetry even though the words may not rhyme. Poetry sometimes depends on how words sound in some languages. This poetry is very hard to translate into other languages. But Bible poetry relies on how thoughts fit together instead of rhyming words. So, Bible poems can be translated into every language of the world.

What is in Psalms?

The psalm poems are about many different things. Here are different kinds of poems you can read in this wonderful Bible book.

(1) *Praise psalms* help us think about God and thank him for who he is. Psalms 33, 103 and 139 are praise psalms.

(2) *Historical psalms* tell what God has done for his people. Psalms 68, 78, 105 and 106 are historical psalms.

(3) *Friendship psalms* are about the loving relationship God has with people who believe in him. Psalms 8, 16, 20 and 23 are friendship psalms.

(4) *Anger psalms* ask God to punish the wicked. Psalms 35, 69, 109 and 137 are psalms which ask God to punish wicked people.

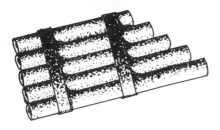

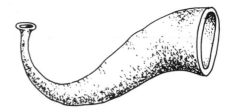

(5) *Confession psalms* tell God how sorry we are about failures and sins. Psalms 6, 32, 51, 102, 130 and 143 are psalms of confession.

(6) *Messianic psalms* are about Jesus, who will come as the promised Messiah (anointed Savior). Psalms that tell us about Jesus are 2, 8, 22, 40, 45, 72, 89, 110 and 132.

(7) *Worship psalms* were used at special holy times when the people of Israel came to worship God at the Temple in Jerusalem. Psalms 30, 92 and 120–134 are worship psalms.

As we read Psalms today we realize that God is glad to have us share all our thoughts and feelings with him. He listens to our fears and troubles. And he listens when we are full of joy. We can share all our feelings with God. And we worship him. Then the Lord helps us to trust him and to find peace.

What is wisdom?

Wisdom is something special in the Old Testament. A person may know many things but not be wise. That is because wisdom is something that comes from God. Wisdom helps us to "understand what is right and honest...and fair...every good path" (Proverb 2:9).

Wisdom literature is made up of sayings that show differences between wise and foolish choices. The wisdom books in the Bible are Job, Proverbs and Ecclesiastes. Several Psalms are also considered wisdom literature (19, 37, 104, 107, 147, 148).

What is in Proverbs?

The whole book of Proverbs is filled with wisdom sayings on many subjects. Here are some of the Proverbs about families.

Writings like Psalms and Proverbs were often done on paper made of papyrus, a plant that grew along the Nile River in Egypt.

Family Proverbs	Proverbs about money

My son, you should listen
   to your father's teaching.
And do not leave your mother's teaching.
<div align="right">Proverb 1:8</div>
	It is the blessing of the Lord
	   that makes you rich.
	And he does not give you trouble
	   with the blessing.
	<div align="right">Proverb 10:22</div>

If a person does not punish his son
   he does not love him.
The person who loves his son is careful
   to correct him.
<div align="right">Proverb 13:24</div>
	It is better to gain just a little the right way
	   than to gain much in an unfair way.
	<div align="right">Proverb 16:8</div>

A wise son makes his father happy.
   But a foolish son makes his mother sad.
<div align="right">Proverb 10:1</div>
	It is much better to get wisdom than gold.
	   And it is better to choose understanding
	     than silver!
	<div align="right">Proverb 16:16</div>

A good person lives an honest life.
   And his children will be happy
     because of him.
<div align="right">Proverb 20:7</div>
	Having a good name is more important
	   than having riches.
	It is better to be well thought of
	   than to have silver or gold.
	<div align="right">Proverb 22:1</div>

The father of a good man is very happy.
   The person who has a wise son
     finds pleasure in him.
<div align="right">Proverb 23:24</div>
	Rich people and poor people share this:
	   The Lord made all of them.
	<div align="right">Proverb 22:2</div>

Proverbs in the Bible help people think about their choices. They help them consider what is really important in life. To the writers of our Bible, having godly children is very important. Having wealth is one of God's blessings. But it is much more important to be a good, wise person than to be rich.

Do good people suffer?
Job

Does God ever let really good people suffer? Many think that if a person does what is right he or she will not have troubles in life. They think when a person suffers, God must be punishing him or her for some sin.

The book of Job is about a man the Bible says was "honest and innocent of wrong" (Job 1:1). Yet terrible things happened to Job. He lost everything he owned. His children were killed. And he came down with a terrible, painful disease (Job 1,2).

Most of the book of Job tells how Job and three of his friends tried to understand why all this had happened. Job's friends said that God must be punishing Job. Job knew he hadn't done wrong. But Job still didn't understand how God could do something to him that seemed so unfair (Job 3-31).

Finally God talked with Job. God didn't explain why he had let Job suffer. God simply helped Job realize that no person can understand all of God's reasons for what he allows to happen (Job 38-40).

In the end, God blessed Job. God gave back Job's health and returned his wealth. And he gave Job another family (Job 42).

Sometimes tragedy comes even to good people. Good people can become sick or have loved ones die. But such suffering doesn't mean that God is punishing us. God has reasons we can't understand for letting his people suffer. Like Job, we need to learn to trust God. In the end, God will bless us as he blessed Job.

Was Solomon always wise?

Ecclesiastes

When Solomon was older he began to worship the false gods and goddesses of his foreign wives. When Solomon forgot God, he was no longer wise.

Solomon must have felt empty and unhappy because he wrote a very sad Bible book. Ecclesiastes tells what Solomon thought and felt when he tried to live without God.

How do we know what Solomon tried to do? He tells us. He says he wanted to explain everything by thinking about what he had seen, instead of looking for answers in God's word (Ecclesiastes 1:12-18). We know that Solomon felt sad. He tells us that, too. All his knowledge only brought him sorrow and grief. And he concluded that life is useless (Ecclesiastes 12:8).

Why is this book in our Bible? It is there to show everyone that even the richest, smartest man who ever lived could not find happiness

Solomon was very wise. When two women both claimed to be the mother of the same baby, he pretended that he was going to divide the baby in half. The real mother stopped him. Then Solomon knew to whom the baby belonged.

without God. If Solomon had been really wise, he would have kept on worshiping and loving God. Then his life would have been happy and full, not sad and empty.

How can we be wise?

Being wise means to make right choices. It means doing what is good and not bad.

God gave us his word so that we would understand what is right. God sent Jesus to give us the strength to do right. And he forgives us when we make bad choices. To be wise, we need to trust in Jesus and do what God tells us in his word is right.

To Think about and Do

1. Can you write Bible poetry? Try to write a poem about your family that is like one kind of Hebrew poetry described here.

2. Many psalms were put to music and sung in worship. Try to make up music to use with one of the Bible's praise psalms. Then sing it to worship the Lord.

3. Choose one of the seven kinds of psalms described in this unit. Read the psalms listed and write down four things you learn about God from them.

4. In Proverbs the "fool" is a person who makes wrong moral choices. He is not a person who doesn't know much or is dumb. Use a concordance to find out what you can about foolish people. How are they different from wise people?

5. Choose one chapter of Proverbs and list the different things the verses tell about. Which of the proverbs in the chapter you chose can guide you in your choices? Make a banner or poster with the proverb that you choose.

Kings and prophets in Israel

After Solomon's death the powerful kingdom he ruled was divided into two kingdoms. Solomon's son Rehoboam (*Re o bō' am*) ruled in Jerusalem over Judah. Ten tribes broke away to follow Jeroboam (*Jer o bō' am*). These tribes kept the name of Israel.

Every king of Israel was evil and led his people away from the Lord. God sent messengers called prophets to warn his people and call them back to him. But Israel refused to turn to the Lord. The evil kingdom was finally destroyed by the Assyrians. And its people were taken away captive.

The good news

▪ God sent his prophets to warn the kings and people of Israel not to sin. God's word warns us about the bad things that will happen if we choose to sin.

▪ God was patient. He gave Israel many chances to change their hearts and lives before he punished the nation.

Was Israel an evil kingdom?

1 Kings 12

The first king of the divided northern kingdom (see map) was Jeroboam. He did not want his people to go to Jerusalem to worship. He was afraid that someday they would leave him and want to be one kingdom again. So Jeroboam set up his own religion in Israel. He

This ancient relief shows Assyrian soldiers attacking the town of Lachish.

invisible god was supposed to ride on the idols. Jeroboam set the calves at Bethel and Dan. But the Lord was to be worshiped only at Jerusalem (Deuteronomy 12:1-7). Jeroboam made priests of people who were not Levites. Jeroboam even set his own worship holidays to replace the special worship times God made. Everything that Jeroboam did was against God's word. The kings of Israel who followed Jeroboam continued his ways. They led their whole nation to sin.

God warned Jeroboam

1 Kings 13,14

When Jeroboam began his evil worship, God sent a prophet to warn him. The prophet shouted out God's judgment. There were evil priests who offered forbidden sacrifices. The prophet said these priests would be burned on Jeroboam's altar!

The furious king pointed at the prophet. He told his soldiers to seize him. But Jeroboam's arm shriveled up, and the king could not move. Then the altar the prophet cursed broke apart!

This story tells us much about the special men the Bible calls prophets.

A prophet was God's special messenger. The prophet gave God's message to the king or people he was sent to. At times false prophets pretended to be God's messengers. How could the Israelites tell the difference between someone pretending to be a prophet and a true prophet? A true prophet spoke in the name of the Lord. And what he said always came true (Deuteronomy 18:21-22). The prophet who spoke to Jeroboam said that the evil altar would break. This was a sign the prophet really was God's messenger. And the altar did break (1 Kings 13:5). When what a prophet said came true, everyone knew his message really was from God.

Jeroboam knew that he had done wrong to set up his own religion. He knew the prophet came from God. But Jeroboam refused to listen to God or his prophet.

Later another prophet told Jeroboam what his punishment would be. Because Jeroboam

refused to obey God, his family would not survive. The Israelites who followed the evil religion of Jeroboam would one day be defeated. A powerful enemy would take them away from their land.

Kings and prophets of Israel

Kings	Prophets	Date
Jeroboam I	Unnamed man of God	930-909 B.C.
	Ahijah	
Nadab		909-908 B.C.
Baasha	Jehu son of Hanani	908-886 B.C.
Elah		886-885 B.C.
Zimri		885 B.C.
Tibni		885-880 B.C.
Omri		880-874 B.C.
Ahab	Elijah	874-853 B.C.
	Elisha	
	An unnamed prophet	
	Micaiah	
	Obadiah (?)	
Ahaziah		853-852 B.C.
Joram	Elisha	852-841 B.C.
Jehu	Elisha	841-814 B.C.
Jehoahaz		814-798 B.C.
Jehoash	Elisha	798-782 B.C.
Jeroboam II	Jonah	793-753 B.C.
	Amos	
	Hosea	
Zechariah		753 B.C.
Shallum		752 B.C.
Menahem	Hosea	752-742 B.C.
Pekah		752-732 B.C.
Pekahiah		742-740 B.C.
Hoshea		732-723 B.C.

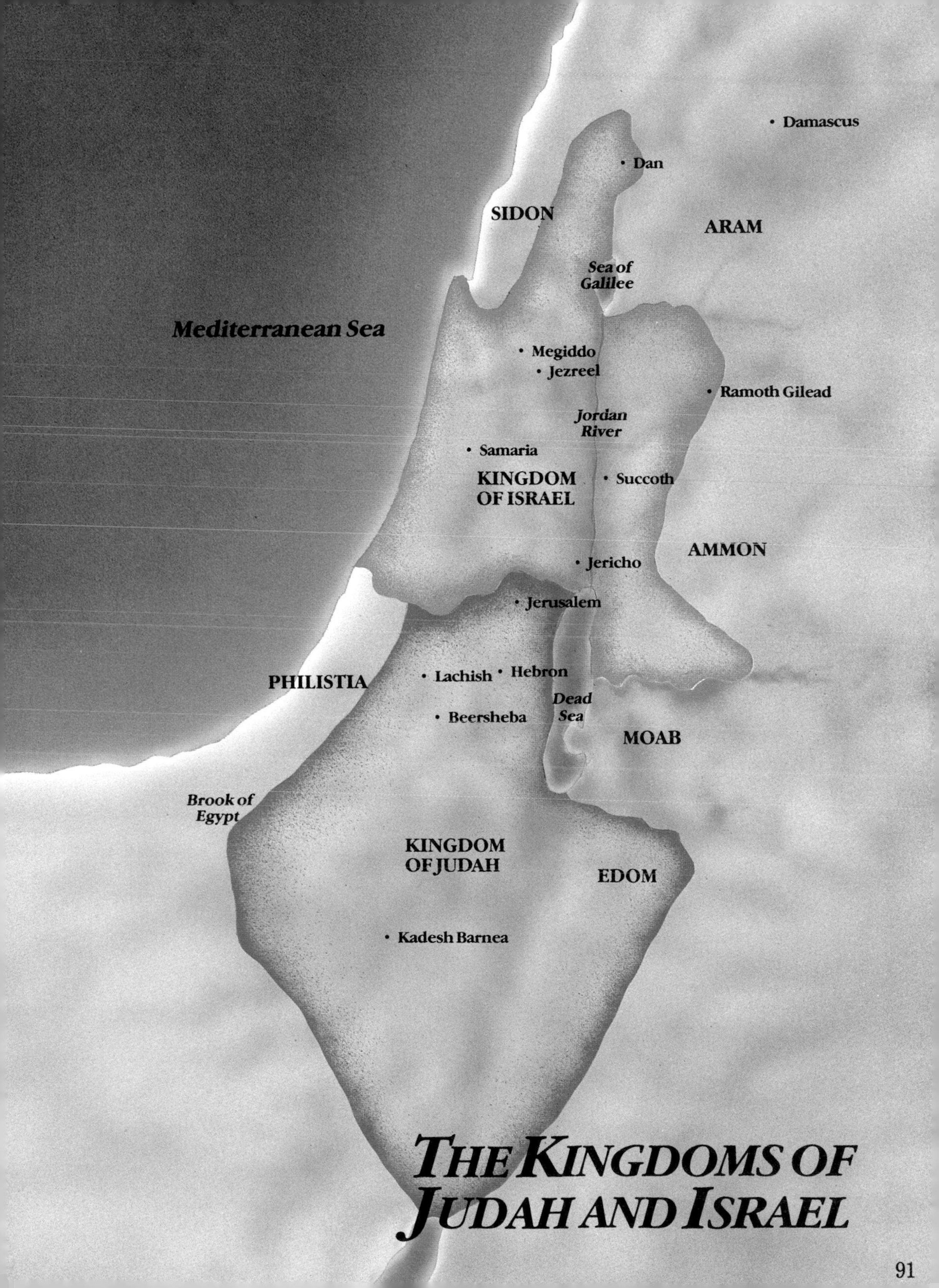

• Damascus

• Dan

SIDON

ARAM

Sea of
Galilee

Mediterranean Sea

• Megiddo
• Jezreel

• Ramoth Gilead

Jordan
River

• Samaria

KINGDOM
OF ISRAEL

• Succoth

AMMON

• Jericho

• Jerusalem

PHILISTIA

• Lachish • Hebron

Dead
Sea

• Beersheba

MOAB

Brook of
Egypt

KINGDOM
OF JUDAH

EDOM

• Kadesh Barnea

THE KINGDOMS OF
JUDAH AND ISRAEL

Israel's most powerful kings

Israel had many enemies and often lost land to them. But Israel also had powerful kings.

Omri (*Ōm ri*) was a strong ruler who set up a new capital city at Samaria (see map, page 91). He conquered the Moabites. And he made an agreement with the Phoenicians (*Fi nish' uns*). His son Ahab ruled for 20 years. Ahab was a strong ruler who won many military battles. But Ahab and his wife Jezebel (*Jez' e bel*) brought the worship of Baal, a false god, into Israel. The prophets Elijah and Elisha led the battle against this false religion.

Jeroboam II was one of Israel's most capable rulers. Under him Israel became a leading nation along the Mediterranean seacoast. Jeroboam II won back nearly all the northern area that David and Solomon had held! In his days Israel was very successful. But the rich people who lived in luxury mistreated and cheated the poor people. God sent the prophets Amos and Hosea to speak against Israel's sins in the days of Jeroboam II. They tried to get Israel to turn to the Lord.

Who were Israel's enemies?

During the 200 years Israel was the northern kingdom, it had many enemies. Sometimes the people of this country even fought their fellow-Israelites of Judah!

At first the Egyptians were Israel's enemies. Shishak (*Shē' shak*), an Egyptian king, took land away from Jeroboam.

The Arameans (*Ar a mē' ans*), whose capital was Damascus, were Israel's enemies during most of this time. Their kings Ben-Hadad I and II (*Ben Hā' dad*) and Hazael (*Hāz ā el*) battled Israel in the days of Omri, Ahab and Jehu.

Assyria was the most powerful enemy of Israel. The capital of Assyria was Nineveh. Assyria was not strong in the days of Jeroboam II. But thirty years after Jeroboam II's death the Assyrians attacked Israel. They destroyed its powerful cities and captured Samaria. Then the Assyrians took all the people of Israel who were left away from their land.

Were ten tribes really lost?

Many people have wondered what happened to the people of Israel. They worried that ten of the Israelite tribes have been "lost." But they were not lost!

Jeroboam I set up his false religion in Israel. But many Israelites who wanted to worship God correctly left Israel and settled in Judah (2 Chronicles 11:13-17). When the kingdom was first divided, Judah had only 180,000 fighting men (1 Kings 12:21). About 20 years later Judah had an army of 400,000 (2 Chronicles 13:3). Thousands from each of the ten tribes had moved to Judah. So the tribes were not "lost" when the Assyrians took Israel's citizens away captive.

What was Obadiah's message?

Obadiah's short message warns a people who live near Israel. Obadiah told them that God would punish them for helping the enemies of God's people. God would keep his promise to bless those who blessed his people. And he would harm those who harmed his people.

What was Jonah's message?
Jonah

In the days of Jeroboam II, God sent Jonah to Nineveh, the capital of Assyria. Jonah was to warn the Assyrians that God was about to destroy the city. Jonah did not want to go. He took a ship going the other way. But God sent a great fish to swallow Jonah and bring him back to shore.

Jonah did go to Nineveh and shout out God's warning. The king and the people of Nineveh repented and turned from their sins. So God did not destroy the city.

Jonah was very upset. The prophet had been afraid that God would spare this enemy who one day would attack his country.

But Jonah's experience in Nineveh was also a message to Israel. Soon God would send the prophets Amos and Hosea to Israel. God showed mercy to Nineveh. That reminded Israel that they could also listen to a prophet's warning.

God made a great fish swallow Jonah when Jonah tried to run away. After three days the fish spit Jonah out onto the shore. Then Jonah did as God had commanded him to.

And they could change their hearts and lives. Then God would have mercy on them, too. And the book of Jonah shows that God loved all people, even the Assyrians.

What was Amos' message?

Amos

Amos lived in Judah. He took care of sheep and sycamore trees. The fruit of the sycamore

tree was eaten by those too poor to buy figs. God told Amos to go to Israel and speak for him and for the poor people.

Amos went to the rich cities of Israel and shouted out God's warning. He told the Israelites that God was going to punish them for their false worship (Amos 4). He would also punish made gold calves for the people to worship. An

them because they showed no concern for the poor. People cared only for themselves and their luxuries. They did not care for others who were hungry (Amos 5,8). But Israel still had hope. If the people would only do good, and not evil, God would have mercy on them. Then they could still live (Amos 5:14).

The people of Nineveh had listened to Jonah. But the people of Israel would not listen to Amos.

Soon the Assyrian armies came. The proud nation of Israel was destroyed, and her sinful rich people were taken away to become slaves.

What was Hosea's message?

Hosea

God also sent the prophet Hosea to Israel. Hosea was a sad prophet. His wife was not faithful to him. Hosea told Israel how sad God was because Israel had not been faithful to him.

Hosea talks about how much God has loved the Israelites. And he tells them how hurt the Lord is that his people will not love him.

Hosea warns Israel, too. God is angry with his people and will surely punish them. When Israel has been punished, the people will turn to God again. Then God will forgive them. And he will love them forever.

It's very sad that Israel would not turn to the Lord before the terrible punishment came! You and I can learn from Israel. And we can learn from the prophets to stop doing wrong and turn to God immediately.

Lost chances

Israel was a nation for just over 200 years. Eight of her 19 kings were murdered or committed suicide. Not one was considered good by God.

God sent prophets to warn Israel and her kings, but the people refused to listen. Finally the Assyrian armies marched into Israel. They destroyed the capital city of Samaria and took the people away as captives. Israel had been given the chance to change their hearts and lives and return to God. The nation would not, and God finally punished Israel, the evil kingdom.

To Think about and Do

1. Pretend to visit two kings of Israel. [Read about them in the Bible: Jeroboam I (1 Kings 12:25 – 14:20) and Jehu (2 Kings 9,10).] Did you like these kings? Would you have liked to live in that country?

2. Check an encyclopedia or books on Bible history to find out these things about the Assyrians.
   - What kind of people were they?
   - What was their religion?
   - How did they make war?
   - What happened to them?
   - What did they look like?

3. People play "Hot and Cold" by telling a player if they are getting closer (hotter) or farther away (colder) from a hidden object. Read the book of Jonah with a friend. When is Jonah closer to God? When is Jonah farther away? Decide together where you would write "hot" and where you would write "cold" in the margin of the book of Jonah.

4. If Amos kept a diary, what important things do you suppose he would have written in it? Read Amos 4 and 5. Then write down three things Amos might have written in his diary.

5. Make a valentine card from God to Israel. To get ideas about what to say on the valentine, and how to decorate it, read Hosea 11 and 14.

Adventures of Elijah and Elisha

Elijah and Elisha lived in the northern kingdom of Israel. Elijah was a prophet in the days of King Ahab, who brought Baal worship into Israel. Elisha was the prophet who continued to struggle against evil. The Bible has many stories about Elijah, Elisha and the evil kings of Israel.

The good news

- God protected the prophets, and others who believed in him, from evil enemies. God protects us today, too.
- God's power made it possible for Elijah and Elisha to win over evil people. God is just as powerful today.

Israel's most evil king

Ahab was Israel's most evil king. Ahab was the son of Omri, who made Israel a powerful kingdom. But Ahab married a woman named Jezebel (*Jez' e bel*). She worshiped Baal. Ahab began to worship Baal, too. And he even built a temple to Baal in the capital city of Samaria.

Elijah may have built an altar similar to this one for the contest with the prophets of Baal.

Here on Mount Carmel the prophet Elijah called down fire from God to destroy the 400 prophets of the false god Baal.

The Bible says he "did more things to make the Lord, the God of Israel, angry than all the other kings before him" (1 Kings 16:33).

Elijah the prophet lived during the 22 years evil King Ahab ruled. Elijah was to battle the evil Baal religion that Ahab and his wife brought into Israel.

What miracles did Elijah do?

God gave Elijah special powers. Then he could battle the false religion of Baal and punish Ahab and the Israelites. The Old Testament reports seven miracles done by Elijah. He stopped rain from falling for three and a half years (1 Kings 17:1). He kept the food of a widow from being used up (17:7-16). He brought the widow's son back to life (17:17-24). He called down fire from heaven to burn up a sacrifice (18:16-40). He brought back rain after the years of no rain (18:41-45). He called down fire on soldiers (2 Kings 1). And he parted the Jordan River (2:1-9).

Elijah proved that God, who sent him, is the true God. And he proved that Baal was a false god. But Ahab and Jezebel did not change.

Read about Elijah and Ahab

1. Elijah is fed by ravens (1 Kings 17:1-6)
2. Elijah saves a widow and her son (1 Kings 17:7-24)
3. Elijah battles the priests of Baal on Mount Carmel (1 Kings 18:16-40)
4. Elijah brings rain (1 Kings 18:41-46)
5. Elijah runs away (1 Kings 19:1-18)
6. Elijah appoints Elisha (1 Kings 19:19-21)
7. Ahab defeats Ben-Hadad (1 Kings 20)
8. Ahab takes Naboth's vineyard (1 Kings 21)
9. Ahab is killed (1 Kings 22:29-40)
10. Elijah is taken up to heaven (2 Kings 2)

Water on Mount Carmel

1 Kings 18

Elijah challenged Ahab's false Baal religion. The people watched. And 450 prophets of Baal begged their god to set fire to wood on which they had laid a sacrifice. The prophets called on their god all day, but no fire came.

Then Elijah prepared his sacrifice to God. He had the wood soaked three times with water. He stepped forward and prayed. Then fire fell

96

from the sky. It burned up the sacrifice, the stones of the altar and the water that soaked everything.

People have wondered where Elijah got the water. Israel had just had three and a half years without rain. When it did not rain, even the streams dried up.

There are two answers. First, people who study old things have found springs and wells below Mount Carmel. These springs do not dry up, even in times without rain. Second, Elijah might have used salt water from the nearby Mediterranean Sea.

But Elijah did soak his sacrifice with water. So the people saw that God could answer prayer and Baal could not. Then they put the 450 false prophets of Baal to death.

Why did Elijah run away?

1 Kings 19

After Elijah's victory at Mount Carmel over the priests of Baal, Queen Jezebel threatened to kill him.

Suddenly Elijah was afraid. And he ran away!

Why would Elijah be afraid? Elijah knew God was with him. Why did Elijah run?

Anyone can be afraid or discouraged at times, even people like Elijah who believe in God. But God was not angry with Elijah. God supplied food to give Elijah strength to run (19:7-9). God spoke to Elijah in a gentle whisper, not loudly (19:10-13). When Elijah felt alone, God told Elijah that there were others in Israel besides himself who worshiped the Lord. Elijah was not alone (19:14,18). Then God gave Elijah an easy job to do (19:15-17). God even gave Elijah a friend to be his companion. His name was Elisha (19:19-21).

God kept on loving and helping Elijah even though he was afraid and ran away.

Who was Ben-Hadad?

1 Kings 20

Ben-Hadad was king of the Arameans, the country we call Syria today. His capital city was Damascus. His country was strong and often went to war with Israel.

In the time of Ahab the Arameans were much stronger than Israel. But God gave Israel victory over Ben-Hadad. The prophet who promised Ahab victory explained why. The Lord had

There are many kinds of vineyards in the East, and the grapes are excellent. They ripen in September and October, which is a season of happiness and celebration.

said, "Then you will know I am the Lord" (1 Kings 20:13).

Ahab had many chances to turn to the Lord. God showed he is the true God on Mount Carmel. God also showed Ahab he is the true God by helping him defeat the much larger Syrian army. But Ahab would not change. He still refused to worship God or to serve the Lord.

Naboth wouldn't sell his vineyard
1 Kings 21

Ahab wanted a vineyard that belonged to a man named Naboth. The field was close to the palace. And Ahab wanted it for a garden. He offered to give Naboth an even better vineyard somewhere else, or to pay him money.

But Naboth refused. So Jezebel paid some evil men to lie about Naboth and had Naboth killed! Then Ahab simply took Naboth's field.

Why didn't Naboth just sell his land to the king? God's law said that his people could not sell the land the Lord gave them! Land was to remain in the family forever (Leviticus 25:14-28) Naboth was a good man who obeyed God. So he refused to sell his land to the evil king. Ahab and Jezebel had no right to Naboth's land. And they did a terrible thing in killing him to get it.

What happened to Ahab and Jezebel?
1 Kings 22, 2 Kings 9

After Naboth's death Elijah found Ahab looking over his new vineyard. The angry prophet announced God's judgment on the evil king and queen.

Wild dogs would lick up the king's blood in the place where Naboth was murdered. And dogs would eat the body of Jezebel outside her palace.

The prophet's words came true. You can read about the death of Israel's most evil king and queen in 1 Kings 22 and 2 Kings 9.

The "double portion of Elijah's spirit"
2 Kings 2

Elijah did not die. Instead, he was taken up alive into heaven by a whirlwind. Just before this happened Elisha begged for a double portion of his spirit. What did he mean?

In Bible times the oldest son in the family was the heir. He would inherit a double share of his father's possessions. Elisha was asking to inherit a share of his master's power. He was not asking for twice as much power as Elijah had.

God granted his request. All his life Elisha was God's chief spokesman to Israel. The Bible even reports twice as many miracles by Elisha (14) as by Elijah (7)!

What were Elisha's miracles?
2 Kings

1. Elisha parts the Jordan River (2:1-8)
2. Elisha purifies water (2:19-22)
3. Elisha curses 42 young men (2:23-25)

As Elisha watched, God took Elijah away in a whirlwind. Whirlwinds are still common today and cause much destruction by their great power.

Leprosy was a name used for many different kinds of harmful skin diseases in Bible times. Some kinds of leprosy still exist today.

4. Elisha provides water to win a battle (3:1-25)
5. Elisha multiplies a widow's oil (4:1-7)
6. Elisha raises a dead son (4:8-37)
7. Elisha purifies poisoned food (4:38-41)
8. Elisha multiplies food (4:42-44)
9. Elisha heals Naaman's leprosy (a harmful skin disease) (5:1-19)
10. Elisha curses Gehazi with leprosy (5:19-27)
11. Elisha makes an axhead float (6:1-7)
12. Elisha enables his servant to see an angel army (6:8-17)
13. Elisha blinds an Aramean army (6:18-23)
14. Elisha promises Jehoash victory (13:10-20)

Elisha curses the young men
2 Kings 2:23-25

Some Bible versions read "lads," as if the persons Elisha cursed were children. But these were not children. They were young men. And they made fun of God. They showed disrespect when Elisha reported that God had taken Elijah up to heaven. So Elisha cursed them because they made fun of God. He did not curse them because they had called him a baldhead.

What was leprosy?
2 Kings 5

The Hebrew word translated "leprosy" was used of many skin diseases. People with leprosy in Israel lived apart from everyone else. And they could not go to the Temple to worship the Lord.

What we call leprosy today begins as a white patch on the skin. As it spreads, ridges develop on the body. In time fingers and toes can wear away.

We have medicines today to use in fighting leprosy. In Bible times only God could cure leprosy.

Naaman was a general of the enemy Arameans. He heard of a prophet who could cure his leprosy. So he hurried to Israel. Elisha did cure Naaman. And the general promised that from then on he would worship only the Lord. He would not worship his people's idols. Only the true God could cure this terrible disease.

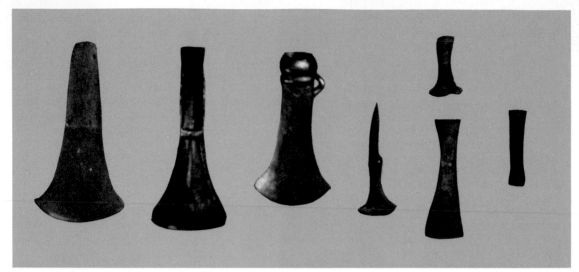

These axheads are from the Bronze Age. They may be very similar to the axhead the prophet Elisha made float on water.

Baal worship in Israel

2 Kings 9–19

Elijah battled Baal worship all his life. He even destroyed 450 priests of Baal. But as long as Ahab and Jezebel lived, the idol worship grew stronger and stronger.

God chose Jehu, an army commander, to be Israel's next king. Jehu killed Jezebel and Ahab's whole family. Jehu then pretended that he would also worship Baal. He called all the ministers of Baal together. Then he had every one killed!

Jehu destroyed Baal worship in Israel. But he kept the false religion established by Jeroboam. Jehu did not try to keep God's law. He had killed Ahab's family and the priests of Baal. But he did it to make his own position more secure, not because he loved God.

To Think about and Do

1. List five ways it might have been fun to be a prophet like Elijah or Elisha. List five ways it might have been hard to be a prophet.

2. Choose one of the 21 miracles listed in this unit. Work with friends to act it out.

3. Sometimes friends feel afraid, as Elijah did (1 Kings 19). What can you learn from the way God helped Elijah that will help your friends?

4. What can you learn about the Arameans and their kings, Ben-Hadad and Hazael (*Házāel*), from a Bible dictionary or encyclopedia? List five facts about each of them.

5. Jehu did the right thing, but for the wrong reason (2 Kings 9,10). Which do you think is more important: 1) to do the right thing or 2) to act for the right reasons? Tell someone about a time you did the right things, but for the wrong reasons.

Kings and prophets in Judah

W hen Solomon's kingdom was divided the southern kingdom was called Judah. Judah had 19 kings. All of them were from King David's family. Eight of the 19 kings were good.

But Judah's people did not remain faithful to God. There were several godly kings. And many prophets warned the people of Judah. But they turned away from God. Finally the Lord sent the Babylonian armies to punish his people. The Babylonians destroyed Jerusalem and the beautiful Temple Solomon built. And they took the people of Judah to Babylon as captives (prisoners).

The good news

• When Judah's kings led their people to obey God, the country was blessed. We will be blessed when we obey God, too.

• God's prophets told Old Testament people how to be faithful to God. We can learn how to be faithful from what they taught.

How long was Judah a nation?

The tribe of Judah remained faithful to David's family. This was when the other tribes broke away in the days of Solomon. They formed their own nation. Judah was ruled by David's descendants from his capital city, Jerusalem (see map, page 91).

The Babylonians destroyed the city of Jerusalem and the beautiful Temple by fire in about the year A.D. 70.

Judah existed as a nation from 930 B.C. to 586 B.C., about 344 years. Israel, the northern nation, was destroyed in 722 B.C., after existing only 208 years.

Why did Judah last so much longer than Israel? Judah had several godly kings. They listened to God's prophets and followed his law. God protected Judah from the enemies who destroyed Israel.

Why was Judah finally destroyed? The people did not remain faithful to God. They chose to worship idols and follow evil ways.

Who were Judah's youngest kings?

Joash (*Jō' ash*) became king when he was only seven years old! His evil grandmother killed his brothers and sisters when Joash was a baby. Joash was hidden and kept safe by the priest Jehoiada (*Je hoi' a da*). You can read about this child-king in 2 Kings 11,12.

Josiah became king of Judah when he was only eight years old. He repaired the Temple of the Lord. While he did this, the people found a

King Hezekiah built an underground waterway into Jerusalem so that if enemies attacked, the Israelites would not have to go outside the city walls to get water. The water collected inside the city as the Pool of Siloam.

Kings and prophets of Judah

Kings ♛	Prophets ♨	Date
☐ Rehoboam		930-913 B.C.
☐ Abijah		913-910 B.C.
☐ Asaᵍ		910-986 B.C.
☐ Jehoshaphatᵍ		872-848 B.C.
☐ Jehoram		853-841 B.C.
☐ Ahaziah		841 B.C.
☐ Athaliah		841-835 B.C.
☐ Joashᵍ	*Joel*	835-796 B.C.
☐ Amaziahᵍ		796-767 B.C.
☐ Azariah (Uzziah)ᵍ	*Isaiah*	792-740 B.C.
☐ Jothamᵍ	*Isaiah* *Micah*	750-732 B.C.
☐ Ahaz	*Micah* *Isaiah*	750-715 B.C.
☐ Hezekiahᵍ	*Isaiah* *Micah*	715-686 B.C.
☐ Manasseh		697-642 B.C.
☐ Amon		642-640 B.C.
☐ Josiahᵍ	*Huldah* *Nahum* *Habakkuk* *Jeremiah*	640-609 B.C.
☐ Jehoahazᵍ	*Zephaniah* *Jeremiah*	609 B.C.
☐ Jehoiakimᵍ	*Jeremiah*	609-598 B.C.
☐ Jehoiachinᵍ	*Jeremiah*	598-597 B.C.
☐ Zedekiahᵍ	*Jeremiah*	597-586 B.C.

Note: Sometimes kings ruled at the same time as their fathers or sons. A ᵍ indicates good kings.

God saved Jerusalem

2 Kings 18,19

The Assyrians who destroyed the northern kingdom of Israel also attacked Judah. King Sennacherib (*Se nak' er ib*) destroyed many cities in Judah. And he sent his army commander to Jerusalem to frighten King Hezekiah. The Assyrians laughed at Hezekiah for depending on God.

Hezekiah asked all of his people to pray. Then Isaiah the prophet gave the king a message. God promised that the Assyrian king "will not enter this city or even shoot an arrow here" (2 Kings 19:32).

God kept his promise. God struck dead 185,000 of the Assyrian soldiers. And Sennacherib went home to be murdered by his own sons!

Sennacherib left a record of his invasion. It was carved in a stone called the Taylor Prism. Sennacherib bragged about taking 46 strong cities of Judah and many prisoners. But all he said about Jerusalem was that he shut Hezekiah up behind its walls "like a bird in a cage."

Sennacherib did not mention the deaths in his army. But a Greek history writer named Herodotus (*Her ōd' ō tus*) did! Herodotus said field mice swarmed into the Assyrian camp. And they ate bow strings and shield handles. Some think that a terrible disease like the Black Plague, carried by the rats and mice, killed the Assyrian soldiers.

God really did protect King Hezekiah and his people when they trusted him. God takes care of us, too, when we trust the Lord.

Babylonian god carved in stone, dating back to 2000 B.C..

copy of the Law. They thought it had been lost. Josiah decided to obey the Law of God completely. He became one of Judah's most godly kings. One of the things Josiah did was to smash false altars and idols throughout Judah. Josiah also fulfilled a 300-year-old prophecy! He burned the bones of false priests on the evil altar Jeroboam had set up at Dan (1 Kings 13). You can read about this child-king in 2 Kings 22,23.

Assyrian warriors

Locusts are insects much like grasshoppers. They eat green plants, and big swarms of them can completely destroy crops.

Joel's message

Joel

Great swarms of grasshopper-like locusts often destroyed crops in Bible lands. One swarm of desert locusts was studied in 1899. This swarm was near the Red Sea and covered 2,000 square miles!

A swarm of locusts darkened the skies in Joel's day. They ate every green thing in the land of Judah. And the prophet recognized them as part of God's judgment. The book of Joel tells about the terrible plague of locusts in the prophet's day (Joel 1:1–2:27). It also warns of terrible punishments to come from God in the future (Joel 2:28–3:8). But Joel makes a promise, too. One day God will come to his people, and there will be peace.

Micah's message

Micah

Micah was very concerned when the people of Israel and Judah did not obey God's law. He warned against idolatry. He also warned against mistreating the poor people. The leaders of Israel and Judah were not protecting the innocent!

Micah pictures God in a courtroom, accusing his people. God will surely punish both countries unless they change their hearts and lives.

One very famous verse in Micah explains what God wants from people who love him. God "has told you what is good. He has told you what he wants from you: Do what is right to other people. Love being kind to others. And live humbly, trusting your God" (Micah 6:8).

The people of Israel did not listen to Micah. And they did not listen to their own prophets. So they were destroyed. King Hezekiah of Judah did listen. And God delayed the punishment that Micah wrote about (Jeremiah 26:17-19).

Isaiah's message

Isaiah

Isaiah was one of the Bible's greatest prophets. He may have been a priest. He was a friend of King Hezekiah. Isaiah's preaching shows us that Hezekiah was a good king. But there was still sin and unfairness in Judah in Hezekiah's time.

What are some of the special things in Isaiah? First of all, Isaiah tells us many wonderful things about God. And he helps us understand what they mean. God is the Holy One (Isaiah 5:16), Lord of heaven's armies (Isaiah 8:13), our salvation (Isaiah 12:2), the everlasting God (Isaiah 44:6), the living God (Isaiah 40:11; 41:10), and Lord of glory (Isaiah 60:1-3).

Second, Isaiah writes often about Jesus long before Jesus was born (John 12:37-40). Some of the passages about Jesus are Isaiah 7:14; 9:1-8; 11:1-12; 53:1-12.

Like the other prophets, Isaiah warns that God will punish his people for their sin. But Isaiah also describes a wonderful time of peace and blessing. God will bring that time to earth after the punishment is past. If you wonder about the good things God brings to his people you can read about them in these verses: Isaiah 35:1-10; Isaiah 49:10-12; Isaiah 54:6-10; Isaiah 60:1-12; Isaiah 62:1-7; Isaiah 65:21-25.

Nahum's message

Nahum

Nahum wrote to comfort the people of Judah. He promised that God would destroy the power of their terrible enemy, Assyria. And he would destroy their capital

Habakkuk's message

Habakkuk

Habakkuk was a prophet in the days of godly King Josiah. Josiah repaired the Temple of God at Jerusalem. Josiah stopped the worship of false gods and goddesses. And he led his people in a promise to keep God's law.

But Habakkuk was still troubled. Even with a godly king, the people of Judah did not keep God's law! There were so many evil people in Judah that terrible wrongs still happened all the time (Habakkuk 1:3,4).

So Habakkuk asked God how he could put up with such evil ways. And God answered him. God would send the Babylonians. They would destroy Jerusalem in a war and punish the people of Judah (Habakkuk 1:5-17).

Habakkuk was not happy with God's answer. But he agreed that the people of Judah should be punished. Habakkuk knew that he, too, would suffer when the Babylonians came (Habakkuk 3:16-17). But Habakkuk remained sure of one thing. God would give him strength for the hard times. And he would rejoice in the Lord his Savior (Habakkuk 3:18-19).

The Babylonian empire was powerful. This is a reproduction of what the Ishtar Gate might have looked like.

Who were the Babylonians?

The city of Babylon was part of the Assyrian empire until 627 B.C. Then it became independent. By 605 B.C. Babylon, led by its greatest king, Nebuchadnezzar (*Neb ū kad nez' er*), defeated the Assyrians. They took over the Assyrian empire!

All the countries of Palestine surrendered to Babylon at that time. Soon Judah turned against Babylon! So Nebuchadnezzar marched his armies back to Judah. He captured Jerusalem in 597 B.C. But the leaders and people of Judah still turned against them! Finally, the last of the people were taken captives to Babylon in 586 B.C.

Babylonians capture enemy cities

Habakkuk describes the terrible Babylonian army. Their "armies march quickly like a whirlwind in the desert" (Habakkuk 1:9). When they come to strong, walled cities "they build dirt roads up to the top of the walls. They capture the cities" (Habakkuk 1:10).

Ancient armies had ways to capture walled cities. Sometimes they would build fires at the base of the walls. The heat cracked the stone. Then it gradually wore away. Sometimes they used catapults (weapons that shot stones) to throw great boulders. Sometimes the catapults shot dead bodies into a city to cause disease. The enemy army might try to dig tunnels under the walls. Or they might try to beat down the city gates with heavy weapons called battering

rams. But the Babylonians put thousands of soldiers and prisoners to work. They simply piled dirt against the city wall. These earth hills were as high as the walls. So the Babylonian soldiers charged up the ramps and took the city.

People in the cities fought back. They shot arrows, threw rocks and poured hot oil on the enemy below them. But no cities could survive an attack by the mighty Babylonians.

Messages of Zephaniah and Jeremiah
Zephaniah, Jeremiah

Zephaniah and Jeremiah were prophets. They began speaking out in the time of Josiah. Both lived through the reign of several of the evil kings who followed the godly Josiah.

Zephaniah delivers a simple message in his three short chapters. Judah's sins are so great that God must surely judge them. Some day God will judge all people. Soon God will judge Judah.

Jeremiah's book has 52 long chapters. The book contains many sermons by this prophet. But the book of Jeremiah also tells the sad story of the prophet himself. Jeremiah spoke God's words of warning. But instead of listening, the kings and people of Judah became angry at him! The prophet was put in jail, and his life was

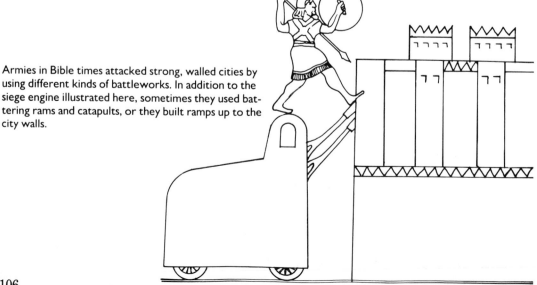

Armies in Bible times attacked strong, walled cities by using different kinds of battleworks. In addition to the siege engine illustrated here, sometimes they used battering rams and catapults, or they built ramps up to the city walls.

A potter makes dishes and utensils from wet clay by molding the clay with his hands as it spins on a wheel. Handmade pottery is still very popular today.

threatened. Still Jeremiah faithfully urged his people to surrender to the Babylonians and live. For over 40 years Jeremiah delivered God's warnings to Judah. Finally Jeremiah saw all his words of warning come true. The Babylonian army burned Jerusalem and the beautiful Temple of the Lord that King Solomon had built.

You can read about the final battle and destruction of Jerusalem in Jeremiah 52.

But you can read good news in Jeremiah, too. God loves his people "with a love that will last forever" (Jeremiah 31:3). God allowed the Babylonians to destroy Judah and take his people from the promised land. But God will bring them back to the land. And his city will be rebuilt (Jeremiah 31:6).

But the best news in Jeremiah is about Jesus.

Jeremiah looks into the distant future. He talks of a time when God will make a new covenant (agreement) with his people. Then God will forgive his people's sins. And he will put his law in his people's hearts (Jeremiah 31:33-34).

When Jesus died, that new covenant was kept. Jesus forgives us. And his Holy Spirit is in our hearts. He helps us to know and to keep God's law (Hebrews 8).

What happened to Judah?

Many of the people of Judah were killed when the Babylonians invaded them. Others died on their way to captivity. But those who lived settled down in the land of their enemy. They would wait until God would keep his promise to bring them back home again.

Many of the people of Judah were taken away as slaves by the Babylonians.

To Think about and Do

1. What can you learn from good kings about being a godly person? Read about four. Then tell how you can be like them.

Asa (1 Kings 15:9-24)
Jehoshaphat (1 Kings 22:41-50)
Joash (2 Kings 11,12)
Amaziah (2 Kings 14:1-22)

Azariah (2 Kings 15:1-7)
Jotham (2 Kings 15:8-32)
Josiah (2 Kings 22,23)

2. Imagine you are a child-king like Joash or Josiah. Draw pictures for your scrapbook. Tell some of the things you plan to command. You can get ideas by reading 2 Kings 11 and 12, or 22 and 23.

3. Pretend you are a lawyer working up a case against Israel and Judah. Read Micah chapter 3. List charges you will bring against these people when the case comes to court.

4. What does Isaiah say about God and Jesus? Look up the verses listed for *one* of these topics (see page 104). What are three things you learn?

5. What was Jeremiah like? Read these verses about him. Now think of five words to describe him.

Jeremiah 1:6-19
Jeremiah 20:1-6
Jeremiah 26:1-15

Jeremiah 28:1-17
Jeremiah 36:1-32
Jeremiah 37:1-21

In a strange land

The people of Judah were taken to Babylon. They settled near the rich and busy capital city of the people who had destroyed their homeland. Life was not hard. And the people were not persecuted (mistreated). But the people began to feel sad for the promised land. Many of them turned to the Lord.

The good news

- God protects his people even among their enemies.

- Godly people can become famous and important.

- God uses even our hard times for good.

What do we know about Babylon?

The city of Babylon was the capital of the Babylonian empire. It was built on the Euphrates River. People who study old things began to explore its ruins almost 100 years ago. Many of

The Ishtar Gate was the entrance to the Processional Street that led to the palace of King Nebuchadnezzar II in Babylonia. This is a representation of how it might have looked.

the careful records the Babylonians kept have been found. These include plans for buildings, descriptions of festivals, records of money spent on public buildings and much literature.

The city of Babylon covered more than 3,000 acres. It was surrounded by walls wide enough for chariot races. One gate from those walls was the Ishtar gate. It was covered with blue tiles and decorated with colorful animal figures.

King Nebuchadnezzar built a famous structure called the Hanging Gardens. It was one of the seven wonders of the ancient world. The gardens were planted on different levels of a great man-made hill. Water was pumped up the hill to keep trees and plants green.

The city of Babylon was surrounded for miles by fields, irrigation canals, homes and businesses. The Israelites were settled by the Kebar River. It was a canal about 60 miles from Nebuchadnezzar's capital city.

Nebuchadnezzar was very proud of the city he built. Old writings found in Babylon report Nebuchadnezzar's bragging words: "Huge cedars from Lebanon, I cut down. With shining gold I covered them, with jewels I decorated them . . . Giant bulls I made of bronze work and clothed them with white marble."

Nebuchadnezzar did accomplish many wonderful things. But his pride led to a terrible judgment from God. Daniel tells of this great king's madness in chapter 4 of his book.

Life in Babylon

Three times groups from Judah were taken to Babylon. The first group was made up of leaders and nobles. Daniel and his three young friends were taken with the first group in 597 B.C. Members of this group probably lived in the capital city itself. That is where Daniel and his three friends were trained to work in Nebuchadnezzar's government.

The final group, taken in 586 B.C., was probably about 70,000 people. The Jews were all settled in their own district. It was called Telabib and was near the Kebar canal. Now called "Jews" (people of Judah), the captives worked on

These were called the Hanging Gardens because they were planted on different levels of a great man-made hill. They were one of the seven wonders of the ancient world.

God sent Ezekiel to the Valley of Dry Bones where Ezekiel saw the bones of dead people come back to life. This was a symbol that God would bring his people back to their homeland.

the king's buildings. And they entered business as merchants. Babylonian business records with Jewish names have been found. At least one successful trading company was owned and run by Jews.

The captives lived on land where much food grows. They raised garden crops (Jeremiah 29:4,7) and may have owned their own homes. The Jewish community even had its own elders and leaders. And it lived under its own laws. The prophet Ezekiel lived in such a community. He gave God's message to the captives.

In fact, life was very good in Babylon. Seventy years later another ruler, Cyrus, told them they could go home! Many of the Jews chose to stay there.

But others were sad for the land they had lost and sins they had done. The Bible book of Lamentations was written in Babylon. It shows the sadness that many of the Jewish people felt. They were away from the land God had promised to Abraham.

Joy is gone from our hearts;
    our dancing has turned to mourning.
The crown has fallen from our head.
    Misery has come to us
        because we have sinned!
Because of this our hearts have become sick.
    And our eyes have become dim
        because of these things.
Mount Zion is a wasteland.
    On Mount Zion foxes prowl about.
                        Lamentations 5:16-18

God's people would be brought back to the promised land one day. But for now, they must remain captives in the foreign land of Babylon.

Ezekiel's message
Ezekiel

Ezekiel may have been taken with the first group of captives. He was a prophet who lived in Babylon 10 years before Jerusalem was destroyed. He was like Jeremiah back in Judah. Ezekiel told his people that God had chosen

The king of Babylon made a law against praying to anyone but him. But Daniel continued to pray to God, so he was thrown into a den of lions. But God saved Daniel from the lions.

Babylon to punish them for their sins.

Several things are special about Ezekiel. He often acted out his messages from God. Ezekiel built a toy army and battle works and attacked a toy Jerusalem. He wasn't just playing soldiers. Ezekiel was showing what would happen in his homeland (Ezekiel 4).

Ezekiel packed a few belongings and left home each day. But he would slip back each night through a hole he dug in the wall. As Ezekiel walked he shook and trembled. This was to show how afraid the people of Judah would be. This would happen when the Babylonians forced them to leave their homes (Ezekiel 12:17-25).

Ezekiel also had many visions. In one he was taken back to Jerusalem. And he saw the leaders of his people. They were worshiping statues and idols right inside the Temple of God! As Ezekiel watched, God's presence left the Temple and Jerusalem. The Lord had left his special city. God would not protect Jerusalem when the Babylonian armies came again (Ezekiel 8-11).

But Ezekiel also had a message of hope. After Jerusalem was actually destroyed, Ezekiel gave the captives wonderful promises. God would bring the people back to their land (Ezekiel 34:25-31) and the Temple would be rebuilt (Ezekiel 40-48).

Daniel in Babylon

Daniel was one of the first captives taken to Babylon. He was trained to be a leader in the Babylonian empire. We know many familiar stories about Daniel. But how old was Daniel when those things happened?

In 605 B.C. Daniel was taken to Babylon and put in the king's school. He was probably 12 or 13 years old. But even as a young boy, Daniel chose to be faithful to God (Daniel 1:8-20).

Four or five years later Daniel was about 18. Then he explained Nebuchadnezzar's dream. Daniel saved the lives of all Babylon's wise men. And he won a high place in the government (Daniel 2:24-45).

Many years later another king of Babylon

came to Daniel. He asked Daniel to explain strange writing that appeared on a wall (Daniel 5:22-30). Daniel was 77 or 78 years old! That night Cyrus from Persia captured Babylon.

Daniel became one of the three highest officers in the Persian empire. Others hated Daniel. They plotted to get rid of him. Daniel, now an old man over eighty, was thrown into a den of lions (Daniel 6). But again God protected this man. Daniel loved and served the Lord in a foreign land.

Daniel was faithful to God and honest all of his long life. He was a member of a captive people. But he became a respected leader in the government of the Babylonian and Persian empires.

Daniel's message

God gave Daniel visions of what would happen to great nations in the future. You can find out about the visions of Daniel and how they came true, in chapter 19 (page 117).

Queen Esther helped her people

Esther

The Babylonians were defeated by Cyrus. He set up a Persian empire. Most of the Jewish people who lived outside the promised land settled in great cities like Babylon.

Esther was an orphan girl who lived with her cousin, Mordecai (*MOR' de ki*). They lived in the Persian capital of Shushan (Susa), in what is now Iran.

The king of that time was Xerxes (*Zurk' séz*). What happened in Esther took place between 483 and 471 B.C.

We know about Xerxes from history. He was the Persian king who tried to invade Greece. But he was defeated in great land and sea battles. The Greek historian Herodotus even tells about a banquet like the one mentioned in Esther 1:1-4. Herodotus explains that it was held to talk over plans for attacking the Greek states.

Esther's story is one of the most interesting in the Bible. It tells how God used the young queen to stop a plot. This plot would have killed all the Jewish people. Today the Jewish people have a special day to remember Esther. It is called the Feast of Purim.

For many years some people said that Esther was simply a story. They said it was made up hundreds of years after it was supposed to have happened. But people who study old things have found out a lot about the Persian

In Bible times people sealed important papers and letters with hot wax. They pressed a special symbol into the wax showing whom it was from. Some seals were worn as signet rings, and others were worn on a cord around the neck.

empire. The book of Esther contains many detailed descriptions of Persian customs. And it gives technical names for government officials. Now everyone agrees that Esther must have been written by a person who was actually in the Persian court. And that person was there at the time Esther was queen.

What good came from captivity?

The Babylonian captivity was punishment from God. But God used the punishment to help his people. Before going to Babylon the Jewish people often worshiped idols. After their captivity, they refused to worship idols. They would not worship them even when foreign rulers tried to make them.

In Babylon the captives began to gather. They would study the Law and worship together. They called the place they met a synagogue (the name for the Jewish church building).

Also, some people in Babylon realized why the captivity had come. It was because their people had not loved God or obeyed God's law. These men decided to study God's word. They would obey it themselves and teach others (Ezra 7:10). These students were called scribes. One of the scribes, Ezra, was a leader of the people when they returned to Judah.

Even punishment can be a good gift when it helps us to stop doing wrong. It helps us to learn to do good. God planned the Babylonian captivity to punish sin. But he brought good to his people as well.

To Think about and Do

1. Why were so many of the captives in Babylon unhappy? Find three reasons in Lamentations 1:16-22.

2. What messages from God did Ezekiel act out?

Ezekiel 4:1-3
Ezekiel 4:4-8
Ezekiel 4:9-17
Ezekiel 5:1-17

Ezekiel 12:1-16
Ezekiel 12:17-20
Ezekiel 24:15-27

What Bible story can you act out for your family?

3. Suppose a friend asks you, "How can I get to be famous and important?" Daniel became very famous and important. Figure out five rules for success from how Daniel behaved (Daniel 1-6).

4. The book of Esther does not mention God or report any miracles. How do you know that God was taking care of Esther and the Jewish people? Ask your mom or dad to read the story of Esther out loud. Then talk about how we know God was taking care of her and the Jews.

5. Who was Xerxes? Why did he want to invade the Greeks? What can you find out from history books about this powerful ruler?

Rebuild Jerusalem – and wait

Cyrus defeated Babylon and established the Persian empire in its place. Then he permitted captive peoples to return to their homelands. Several thousand Jews went back to the promised land. They were eager to rebuild the Temple of God and the city of Jerusalem.

The good news

- People who listen to God's word and obey it are blessed.
- The prophet Haggai taught the Jews to put God first. We can put God first in our life. Then we will be blessed as they were.

The people return

Before Jerusalem was destroyed Jeremiah had prophesied that the Jews' captivity would last 70 years (Jeremiah 25:11-12; Jeremiah 29:10). When Cyrus defeated Babylon he set up a Persian empire in 538 B.C. He immediately

Nehemiah supervised the men who rebuilt the walls of the city of Jerusalem.

ordered a return of the Jews. Cyrus also ordered the Jews to rebuild the Temple in Jerusalem. The cost of rebuilding was to be paid by the Persians. The gold and silver tools the Babylonians had taken from Solomon's Temple were to be returned!

Ezra 1–6 tells of the first group's exciting return. The people who lived near their land did not want the Jews to succeed. They tried to frighten them away. But God helped the Jews overcome their neighbors.

This first group of 42,360 settlers returned to Judah in 537 B.C. A second group followed eighty years later in 458 B.C. And a smaller, third group returned in 444 B.C.

Haggai's message
Haggai

The Jews who returned to Judah were supposed to rebuild the Temple in Jerusalem. They did lay the foundation. But they did not finish the building.

The captives had heard stories of a land where much food grows. But Judah had been ruined by Nebuchadnezzar's armies. Its fields were now filled with weeds. The people had to struggle to clear the land, plant crops and build homes. They thought they had no time to give to build the Temple of the Lord. They worked hard, but each year things seemed worse.

The prophet Haggai preached sermons telling the people to finish the Temple. His first sermon is found in Haggai 1:1-15. Haggai told the Jews that they did not care about God. And he said they should finish the Temple of the Lord. The leaders and people listened to Haggai. They began work right away.

Haggai preached other sermons (Haggai 2:1-9,10-19,20-23). In these sermons Haggai gave them a special promise from God. The people had obeyed the Lord. Haggai promised that from now on God would bless them.

God does bless all who are faithful to him.

After the Temple was completed, Ezra led the second group that returned to Judah (Ezra 7-10). Ezra was given a very special privilege by the Persian emperor. Ezra was to appoint judges. These judges would rule Judah but not by Persian law. They would rule by the law of the Lord. God's people must still pay taxes to Persia. They would not have their own king or nation. But the people of God would be ruled by the law of the Lord.

Who was Nehemiah?
Nehemiah

Nehemiah (*Ne he mi' ah*) was a high officer in the Persian emperor's court. He was upset when he heard that the walls of Jerusalem were still broken down. This was in 444 B.C. He led a small group to Jerusalem to help the people rebuild their city walls.

The book of Nehemiah is his own story. Nehemiah faced many bad feelings from neighbors. He also had to battle the rich in Judah who were cheating the poor people. Nehemiah found that many people were breaking God's laws. Even priests had married women who worshiped idols.

Nehemiah did rebuild Jerusalem's walls, in spite of all his enemies. He served two terms as governor in Judah. During Nehemiah's life he made his people obey God's law. But after Nehemiah died, the people of Judah again disobeyed God.

Zechariah's message
Zechariah

Zechariah (*Zek a rī ah*) lived at the same time as Haggai. In fact, Zechariah preached his first sermon (Zechariah 1:1-6) on the day of Haggai's second sermon.

The first part of Zechariah reports visions (special messages) God gave the prophet. The last part of Zechariah tells what will happen when the Lord comes at last to save his people. There will be great battles, but "then the Lord my God will come, and all the holy ones will be with him" (Zechariah 14:5).

Zechariah's message was important. This was because the people of Judah would have to wait hundreds of years before God acted again. Zechariah and Daniel both warned the Jewish

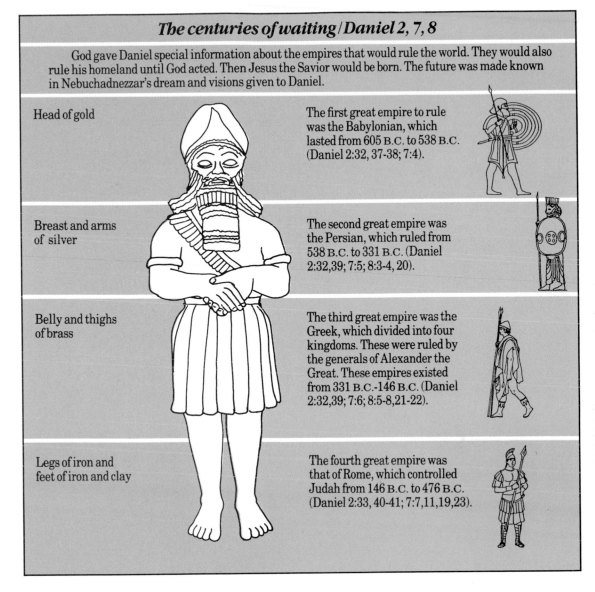

The centuries of waiting / Daniel 2, 7, 8

God gave Daniel special information about the empires that would rule the world. They would also rule his homeland until God acted. Then Jesus the Savior would be born. The future was made known in Nebuchadnezzar's dream and visions given to Daniel.

Head of gold

The first great empire to rule was the Babylonian, which lasted from 605 B.C. to 538 B.C. (Daniel 2:32, 37-38; 7:4).

Breast and arms of silver

The second great empire was the Persian, which ruled from 538 B.C. to 331 B.C. (Daniel 2:32,39; 7:5; 8:3-4, 20).

Belly and thighs of brass

The third great empire was the Greek, which divided into four kingdoms. These were ruled by the generals of Alexander the Great. These empires existed from 331 B.C.-146 B.C. (Daniel 2:32,39; 7:6; 8:5-8,21-22).

Legs of iron and feet of iron and clay

The fourth great empire was that of Rome, which controlled Judah from 146 B.C. to 476 B.C. (Daniel 2:33, 40-41; 7:7,11,19,23).

people of a long wait. They told them something of what would happen during the coming centuries. The chart on this page shows events Daniel told about before they happened.

Malachi's message

Malachi

Malachi is the last book of the Old Testament. It was written over 400 years before Jesus came.

Daniel and Zechariah both told the Jewish people that God would not forget them. This was even though centuries would pass before God acted again. God would not forget. But would God's people remember him? And would they be faithful to the Lord?

Malachi tells how quickly the people of Judah forgot the Lord and turned away from him. Just a few years after Nehemiah's death the people of Judah stopped worshiping God (Malachi 1:6–2:9). And they broke promises (Malachi 2:10-16). They doubted the Lord (Malachi 2:17—3:5). And they no longer believed he was important (Malachi 3:6–4:3).

The book of Malachi closes with a warning. The evil people will be punished when God does act. But those who love God and honor him will be his own special treasure. God will spare the people who love him when he comes (Malachi 3:16-18).

Did Daniel tell the future?

Daniel

Daniel's prophecy told of all the world empires that would follow each other. They would rule from his time to the birth of Christ (see chart). Every detail was accurate. Daniel even wrote of the death of the great Greek conqueror Alexander. Daniel even told how his four generals would divide up the empire he won (Daniel 8:5-8, 21-22).

At one time people said that such an accurate account must have been written after each empire came. They said it could not have been written hundreds of years before. They argued that the writer of Daniel had made

mistakes. They said Nabonidus (*Na bon i dus*), not Belshazzar, was ruler when Babylon fell.

But people who study old things have shown that Daniel *was* right! Belshazzar was king with his father Nabonidus. Nabonidus was in Arabia when Babylon fell! Many other details of Daniel show that the book was written by a person of Daniel's time. This person knew about the Babylonian and Persian courts. And a man high in the government would have known these same things.

How then could Daniel have told what would happen hundreds of years ahead of time? God, who knows the future, made these things known to Daniel.

God wanted the Jewish people to know through the centuries of waiting that what was happening to them was part of God's plan. God was still in control of history. When the time came God would act again.

And God did act. When it was just the right time, God sent Jesus into the world to become our Savior.

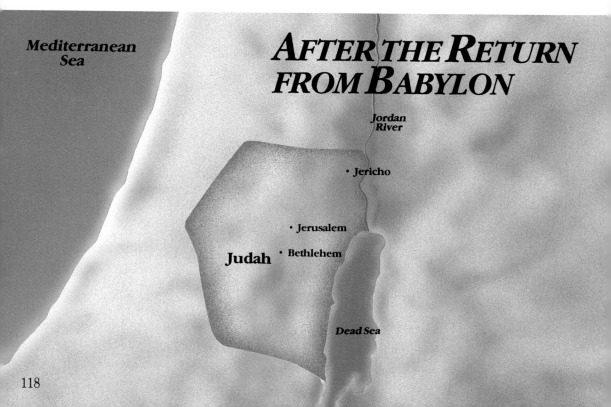

Mediterranean
Sea

AFTER THE RETURN FROM BABYLON

Jordan
River

• Jericho

• Jerusalem

Judah • Bethlehem

Dead Sea

This is a seal of Darius, king of the Persian empire. It shows him hunting a lion from his chariot.

To Think about and Do

1. The people of Judah listened to Haggai's sermon. They went to work finishing the Temple. God blessed them when they obeyed. Listen to a sermon in your church. How can you obey the Lord?

2. Nehemiah gave each person rebuilding the wall his own job (Nehemiah 3). Plan a class or family work project to help someone in your church or community. Plan ahead of time what each of you will do to help.

3. Nehemiah's enemies tried to keep him from succeeding. What tricks did the enemy use?

Nehemiah 4:1-6   Nehemiah 4:16-23   Nehemiah 6:10-13
Nehemiah 4:7-15   Nehemiah 6:1-9

What can we learn from Nehemiah to make sure we have success?

4. How did the people in Malachi's time show God was not important to them? Read these passages. Then tell your parents how you can show that God *is* important to you!

Malachi 1:6-9   Malachi 3:10-16   Malachi 3:6-12
Malachi 1:11-14   Malachi 2:17   Malachi 3:14-18

5. What can you learn about Alexander the Great and the Greeks who conquered Persia? What can you learn about the Roman armies? Check your church or school library and write five facts about each on a 3″ × 5″ card. Compare your cards with the cards others have made.

The world of Jesus

Jesus was born in Bethlehem, about five miles south of Jerusalem. It was in the land God promised to Abraham's children. In those days the land of the Jews was just a tiny part of the great Roman Empire. No one thought that anything important could happen there. But for hundreds of years God had been preparing the land, and the whole world. Now everything was ready for the birth of God's Son, Jesus!

The good news

- God prepared the world so everything was ready for the birth of his Son.
- At just the right time, God sent his Son Jesus to be our Savior. And he would reveal God's love to everyone.

What the world was like

The promised land when Jesus was born

When Jesus was born, the promised land was a small province (area) in the great Roman Empire. There were about 4,000,000 Jews in the world. But only about 700,000 lived in their homeland.

Many of these Jews lived in Galilee or Judea. These are two areas we read about in the New Testament. More lived in Perea (see map, page 134). Jews did not like to live in Samaria, which separated these areas.

How big was the Roman Empire?

In the time of Jesus, the Roman emperor Augustus ruled a large area. He controlled all the lands along the Mediterranean Sea and the island of Britain.

Roman armies, organized into well-armed "legions," were the most powerful in the world. The Romans had built roads paved with stone throughout their empire. Then their armies

ISLAND OF BRITAIN

THE ROMAN EMPIRE IN NEW TESTAMENT TIMES

GALLIA — Rhine River

Danube River

ITALY — Black Sea

HISPANIA

CORSICA — Rome — MACEDONIA — Byzantium — CAPPADOCIA

SARDINIA — PHRYGIA — GALATIA — Tigris River — Euphrates River

Corinth — Athens — LYCIA AND PAMPHYLIA — CILICIA

SICILIA

Carthage — CRETE

Mediterranean Sea — MESOPOTAMIA — JUDEA

AFRICA — CYRENE — Alexandria — Jerusalem

could march quickly wherever they were needed. The Romans also destroyed the pirates that once made sea travel dangerous. The Roman armies made travel on land and sea safe. This helped Christian missionaries travel all over the world telling people about Jesus.

The Romans sometimes let the people they conquered rule themselves. The Jews were ruled by local courts and by the Sanhedrin. The Sanhedrin was a council of leaders. The Sanhedrin was to use God's law to rule God's people.

In Jesus' time a Roman governor was over the Sanhedrin in Judea. And a son of a king called Herod the Great ruled for the Romans in Galilee and Perea.

When Jesus was born, Herod the Great was still alive. He ruled all these areas. Herod the Great is the king who tried to have the baby Jesus killed. Herod was a cruel and wicked man. He killed his own wife and children when he thought they wanted his kingdom. Herod was called "the Great" because he built many cities and palaces. Herod also had the Temple of God in Jerusalem made larger and more beautiful.

When Herod the Great died, terrible battles were fought in Judea and Galilee. Thousands were killed. The Roman army stopped the fighting. Things were peaceful again for some twenty years under three different Roman governors. Then Pontius Pilate became governor of Judea. There was more violence and executions.

Jewish people and Roman rule

People do not like foreigners to rule them. In 167 B.C. the Jews had turned against a different foreign ruler. He had ordered them to worship false gods. The Jews were led by Judas Maccabeus, nicknamed "the Hammer." He established a Jewish kingdom.

The little Jewish kingdom was taken by the Romans. It was turned over to the father of Herod the Great. This happened about 60 years before Jesus was born.

Many of the Jewish people dreamed of a time they would be free again. Different political groups in Judea argued about how that freedom would come. The Zealots wanted to turn against

Rome and go to war. The Sadducees controlled the priesthood in Jesus' day. They thought it was best to get along with the Romans. They also wanted to keep their own political power. The Pharisees were a small group of about 6,000 men. They only wanted to keep God's law carefully. They were waiting for God's promised Messiah to bring freedom.

The word Messiah means "anointed one." In Bible times a person was often appointed for a special task by being anointed. Sweet-smelling olive oil was poured on that person's head. The Old Testament promised that one day God would send his people a Savior. The Savior would be appointed by God for his special task. So he was called the Messiah. In the troubled times that Jesus lived, most of the Jewish people hoped the Messiah would come soon. They looked for God's

A Roman soldier in uniform.

Many homes in Palestine today are like homes of Bible times.

Messiah to set them free from the Romans. And they wanted him to make Judah a powerful kingdom again.

The people of Jesus' day did not think about other Old Testament promises about the Messiah. He would deliver them from sin, not just from foreign rulers. They looked for a powerful ruler. So, many people refused to believe that the carpenter from Nazareth could be the Savior promised to them by God.

What life was like

What language did people speak?

Most people who lived east of the Mediterranean Sea in the Roman Empire spoke Greek.

The Jewish people used both Hebrew, their first language, and Aramaic. Jesus and his disciples probably spoke all three languages.

What were houses like?

Houses in the land of Jesus were usually built of sun-dried brick. In the cities, poorer and middle class people often rented single rooms in large apartment buildings.

The houses of wealthy people were very comfortable. They had many rooms and were built around an open courtyard. Some houses even had furnaces. Hot air was carried to parts of the house by pipes. Some houses also had running water.

Most houses in Galilee and Judea were one

story. The roof was flat. It was made of tiles or layers of branches and mud. Stairs on the outside of the house led to the roof. People often ate and slept there. A low wall around the roof kept people from falling off.

What did people eat?

The Jews ate two regular meals, at noon and in the evening. Most people ate fruits and vegetables and sometimes fish and cheeses. Meat was usually eaten only on festival days. Bread, cooked in flat, round loaves, was a basic food.

What were clothes like?

Jewish men wore white tunics. A tunic was something like a long shirt, about knee length. They also wore a belt, called a girdle in some Bible versions. And they wore shoes or sandals on their feet. The men wore their hair shorter than the men of some other nations. And they grew beards. Women wore short tunics under a brighter colored outer tunic that came to their feet. A Jewish woman wore a veil that covered her head, but not her face.

What work did people do?

In the Roman Empire as a whole there were probably more slaves than free men. There were fewer slaves in the little land of the Jews.

People did many things to earn a living. Many worked on small farms or herded sheep. Some had little shops or small businesses. There were fishermen, men who made animal hides into leather, tentmakers and carpenters. Each of these four last occupations is mentioned in the New Testament.

There was also the occupation of tax collecting. The Romans made the people of the lands they ruled pay many taxes. The Jews hated the

In the East, stairs on the outside of houses led to the flat roof where people often ate, slept or sat in the cool of the evening.

tax collectors. They sent money they collected to Rome. But they often stole extra money for themselves. Few Jews were friends with tax collectors, even though they were Jews, too.

Did children go to school?

The Jewish people in Jesus' time thought education was very important for boys. Jewish boys began to go to school in their local synagogue (place of worship) at age six. They were taught to read and write from the Old Testament. They also learned simple arithmetic and religious rituals (customs).

Every Jewish boy also learned a skill. Then he would be able to work and provide for himself and his family.

Only a few Jewish boys continued to study when they grew older. They studied with a rabbi (Jewish teacher), hoping to learn from him. The goal of higher education was to help the student become an expert in the Old Testament.

Jewish worship

Cities and towns throughout the Roman Empire had synagogues, or Jewish churches. On the Sabbath (Saturday), the Jewish people gathered there to read the Old Testament and pray.

In Jerusalem, the priests offered animal sacrifices. The people brought these to the Lord at the beautiful Temple.

Also, Jews from all over the world traveled to Jerusalem for special religious holidays.

At Passover the Jews celebrated the time God brought the Israelites out of Egypt. Pentecost celebrated harvest time. Rosh Hashanah was the New Year. On the Day of Atonement (Cleansing) the people were to be sorry for their sins. And a special sacrifice was made for sin. The Feast of Shelters was a very happy festival. Families lived outdoors in tent-like shelters made of branches. Then they remembered Israel's journey from Egypt to the promised land.

To Think about and Do

1. How big was the Roman Empire? Compare a modern map with the map on page 120. What modern countries were part of the great Roman Empire?

2. To learn about the world of Jesus' time, prepare reports on the following subjects. You may write your report, draw it, or be ready to tell about it. Think about working with a friend.

- Roman roads
- Augustus
- Pontius Pilate
- Roman legions
- Herod
- Herod's temple
- Sadducees
- Pharisees

3. Why did the people in Jesus' day think the Messiah would be a powerful ruler and free them from the Romans? Look up these verses about the Messiah in the Old Testament:

Isaiah 11:1-11   Jeremiah 23:5,65   Zechariah 9:9-17

Tell someone how you would answer the question.

4. Plan and prepare a Bible times meal for your family or your class. What will you serve? (Figs, grapes and other fruit. Flat pita bread is available in many stores. Cheese and perhaps some boiled or broiled fish.)

5. Yearly festivals helped the Jewish people remember God and what he had done for them. List each festival, and tell what it helped them to remember. What can we learn about God from these festivals?

Jesus' birth and boyhood

The first four books of the New Testament are called the Gospels. They tell about Jesus' birth and his life on earth. What the Gospels tell about Jesus' birth makes it clear that Jesus was a very special person.

The good news

• Jesus is God's own Son. He was born as a human being to become our Savior.

How do we know about Jesus?

The four Gospels were written to tell the world about the life and death of Jesus and that he was raised from death. The Gospel of Matthew and the Gospel of John were written by two of Jesus' own disciples. They told what they saw themselves. Most people believe the Gospel of Mark was written by a young man who reported what he learned from the disciple Peter. Luke did not meet Jesus while he was alive. But Luke says he has reported what he learned from "the people who saw those things from the beginning" (Luke 1:2).

Cave near Bethlehem, probably like the one in which Jesus was born.

The town of Nazareth was the hometown of Jesus. Nazareth still exists in southern Galilee today.

What we have in the Gospels is the story of Jesus. It was reported by people who lived in Jesus' own day. They tell us what they themselves saw and heard.

When was Jesus born?

Luke 2:1-5

Scholars have studied old records to determine just when the census Luke mentions was taken (Luke 2:1-2). And just when did Herod the Great die (Matthew 2:19)? Most believe that Jesus was probably born in 5 B.C. Why 5 B.C.? The calendar we use today was not invented until A.D. 525. The person who prepared that calendar was named Dionysius. He missed the actual date of Jesus' birth by five years.

So if you want to know just how long ago Jesus was born, add five years to what your calendar says!

Jesus' birth was special

Jesus was born as any normal child is born into the world. But there were special things about Jesus' birth that make him different from every other person.

Life begins for human beings at conception. This is when a father's sperm and mother's egg combine to start a new life. But Jesus existed as God before conception! The Bible says that Jesus was "with God in the beginning" and that he "was God" (John 1:1-13). This Bible teaching is called the "pre-existence" of Jesus. Only Jesus lived before he was conceived or born.

Jesus is special because he had no human father. Joseph was engaged to Jesus' mother Mary. But he had not married her when Jesus was born. God himself was the father of Jesus (Matthew 1:18).

Jesus is special because his birth was announced by angels. An angel from God told both Mary and Joseph about the child before Jesus was born. God had announced the birth of other children like Isaac and Samson beforehand. But only about Jesus did angels say the baby would be the Son of God. Only Jesus would save his people from their sins (Matthew 1:21). And a whole chorus of angels announced Jesus' birth to shepherds (Luke 2:8-20).

Jesus is special because his birth was marked by a special star in the heavens. Astrono-

126

mers in Europe learned hundreds of years ago the planets Jupiter, Mars and Saturn had lined up with each other to make a single bright star in 6 B.C. Records of Chinese astronomers tell of a bright star, perhaps a comet, that appeared about the time Jesus was born! But none of these bright stars was like the very special star God made shine to mark the birth of his own Son.

All these things help us realize that the birth of Jesus was very special. God's Son had come to earth and was born as a human baby. The baby would grow up and teach his followers. Then as a man Jesus would die to pay for our sins.

Who were Mary and Joseph?
Matthew 1, Luke 1,3

Mary and Joseph were both ordinary Jewish people, living ordinary lives. Joseph was a poor carpenter. He could not even afford to buy a lamb to offer when the family went to the Temple to make offerings required in God's Law. Only the poor offered two doves or young pigeons (Luke 2:24; Leviticus 12:8).

Joseph and Mary were poor. But they were special in two ways. First, each was a descendant of King David. Their child could be king of Israel! Their family history is recorded in Matthew 1 and Luke 3.

Mary and Joseph also loved God and were willing to obey him. Mary showed her love for God by her obedience and in her praise (Luke 1:26-38, 46-56). Joseph showed his love for God by obeying the angel. He told Joseph to marry his pregnant fiancee.

We know Mary and Joseph were good people who loved God. They must have been good parents as baby Jesus grew up.

Where was Jesus born?
Luke 2:1-7

Joseph lived in the town of Nazareth, in Galilee. Even though Mary was pregnant, both of them had to travel to Bethlehem in Judea to register in a census (count) ordered by the Romans (see map, Cities of Jesus, page 134).

Joseph and Mary were in Bethlehem to register for the census when Jesus was born. Because there were so many people there to register, no rooms were left in the inns. So Jesus was born in a stable and slept in the animals' feedbox.

They had to go to Bethlehem because Roman law said "whoever has property [land] in another city must give his tax report in that city." Joseph and Mary were each in David's family line, and the family property was in Bethlehem. So Roman law said both had to travel there at census time.

Many others traveled to Bethlehem for the census, too. When Joseph and Mary arrived, there was no room at the local inn. Jesus was probably born in a cave behind the inn. In those days caves were used as stables for animals.

The shepherds hear about Jesus
Luke 2:8-21

Jesus was born in the time of year when shepherds brought their flocks to the hills near Bethlehem. Angels appeared to some shepherds in those hills. The angels were singing and praising God. The shepherds found out that God's Son had just been born. So they hurried into town to see the baby Jesus.

Who were the wise men?
Matthew 2:1-12

The name given the wise men is Magi. This title was used for hundreds of years in the government of Persia. The Magi were highly trained advisers to the ruler. David was one of the Magi in the days of Cyrus and the great Persian empire. This was nearly 500 years before Jesus was born.

The Magi saw an unusual star in the sky. Then they may have remembered the teaching of Daniel and the promise of a star in Numbers 24:17. The wise Magi hurried to Judah. They wanted to honor the new king of the Jews. He would save the world from war and suffering.

The Magi came to Jerusalem and asked King Herod about Jesus. Herod sent them to look for the young ruler. This was because Herod wanted to kill him. God guided the Magi to Bethlehem. There they found Jesus and worshiped him.

Why did Herod kill children?
Matthew 2:1-12

Herod the Great was dying of a painful illness when the Magi came to Jerusalem. In just two or three months Herod would be dead (he died in March of 4 B.C.)! But this cruel and jealous king had killed his own wife and sons. This was because he thought they wanted his throne. [The Roman emperor joked that it was safer to be Herod's pig (hus) than his son (huios)!]

God warned the Magi after they found Jesus not to return to Jerusalem. But the Magi had told Herod when they first saw the star. The wise men did not return. But Herod learned from the Old Testament that the promised ruler was to be born in Bethlehem (Micah 5:2). So Herod gave an order. All boy children two years old and younger around Bethlehem should be put to death! He was going to kill anyone who might take his place as king.

Joseph's money for travel
Matthew 2:13-18

Herod's soldiers arrived in Bethlehem. But before they came, an angel warned Joseph to

A model of King Herod's palace in Jerusalem.

take Mary and Jesus and escape to Egypt. In those days travel was expensive. And we know that Joseph and Mary were poor.

But the wise men had brought gifts to Jesus. These were gifts usually given to kings: gold, and the expensive perfumes frankincense and myrrh. It could have been with money from these gifts that Joseph was able to take his family to safety.

Where is Nazareth?

After Herod died God's angel told Joseph it was safe to return. But the family was sent to Nazareth. It is a beautiful hilly town in Galilee, where Jesus grew up (see map, Cities of Jesus, page 134).

Here Jesus played as a child. And later he worked as a carpenter with Joseph.

Jesus' childhood

Luke 2:41-52

The Bible says very little about Jesus' childhood.

It does say that when Jesus was 12 years old a very special thing happened. Like other Jewish boys, at 12 Jesus became a "son of the law." He was old enough to be responsible to keep God's law. That year Jesus went with his parents to Jerusalem. They went for Passover and the seven-day celebration that followed it. On festival days religious teachers held public classes in the Temple. Jesus stayed there, asking and answering questions.

We learn two important things from this. First, the teachers were amazed at Jesus' understanding. Second, when his parents found Jesus he told them, "I must be where my Father's work is" (Luke 2:49).

Even as a boy, Jesus knew that he was God's own Son. And he understood what the Bible teaches.

Then Jesus went back home to Nazareth. The Bible simply says that he obeyed his parents. He continued to learn, and he grew taller. Other people liked Jesus. But most important, everything Jesus did pleased God.

To Think about and Do

1. Jesus' birth was special to the whole world. Your birth was special to your own family. Tell your parents what made Jesus' birth special. Ask your mother and father to tell you about when you were born.

2. What else does the Bible tell us that shows how special Jesus is? Find out in Philippians 2:5-8, Colossians 1:5-19 and Hebrews 1:1-13.

3. Why is Jesus special to you and your family? Ask your parents what makes Jesus special to them. Tell someone what makes Jesus special to you.

4. Joseph and Mary were good parents. What are some of the things that your parents do that you think Mary and Joseph did?

5. Even as a child Jesus did what was right. He obeyed his parents, learned and grew and pleased God. People liked Jesus. What are some of the things you do that help people like you? What are some of the things you do to please God? Make a list of things you can do to please people who are important to you. And make a list of things you can do to please God.

Jesus' baptism and temptation

When Jesus was about 30 years old, his friend, John the Baptist, began to preach in Judah. John called on the Jews to repent. He told them to get ready for the promised Messiah. Jesus was baptized by John. Then he was tempted by Satan. When Jesus defeated Satan, Jesus himself began to preach to the people.

The good news

- We can follow our Lord and be baptized as he was.
- We can overcome our temptations in the strength God gives us from his Word.

Who was John the Baptist?

Luke 1, Matthew 3

John was Jesus' childhood friend. God sent John to speak to his people. He was to prepare their hearts for the coming of God's Son.

John the Baptist was a rugged man who lived in the desert and wore camel hair clothes. He ate natural foods like locusts and wild honey. His job was to prepare the people for Jesus' coming.

130

John lived in the wilderness. He dressed in rough clothing. He ate only the simplest foods. In this, John was like the prophet Elijah (2 Kings 1:8). About 400 years before, Malachi had said someone like Elijah would come. He would come just before the Messiah, the Savior promised by God (Malachi 4:5).

John began to preach in the desert by the Jordan River (see map, Cities of Jesus, page 134). Some people thought John was the Christ. John corrected them. "I am the voice of a person shouting in the desert," John said (John 1:23).

John's purpose was to get the Jewish people ready to listen to Jesus. Jesus was the one the people of Israel were waiting for.

What was John's message?

Matthew 1, Luke 3

John preached bad news and good news. The bad news was that God saw his people's sins. God was angry with them. Religious leaders pretended to love God. But they were really interested in money and power. People were selfish and unwilling to share with needy people. Tax collectors cheated others. And soldiers forced people to give them money.

But John had good news, too. He told people they could repent. They could change their hearts and lives. Soon God's promised Messiah would come. And their sins would be forgiven.

But John warned his listeners. People who turn to God must truly repent. They must show by good lives that there has been a real change in their hearts.

What good news this was! Christ, the anointed (special) one God had promised to send his people, was coming soon. People whose hearts were open to God would know him. They would have their sins forgiven.

Why did John baptize?

John baptized people in the Jordan River. In Old Testament times washing with water was a sign of cleansing (Leviticus 14:7-8; 2 Kings 3:11; 5:14). John's baptism was different. It showed that the people who were baptized

Jesus may have been baptized near here in the Jordan River.

turned from their sin to God. They were seeking forgiveness from God. John's baptism was for repentance. It showed that a person was ready to change his heart and his life.

131

After Jesus was baptized by John the Baptist, he went into the desert. There the devil tried to tempt Jesus to sin. This is sometimes called the Wilderness of Temptation.

Why didn't John want to baptize Jesus?

One day Jesus joined the crowds that listened to John the Baptist preach. Jesus came to the water to be baptized. But John tried to stop him. Why?

John did not realize yet that his friend was the Christ (John 1:31). But John did know that Jesus didn't sin. So Jesus did not need to repent (Matthew 3:14). But Jesus insisted. He said, "We should do all things that are right" (Matthew 3:15).

Why was it right for Jesus to be baptized? By being baptized, Jesus showed that he agreed with the message of John. By being baptized, Jesus showed that he trusted the promises of God. By being baptized, Jesus showed that he promised to obey God.

Being baptized was the right thing for Jesus to do. Being baptized is the right thing for us to do, too. If a person trusts Jesus as Savior, and is ready to obey God, he or she can be baptized as Jesus was.

What happened at Jesus' baptism?
Matthew 3:13-17; John 1:29-34

When Jesus was baptized, the Holy Spirit came down on Jesus like a dove. God's voice spoke from heaven. God said, "This is my Son and I love him. I am very pleased with him" (Matthew 3:17).

Then John the Baptist realized that Jesus was the promised Savior!

From then on John told people about Jesus, saying, "He is the Son of God" (John 1:34).

Was Jesus really tempted?
Matthew 4; Luke 4

What is *temptation*? A temptation is anything that seems attractive or worth having, but is wrong.

After Jesus was baptized, the Holy Spirit led him into an empty wilderness. Jesus did not eat for 40 days. When he was weak and hungry, Satan himself came to tempt Jesus.

What Satan suggested seemed good and

worth having. But doing it would have been wrong. So Jesus really was tempted. Jesus was hungry. So making bread from stones must have seemed like a good thing. God loved Jesus. So jumping from the top of a Temple wall and letting God show his love by saving Jesus might have seemed good. Someday Jesus will rule the whole world. So when Satan offered to give Jesus the kingdoms of the world right away, that might seem good, too. But doing any of these things would have been wrong!

Why were they wrong? God had not told Jesus it was time to eat again. So he did not make bread. God wants people to trust his love, not to ask God to prove his love. So jumping from the Temple would have been wrong. Jesus will rule someday, but first Jesus had to die to give forgiveness to people who believe in him.

Jesus really was tempted. What Satan offered did seem attractive and worth having. But Jesus could see the wrong in everything Satan suggested.

How did Jesus overcome temptation?

Each time Jesus was tempted, he remembered a passage from the Old Testament. Jesus chose to do what the word of God says instead of giving in to temptation.

Choosing to obey God's word is the way we can win over temptations, too. Jesus won over temptation. Jesus will help those who trust and obey him overcome their temptations, too.

After Jesus' baptism and temptation

Jesus did not go back to being a carpenter. From this time on Jesus taught. He chose twelve men to be his followers (disciples). Jesus also healed people and performed miracles. He did these as he taught everyone who would listen how to live to please God.

You can learn about Jesus' miracles in chapter 23 of this book. You can learn about Jesus' parables and teaching in chapter 24.

The high corner of the wall around the Temple was called the Pinnacle.

Chapter 25 tells about Jesus' disciples, and chapter 26 tells about Jesus' enemies.

Jesus' first miracle

In Jesus' time, wedding celebrations lasted from two to seven days. Jesus went to a wedding party in Cana, in Galilee. But the wine had just run out. So Jesus turned more than a hundred gallons of water into wine (John 2:1-11)!

In Jesus' day people made water safe to drink by mixing it with wine. Writings from Bible times tell us that people usually mixed three parts water with each part of wine. The rabbis, or religious teachers, said that wine not mixed with water was unclean. And it could not be drunk. Some rabbis even demanded that wine be mixed with ten parts of water before it could be drunk.

So the wine that Jesus made at the wedding was not like what we call wine today. It was real wine. But it was mixed with water.

CITIES OF JESUS

Mediterranean
Sea

• Tyre

• Caesarea Philippi

SYRIA

• Korazin

Capernaum •

• Bethsaida

GALILEE

• Cana

Sea of
Galilee

• Nazareth

• Gadara

• Nain

DECAPOLIS

• Caesarea

Jordan
River

• Sychar

SAMARIA

• Arimathea?

PEREA

• Emmaus

• Jericho

JUDEA

• Jerusalem

• Bethany

• Bethlehem

IDUMEA

Dead Sea

This mountain is very near where Jesus preached the Sermon on the Mount in which he gave the Beatitudes.

Jesus' first sermon

Matthew 5:1-12

The first teaching of Jesus found in Matthew's Gospel is called the Beatitudes. These verses tell us how to be truly happy.

Having wealth or many possessions, or having a good time will not make people really happy. There are people who find true happiness. They are the ones who want to do right more than anything else. Happy people show mercy to others. They are pure in their thinking. And they work to bring peace. These things are important to God.

We are truly happy when what is important to God is important to us, too.

How wonderful that Jesus came. He helps us win over our temptations. He shows us how to live a happy life.

To Think about and Do

1. Read Luke 3. What does it mean for people to repent (change their heart and life) today? How can people show they have changed?

2. Invite a church leader to explain baptism. Ask him to tell the importance of baptism today.

3. Make a list of your own temptations. Talk about your temptations with your parents or a grown up friend. Why do they seem good and worth having? What makes them wrong?

4. Look up 1 Corinthians 10:13 in a children's Bible. Memorize the part of the verse which helps you know that you can win over your temptations.

5. What kinds of things make you happy? Read the Beatitudes in the *International Children's Bible* (Matthew 5:1-12). What things does Jesus say are important? How can they make you happy?

The power and love of Jesus

Jesus is the Son of God. When Jesus was on earth, he performed many miracles that showed his power. Jesus' miracles always helped others. He never hurt them. Jesus' miracles proved he was sent by God. They also showed the love of our God.

The good news

- Jesus has power over nature, sickness, evil spirits and even over death.
- Jesus uses his power to help those who have needs. He helps people who have faith in him.
- We can trust Jesus to use his power to help you and me.

Are miracles magic?

In Jesus' time people who worshiped idols believed in magic. They tried to use spells and witchcraft to control their gods or other people. They thought magic could make another person love them. And they thought magic could hurt or punish their enemies. The Old Testament says that magic practices are wrong (Deuter-

This pool was surrounded by five porches where sick people lay. The water in the pool was sometimes stirred up. Many people believed the first person into the troubled water would be healed.

Stormy winds come up quickly on Lake Galilee. Many of Jesus' miracles were done on and around this lake.

onomy 18:9-12). When people became Christians, they burned their books of magic (Acts 19:19).

But even people who believed in magic were amazed at Jesus' miracles. What Jesus did was much greater and more wonderful than any magic people knew. Jesus' miracles clearly showed the power of God.

Jesus did not use magic words or rituals. Jesus just spoke, and what he said happened.

Jesus never used his power to hurt or control people. Jesus used his power to heal the sick or feed the hungry. Or he helped in some other way. Jesus' miracles not only proved that Jesus came from God. His miracles showed how much God loves all people.

Kinds of Jesus' miracles

The New Testament tells us about four kinds of miracles Jesus performed.

One kind of miracle showed Jesus has power over nature. He stopped the storm. He walked on the water. And he made just a little bread become enough to feed thousands of hungry people.

One kind of miracle showed Jesus' power over sickness. He healed the lame and even made blind people see.

One kind of miracle showed Jesus' power over evil spirits. He commanded demons who were hurting people to leave them alone. And the demons had to obey him.

One kind of miracle showed Jesus' power over death itself. Jesus brought people who had died back to life.

There is nothing too hard for Jesus. Jesus, who loves you and me, can do all things.

Jesus has power over nature

Why were the disciples afraid?
Matthew 8:23-27

Wild winds can suddenly sweep down the Jordan River valley and cause terrible storms on the Sea of Galilee. Several of Jesus' disciples were fishermen. They were used to rough water and storms. Why were they so afraid? The Bible word used to describe the storm means "earthquake." The sea was shaking and heaving. And foaming waves broke over the sides of the small boat. The boat was filling with water when the terrified disciples woke Jesus up. They were sure the boat would sink.

But really, did the disciples need to be afraid? Jesus was in the boat, and Jesus was God's Son. Jesus told the storm to stop, and it did. Even more, the water immediately became calm!

The disciples learned from this miracle to trust Jesus. They learned that Jesus is in control even in dangerous conditions.

Power over sickness
Jesus' healing miracles

Jesus did more healing miracles than any other kind. What can we learn from them?

First, many healings were done as a response to faith. People came to Jesus because they believed Jesus could help.

Second, Jesus' healings show how much he loves people. Never once did Jesus make a person sick—not even people who hated him

The miracles of Jesus

Miracle	Scripture	Where performed	What it shows
Power over nature			
Turns water to wine	John 2:1-11	Cana	Jesus is God's Son
First catch of fish	Luke 5:1-11	Sea of Galilee	Shows Peter that Jesus is Lord
Stills the storm	Matthew 8:23-27 Mark 4:35-41 Luke 8:22-25	Sea of Galilee	Teach disciples to trust Jesus
Feeds 5,000	Matthew 14:15-21 Mark 6:35-44 Luke 9:12-17 John 6:5-15	near Bethsaida	Jesus cares about people in need
Walks on sea	Matthew 14:22-33 Mark 6:45-52 John 6:16-21	Sea of Galilee	Shows disciples Jesus' power
Feeds 4,000	Matthew 15:32-39 Mark 8:1-9	near Bethsaida	Jesus cares about the hungry
Money from fish	Matthew 17:24-27	Capernaum	Pay Peter's tax
Withers fig tree	Matthew 21:17-22 Mark 11:12-14; 20-25	Jerusalem	To teach faith
Second catch of fish	John 21:1-14	Sea of Tiberias	Reveal Jesus to disciples
Power over sickness			
Heals nobleman's son	John 4:46-54	Cana	Faith
Cures man with harmful skin disease	Matthew 8:1-4 Mark 1:40-45 Luke 5:12-15	Galilean city	Faith, caring
Heals soldier's servant	Matthew 8:5-13 Luke 7:1-10	Capernaum	Faith
Heals Peter's mother-in-law	Matthew 8:14-17 Mark 1:29-31 Luke 4:38-39	Capernaum	Friendship
Heals paralyzed man	Matthew 9:1-8 Mark 2:1-12 Luke 5:17-26	Capernaum	Jesus has power and can forgive sins
Cures woman of bleeding	Matthew 9:20-22 Mark 5:25-34 Luke 8:43-48	Capernaum	Faith
Gives blind their sight	Matthew 9:27-31	Capernaum	Faith

Miracle	Scripture	Where performed	What it shows
Heals crippled hand	Matthew 12:9-14 Mark 3:1-6 Luke 6:6-11	Galilee	God cares for people more than for religion
Heals non-Jewish girl	Matthew 15:21-28 Mark 7:24-30	Tyre	God loves all peoples
Heals deaf man who cannot talk	Mark 7:31-37	Decapolis	Bring friends to Jesus
Heals a man at a pool	John 5:1-18	Bethesda	Faith
Gives back sight	Mark 8:22-26	Bethesda	Bring friends to Jesus
Gives sight to man born blind	John 9:1-41	Jerusalem	God's power
Heals man with dropsy	Luke 14:1-6	Jerusalem	God loves people more than religion
Heals ten of harmful skin disease	Luke 17:11-19	Galilee	Need to be grateful
Replaces ear of high priest's servant	Luke 22:49-51 John 18:10-11	Garden of Gethsemane	Jesus' deep love for enemies
Power over evil spirits			
Heals man who could not talk because of demon	Matthew 9:32-34	Capernaum	Jesus' power is from God
Sends evil spirit from man	Mark 1:23-27 Luke 4:33-36	Capernaum	Jesus has power over the Devil
Heals man who was blind and could not talk	Matthew 12:22 Luke 11:14	Galilee	Jesus' power is from God
Heals child with demon	Matthew 17:14-20 Mark 9:14-29	Mt. Tabor	Faith is greater than Satan
Heals woman crippled for 18 years	Luke 13:10-17	Jerusalem	God loves people, not religion
Power over death			
Raises Jairus' daughter	Matthew 9:18-26 Mark 5:35-43 Luke 8:41-42, 49-56	Capernaum	Faith
Raises widow's only son	Luke 7:11-16	Nain	Caring
Raises Lazarus	John 11:1-45	Bethany	Jesus has power over death

and were his enemies. Jesus used his power to help and not harm.

Three times Jesus made people well on the Sabbath (Matthew 12:9-14, Luke 13:10-17; 14:1-6). Some religious leaders were angry because they thought healing was work. And work should not be done on the Sabbath. But Jesus said that it is never against God's law to do good on the Sabbath (Matthew 12:12). Jesus' healing miracles show us that Jesus wants only to do good for us.

The healing miracles of Jesus did show his power. They proved that Jesus was sent by God. They also teach us that we can come to Jesus and ask him when we need help.

Why isn't everyone made well?

The Bible tells us that when we have troubles or are sick we are to pray as well as use medicine (James 5:13-18). God can heal us when we trust him and pray.

Sometimes, though, God says "no" when Christians ask for healing. We may not get well right away. Timothy had stomach trouble and was often sick (1 Timothy 5:23). Paul had a serious sickness. But when he prayed, God told Paul he would not make him well (2 Corinthians 12:7-10). Paul was not discouraged, though. Paul knew that God would give him the strength he needed in spite of his weakness.

God wants only good for us. And the Bible promises that "in everything God works for the good of those who love him" (Romans 8:28). Usually getting well is his good for us. Usually when we ask Jesus for help we will be healed. But if we are not made well right away, we can still trust God. He loves us and uses even sickness for good.

Power over evil spirits

What are demons or evil spirits?

Demons are real spiritual beings. Some people believe demons are evil angels, who chose to follow Satan.

The Gospels tell many stories about demons. When Jesus came to earth, Satan arranged all his forces to battle him. So demons were very active then. But whenever Jesus met demons, he drove them away.

Demons, like Satan, are the enemies of God and people. Demons in Jesus' day showed their presence by making people sick or mentally ill. Jesus helped people; demons hurt people.

The demons and evil spirits the Bible speaks about truly are wicked and evil.

Can demons hurt us today?

Some people are afraid of demons and evil spirits. Demons are evil. No one should ever go to people who claim to be able to talk with spirits.

But if demons are powerful, Jesus is even more powerful! Every time Jesus met a person with a demon, Jesus sent the demon out of that person.

When anyone has Jesus as his Savior, Jesus is a part of his or her life. Jesus still is more powerful than any demons. If Jesus is your Savior, you can trust in him. You do not need to be afraid of evil spirits.

Power over death

People Jesus raised from the dead

The New Testament tells of three people Jesus brought back to life.

This is the tomb many believe Lazarus lay in when Jesus raised him from the dead.

In Bible times there was no way to preserve bodies from decay. So people who died were buried almost immediately. Two of the people Jesus brought back to life must have just died (Jairus' daughter, Matthew 9:18-26; a widow's son, Luke 7:11-16). Jesus' friend Lazarus had been dead and buried for four days (John 11:1-45). Jesus was able to give life back to people who had died.

Jesus' power over death

John 11:1-45 tells about Lazarus (*Laz' a rus*). Jesus came to Bethany where his friend was buried. He reminded Lazarus' sisters, "I am the resurrection and the life. He who believes in me will have life even if he dies" (John 11:25).

Then Jesus proved that he has power to give life to the dead. He did this by giving life to Lazarus.

Christians rejoice in this special power of Jesus. Because Jesus is our Savior, we know that loved ones who have died live again. We know that when we die, we will be given life again by Jesus, too.

What else proves Jesus' power over death?

Jesus had taught and healed people for three years. Then Jesus himself died on the cross and was buried. But Jesus did not stay in the grave. God raised Jesus to life again.

The Bible says that Jesus "was shown to be God's Son with great power by rising from death" (Romans 1:4).

Jesus often healed people like this blind woman.

To Think about and Do

1. Draw a large map of the land of Jesus (see map, Cities of Jesus, page 134). Locate the places Jesus did his miracles. Use four different colored tacks or pens to make four kinds of miracles. Do you think there was anyone who might not have heard of or seen Jesus' miracles?

2. Choose a favorite miracle of Jesus and tell why it is your favorite.

3. Read about Jesus' stopping the storm (Matthew 8:23-27). Draw a picture of your favorite part. Tell why that part is your favorite.

4. Draw a picture that shows when you are most happy that Jesus is with you. He is with you as he was with the men in the boat.

5. How did different people react to Jesus' miracles?
   - Jesus' disciples (John 2:11; 4:46-54)
   - The crowds (Matthew 8:28-34; Luke 7:11-16)
   - Jesus' enemies (John 3:2; Luke 10:17; John 11:45-53)

How do you think you would have felt if you had been there when Jesus did his miracles? Write a letter to a friend to describe your feelings.

The parables and teachings of Jesus

As Jesus traveled and healed people, he also taught about God. Often Jesus told stories to help his listeners understand important truths about God's love. Today the stories and teachings of Jesus still help us to understand who God is and how we can live to please him.

The good news

- God loves us very much. He sent us his Son so we could have eternal life.
- God takes care of us and answers our prayers.
- God gives us instructions for living in his word.
- God keeps us close to him as we listen to and obey his word.

Where did Jesus teach?

Jesus did not teach in a school. Jesus taught wherever people gathered. One of Jesus' most famous lessons, called the Sermon on the Mount, was taught on a hillside. Another time the crowds were so great that Jesus got in a small boat. He pushed it out from the shore. That time Jesus taught the people on the shore

Jesus told a story about a Samaritan who helped a Jewish man who had been beaten by robbers. The story encourages us to do good to all who need help. See the chart of stories Jesus told, found on page 145.

This narrow road led between Jericho and Jerusalem.

while he stood in a fisherman's boat.

When Jesus taught, he often used stories about familiar things. These stories helped Jesus' listeners understand his message about God. Some of Jesus' stories are retold on the next page. Where do you suppose Jesus might have been as he told each story?

Matthew 13:1-8, 18-23. To plant their crops, farmers in Jesus' time took handfuls of seed. Then they tossed it out on the ground. Some of the seed fell on ground the farmer had prepared. But some fell on rocky places. Jesus used this familiar scene to warn everyone who heard him. He told them they must not let their hearts be stubborn when they hear God's word. We who hear God's word must listen carefully. Then what God says can grow in our lives.

Luke 15:8-10. When women married, their fathers gave them presents, called dowries. Usually the present was money: coins hung together on a string. These coins were very important to women of Jesus' day.

The woman in Jesus' story had 10 coins. Perhaps they were her dowry. They weren't worth more than five dollars. And the coin the woman lost was worth only about 18 cents! But that coin was important to the woman, and she looked hard for it. When she did find it, she was so happy she ran and told all her neighbors she had found her coin.

Some might not think that a single person is worth much to God. Jesus' story helped his hearers understand that God loves even the least important person. God is filled with joy

143

when any person obeys Jesus.

Luke 10:30-37. What does it mean to love your neighbor? Jesus told about a "Good Samaritan" to answer that question. In Jesus' time, the Jews did not like Samaritans. Many Jews traveling from Judea to Galilee would even cross the Jordan River. They would take the long road through Perea (see map, page 134) just to avoid traveling in Samaria.

Jesus' familiar story tells about a Jewish man who was beaten and robbed in Judea. He was on the road between Jericho and Jerusalem. Other people traveling the road hurried by the hurt man, afraid the robbers might get them, too. But a Samaritan cared enough about the hurt man to stop and help him.

Jesus helped his listeners understand that the "neighbor" God tells us to love isn't just a friend. Our neighbor is anyone we can help.

Matthew 7:24-28. The land where Jesus lived is rocky and hilly. When rains come, the water does not sink into the ground. But it races downhill, flooding along the creeks and valleys. No wise person would build a house on sandy ground where the floods rushed by.

But Jesus told a story about a foolish man who did build on sandy ground. And he told about a wise man who built his house on a solid, rock foundation. When the rains came and the valleys flooded, the foolish man's house fell down. But the house of the wise man stood firm on its safe, rocky foundation.

Jesus told his listeners they, too, must choose to be wise or foolish. A wise person will listen and do what Jesus says. The person who hears and obeys Jesus will always be safe.

But the foolish person hears what Jesus says but will not do it. He is in great danger.

What did Jesus teach?

Jesus taught about the most important things in the world! Jesus talked about God's love, himself, eternal life, God's word, prayer and even you and me.

Often Jesus taught in stories called *parables*. The word parable means an illustration "set alongside," to make something plain.

Some of Jesus' parables were ordinary stories. They helped his listeners understand what Jesus meant. Other stories were hard to understand. On page 145 is a list of all of the stories Jesus told. It explains what Jesus is teaching in each one.

We want to listen carefully to Jesus. What he says to us really is the most important thing we can ever hear or learn.

Jesus' teaching about God's love

Once when Jesus was teaching in the fields, he pointed out birds and wildflowers that brightened the hills. Jesus reminded his listeners that God provides food for the birds. And he dresses the flowers in beautiful petals. God, who is a father to his people, will surely take care of us. People are much more important to God than birds and flowers are (Matthew 6:25-34).

Jesus' teaching about himself

Jesus said many things about himself. He called himself the Bread of Life (John 6:35-68). In Bible times bread was the most important food in a person's diet. Jesus was saying that he is the source of life to everyone who believes in him.

Jesus called himself a Good Shepherd (John 10). Shepherds in Jesus' day lived with and protected their sheep. At night the sheep were placed inside safe walls. The shepherd often slept by the one door. This was so no wild animals could get by him to attack the sheep. A good shepherd was ready to fight for his sheep, even if he were killed protecting them. Jesus called himself the Good Shepherd to let us know that he was willing to die for us. And he will always protect us.

Jesus called himself the Vine and called us branches (John 15:1-11). Grapes grew on the low vines of Jesus' land. They were one of its most important crops. Jesus wanted us to know that he will give us strength to do good things. This is like the sap flowing through a vine that gives its branches strength to produce grapes. As long as we love Jesus and obey him, he will give us strength to do good.

144

Stories Jesus told

Parable	Passage	Subject	Lesson
New winebags	Matthew 9:16-17	Jesus' message	Jesus has a new message from God
Farmer and the seed	Matthew 13:1-8 Mark 4:3-8 Luke 8:5-8	God's word	We must hear and obey God's word
Weeds	Matthew 13:24-30	God's people	The good and bad will be separated
Mustard seed	Matthew 13:31-32 Mark 4:30-32 Luke 13:18-19	God's people	Small beginnings can lead to big things
Yeast	Matthew 13:33 Luke 13:20-21	God's people	Small beginnings can lead to big things
Hidden treasure	Matthew 13:44	God's people	Choose what is truly valuable in life
Very valuable pearl	Matthew 13:45-46	God's people	Choose what is truly valuable in life
Fishing net	Matthew 13:47-50	God's people	The good and bad will be separated
Lost sheep	Matthew 18:12-14 Luke 15:3-7	God's love	God loves each person deeply
Servant who would not forgive	Matthew 18:23-25	God's people	We forgive because God forgave us
Workers in a vineyard	Matthew 20:1-16	Service	God rewards us generously
Two sons	Matthew 21:28-32	God's love	God welcomes the sinner who comes to him
Evil renters	Matthew 21:33-46 Mark 12:1-12	Punishment	People who hate God's Son will be punished
Wedding dinner	Matthew 22:1-14	Punishment	People who do not accept God's invitation will be punished
Ten virgins	Matthew 25:1-13	Jesus' return	We must be ready when he comes back
Talents	Matthew 25:14-30	Service	We must use our abilities to serve God
Wise and evil servants	Matthew 24:45-51 Luke 12:42-48	Service	We are to serve God and others as we wait for Jesus to return
Two men who owed money	Luke 7:41-43	God's people	We love God more when we realize we are sinners
Good Samaritan	Luke 10:30-37	Service	Do good to all in need
Friend at midnight	Luke 11:5-8	God's love	God is always willing to help
Unimportant seat at party	Luke 14:7-11	Humility	Don't be proud: let God reward
Lost coin	Luke 15:8-10	God's love	Each one is important to God
Son who left home	Luke 15:11-32	God's love	God forgives all who change their hearts and minds and return to him
Clever manager	Luke 16:1-10	God's people	We are to use money to do good and prepare for the future
Rich man and Lazarus	Luke 16:19-31	Punishment	People who love money more than God are foolish
Unworthy servants	Luke 17:7-10	Service	Serve God because we are thankful
Unfair judge	Luke 18:1-8	God's love	God will answer our prayers if we ask him
Pharisee and tax collector	Luke 18:9-14	God's love	Anyone who changes his heart and life can be forgiven
Bags of money	Luke 19:11-27	Service	Use our talents to serve God

Jesus did not always use stories to teach. Many times he spoke plainly. Jesus said he came from God and speaks only his father's words (John 8:42-59). Jesus said that he is the only way a person can come to God (John 14:1-6). This is because Jesus truly is the Son of God (Matthew 26:63-68).

Jesus' teaching about his words

Jesus taught that his words are to be obeyed. If we live by Jesus' words we will be set free from sin (John 8:31-36). What Jesus teaches is a firm foundation for our life. And we are wise if we build our lives on his words (Matthew 7:24-38).

Jesus also taught that if we love him, we will do what he says. When we love Jesus and obey his words, God is very close to us (John 14:15-24).

Jesus' teaching about eternal life

Jesus taught that God loves people so much that he gave his one and only Son. Jesus said, "God gave his Son so that whoever believes in him may not be lost, but have eternal life" (John 3:16). Jesus made this promise other times as well. Jesus gives us eternal life (John 5:24-29). When Jesus returns, he will raise people back to life who have died (John 11:17-26).

We can trust Jesus as our Savior, because he is the one who brings us life that will last forever.

Jesus' teaching about prayer

Jesus promised that God will hear and answer our prayers. You can read some of these prayer promises in Matthew 6:5-15 and John 16:23-24.

Jesus also taught his disciples how to pray. This special prayer is one we call the Lord's Prayer. It teaches us many things about living close to God (Matthew 6:9f).

When we pray daily, we will be helped to remember God and his ways. God will answer this prayer, just as he answers our other prayers.

What Jesus taught his disciples to say	What it means
Our Father in heaven	We are to think of God as a good and loving father
we pray that your name will always be kept holy.	We are to think of God as real and very important to us.
We pray that your kingdom will come, and that the things you want will be done, here on earth and also in heaven.	We ask God to help us obey him each day so we will be good citizens in Jesus' kingdom.
Give us the food we need for each day.	We depend on God to take care of us each day.
Forgive us the sins we have done, just as we have forgiven those who did wrong to us.	We know we need to be forgiven for our sin. And we need to forgive others who sin.
Do not cause us to be tested, but save us from the Evil One.	We ask God to keep us from wanting to do wrong and following Satan's evil ways.

Jesus' teaching about you and me

Jesus had many things to say about people. For one thing, Jesus taught that little children are very important to God (Matthew 19:13-15; Mark 10:13-16).

Jesus had special names for his people. He called them lights (Matthew 5:14-16; Luke 8:16-18). In Jesus' day lamps were like shallow cups. Pure olive oil was put in the lamps. They had a bit of flax for a wick. Even these dim lamps could always be seen in a dark house. People who love Jesus are like this. The light of our good lives shows up when others around us do evil.

146

There were many kinds of oil lamps in Bible times. Jesus said that his followers are like a light to a dark world.

What can we do to be lamps? Some of Jesus' instructions tell us. We are to love God and our neighbors (Mark 12:28-34). We are even to love our enemies (Matthew 5:43-48). It is better to love others than to judge them guilty (Matthew 7:1-6; Luke 6:37-42).

To Think about and Do

1. Make a mural showing Jesus' teaching. On your mural have pictures of some of the things Jesus told stories about.

2. Read about the Good Samaritan. It is in Luke 10:30-37. Pretend Jesus visited your school to tell this story today. Write down how you think he might tell it now.

3. Read three of the stories Jesus told. Which is easiest to understand? Try to explain it to a friend. Which is hardest to understand? Ask your parents or a teacher to help you understand it.

4. Look up "sheep" and "shepherd" in a concordance. Then read some of the verses in your Bible. How do you think God is like a shepherd? Do you like being one of his sheep? Why?

5. Make a Bible time lamp in your kitchen. You will need pure cooking oil and a bit of cotton cloth for a wick. Pour some oil in a cup or saucer. Drop the cotton wick in it. Light the wick. Turn off all the lights in your house. The lamp light is dim, but it shows up in the darkness.

Disciples and followers of Jesus

Many people who saw Jesus' miracles and heard his teaching decided to follow him. These people were called his disciples, or followers. Jesus chose twelve men to be his special disciples. The Bible tells us about the first twelve disciples. And it teaches us how we can become Jesus' followers, too.

The good news

• Jesus invites those who believe in him to be disciples.

• Jesus' disciples promise to follow Jesus.

• Jesus' disciples have a happy and meaningful life.

What is a disciple?

In Jesus' day a person who wanted to become a leader first became a disciple. That person went to live with a rabbi (a Jewish teacher of God's word). The disciple listened to everything his teacher said. And he watched the

A fishing boat on the Sea of Galilee.

Jesus called Simon Peter and his brother, Andrew, to be fishers of men.

way his teacher lived. The disciple did not want just to learn what his teacher knew. The disciple, as Jesus said, wanted to "be like his teacher" (Luke 6:40).

People who are disciples of Jesus want to learn everything they can from Jesus' words. But Jesus' disciples also want to become more and more like him.

Who were Jesus' disciples?
Matthew 10:2-4; Mark 3:16-18; Luke 6:12-16

Sometimes in the Bible *disciple* just means a follower of Jesus. This was someone who believed in him (John 8:31). But Jesus also chose twelve men to be his special disciples. The twelve disciples traveled with Jesus everywhere he went. They watched his miracles, listened to his teaching and asked him questions. Then Jesus sent them out to teach and preach.

Who were the twelve disciples?

Their names were Simon (Peter), Andrew, James, John, Philip, Bartholomew, Matthew, Thomas, James ("the less"), Thaddaeus, Simon the Zealot and Judas.

Meet the twelve disciples
Simon Peter

I was a tough fisherman when Jesus called me to follow him. It was hard for me to be a disciple. I kept on saying the wrong thing. But Jesus stayed with me. I was the first disciple to preach the Gospel after Jesus was raised from death. I was the first to do a miracle, preach to Gentiles and raise the dead. I am mentioned more in the Gospels and Acts than any other disciple. You can read about me in Luke 5:1-11; Matthew 16:13-26; Matthew 26:31-35, 69-75; John 21:15-19; Acts 1:15-26.

Andrew

I am Peter's brother. Like Peter, I was a fisherman. I heard John the Baptist say that Jesus is the Lamb of God, our Savior. So I quickly ran after Jesus and asked if I could stay with him. After that first day I knew that Jesus was the Christ. And I hurried and told my brother Peter. You can read about me in Matthew 4:18; Mark 1:16-18,29; Mark 13:3; John 1:40,44; 6:8; 12:22; Acts 1:13.

James

Until we met Jesus, my brother John and I ran a fishing business for our dad, Zebedee. Then we left everything to travel everywhere with Jesus. John and I were both rather hot-tempered. In fact, Jesus called us his "Sons of Thunder." You can see why when you read that once we wanted to call down fire on some villagers. They wouldn't let us stay overnight. John, Peter and I were closest to Jesus. We three were there when Jesus cried in Gethsemane. And when Jesus was changed on a mountain we were there, too. Even his clothes shined brightly. You can read about these things and more about me, in Matthew 4:21; Matthew 17:1; Mark 5:37; Mark 9:2; Mark 10:35,41; Mark 13:3; Mark 14:33; Luke 5:10; Luke 8:51; Luke 9:28; Acts 1:13; 12:2.

John

Like my brother James, I was hot-tempered. But I changed. In fact, I'm the "disciple Jesus loved." The New Testament letters that I wrote are about love. When Jesus was killed on a cross, he asked me to take care of his mother. I lived many years after Jesus returned to heaven. and I saw Jesus' church spread across the Mediterranean world. One of the Roman emperors sent me to a lonely island. This is where I wrote Revelation, the last book of the Bible. You can read about my days with Jesus and the Twelve in Matthew 4:21; Matthew 17:1; Mark 1:19,29; Mark 5:37; Mark 9:2,38; Mark 10:35,41; Mark 13:3; Mark 14:33; Luke 5:10; Luke 8:51; Luke 9:28,49,54; Luke 22:8; Acts 1:13; Acts 3:1,3,4,11; Acts 4:13,19; Acts 8:14; Acts 12:2; Galatians 2:9; Revelation 1:1,4,9.

Philip

I suppose my greatest work is my eagerness to introduce people to Jesus. I told my friend Nathanael about Jesus. When some Greek travelers wanted to meet Jesus, I was the one who tried to arrange it. I am mentioned in John 1:43-49; John 6:5,7; John 12:21-22; John 14:8-9; Acts 1:13.

Nathanael

I'm the Nathanael that Philip told about Jesus. My other name is Bartholomew. Jesus told me he saw me under a fig tree. I knew then Jesus was the Son of God. Jesus seemed surprised that I believed in him so quickly. He promised that I would see many wonderful things as I followed him. You can read about me in John 1:45-49; John 21:2; Acts 1:13.

There were many fig trees in the East. A fig is an olive green, oval-shaped fruit with a fuzzy skin like a peach.

Matthew

Sometimes I'm called "Levi" in the Bible. In my own day I was called all sorts of names. You see, I collected taxes. I usually collected extra for myself. All of us did it. So most folks hated us tax collectors. They looked on us as great sinners. But Jesus came up to my tax office one day and told me to follow him. And I did. You can read about me and the feast I held for Jesus. I am in the Gospel I wrote and in the other Gospels, too. Just find and read Matthew 9:9; Matthew 10:3; Mark 2:14; Mark 3:18; Luke 5:27,29; Luke 6:15; Acts 1:13.

Tax collectors were very unpopular because they made the people pay taxes to the Roman government.

Thomas

I've been called Doubting Thomas all these years. I wasn't there, you see, when the others first saw Jesus after he was raised from the dead. I didn't believe my friends. I had to see for myself. Later, the moment I saw Jesus, I fell on my knees and worshiped him. Read about me in John 11:16; John 14:5; John 20:23-28; Acts 1:13.

James (the Less), Thaddaeus, Simon

We three aren't very well known. James is usually mixed up with the other Jameses in the New Testament. By the way, he's called "the less" because he's younger than the better known James. It is not because he's smaller. As for me, Thaddaeus, my other name was Judas. I just had to keep on saying "not Iscariot" so folks wouldn't confuse me with the traitor who betrayed Jesus. Simon is called "the Zealot" because he wanted to turn against the Romans who ruled our country. We're not well known, as I said. But we followed Jesus faithfully. And after he was raised from death we went out to preach the Gospel. You can read about us in Matthew 27:56; Mark 15:40; Mark 16:1; Luke 24:10; John 14:22.

Judas Iscariot

Yes, I'm the one. I betrayed Jesus for money. Money was always important to me. I was the treasurer for our group of disciples. I kept our money—and I took some of it for myself. People have tried to make excuses for what I did. I don't want excuses. I sold Jesus out because that's the kind of person I am. Even being around Jesus for years didn't change me. That was because I didn't want to change. You can read about me in Matthew 26:14,25,47; Matthew 27:3,5; Mark 14:10,43; Luke 22:3,47,48; John 6:71; John 12:4; John 13:2,26-29; John 18:2,3,5; Acts 1:16,18,25.

Can we become Jesus' disciples?
John 1:43-49

Being disciples begins by believing in Jesus. Before Jesus began to teach or had performed any miracles, Philip brought his friend Nathanael to meet Jesus. When they had talked for a few minutes, Nathanael said to Jesus, "You are the Son of God" (John 1:49).

Nathanael already believed that Jesus is God's Son. To become a disciple of Jesus, a person must also trust Jesus as Savior. And he must obey him as Lord, as Nathanael did.

How do disciples serve Jesus?
Matthew 9:35—10:42; Luke 9:1-6

Jesus traveled through towns and villages, teaching and healing the people. Everywhere Jesus went he found people who were worried

Today, too, people who love Jesus travel to all parts of the world to teach people about him.

and helpless. And Jesus felt sorry for them.

Jesus told his twelve followers to pray for workers who would travel as he did to help others.

Then Jesus sent his disciples out to preach and heal. Jesus promised his followers that God's Spirit would speak through them. And then they would be able to help others.

Today, too, there are many people in the world who are worried and helpless. They have no one to help them. Some live in our towns and go to our own schools. Many live in other parts of the world. Today, too, disciples serve Jesus. They do this by caring for the helpless and teaching them about Jesus.

How do disciples live?
Luke 12, 17

The Bible shows us how we are to live to be Jesus' disciples. Here are some of the things Jesus taught his followers to do.

Disciples tell others about Jesus / Luke 12:1-12. Jesus taught that we should not be afraid of what others might think or say. God is the one we want to please. Disciples are not ashamed of Jesus. We are to "stand before others" and say we belong to him. We are not to worry about what we will say to others. Jesus promised his twelve disciples that God's Holy Spirit will "teach you what you must say."

Disciples trust God completely / Luke 12:13-34. Many people worry about money and work hard to get rich. Jesus told his followers not to worry even about food and clothes. God takes care of the birds and the flowers of the field. We are much more important to God than birds and flowers are. God is a good father to Jesus' followers. So disciples trust God completely. What Jesus' followers want most is to do what pleases God. We trust God to meet all our needs as we live to please him.

Disciples serve others faithfully / Luke 12:35-48. Jesus' disciples are all servants. We are supposed to love and help each other. This is what Jesus asks us to do. While Jesus is in heaven, we are to spend our lives helping each other.

*Jesus' disciples forgive each other freely /
Luke 17:1-10.* Even people who love Jesus sometimes do wrong and sin against others. If someone does something bad to a disciple, Jesus'
follower is to tell him he is wrong. If he is sorry,
we are to forgive him.

Jesus' twelve disciples thought this was
very hard. And they asked Jesus to give them
more faith. But Jesus reminded them that his
followers are servants. Jesus is our Lord, and we
are to obey him. It does not take extra faith to
forgive others. We forgive because Jesus tells us
to.

*Disciples expect Jesus to return / Luke
17:20-37.* Jesus promised that he will come
again. Most people on earth will not expect
Jesus. They will be busy with everyday activities. We expect Jesus to come back at any time.
We disciples look for Jesus. And we try each day
to do the things that please him.

Disciples are special people because a
disciple follows Jesus. And he tries to please
him. People who are good disciples tell others
about Jesus. They trust God, serve others, forgive each other and expect Jesus to return soon.

The greatest disciples of all
Matthew 20:20-28

Once the mother of James and John asked
Jesus if they could be the most powerful people
in Christ's kingdom. The rest of the twelve
disciples heard this. They became upset and
angry. Each of them wanted to be great!

Jesus called his twelve followers together
and told them how a disciple can be great. Here
is what Jesus said. "If one of you wants to become
great, then he must serve the rest of you like a
servant" (Matthew 20:26).

Why is this the way to become a great
follower of Jesus? Jesus himself came to earth
to serve others. Jesus even gave his life to save
us. A disciple, who wants to be like his teacher,
will choose to serve others as Jesus did.

To Think about and Do

1. Which of the twelve disciples would you like most to be like? Read some verses about him,
and tell why he is a good example for you.

2. Make and play a "name the disciple" game. Write a single fact about a disciple on one side of
a 3" × 5" card. Put the disciple's name on the other side. Make up as many cards as you can. Divide
into teams, and have one person draw a card and read the clue. The first team to name the
disciple correctly receives five points.

3. Today, missionaries go all over the world to tell others about Jesus and to help them. They
are very much like the twelve disciples Jesus sent out. Ask someone from your church's missionary committee to tell you about the missionaries your congregation helps to support.

4. How can you be a disciple of Jesus? Pick one of the five things disciples do:

- tell others about Jesus
- serve others
- expect Jesus to return
- trust God
- forgive freely

Do something this week to be like one of Jesus' disciples. Then tell someone what you did.

5. Act out something one of Jesus' disciples did. Let your friends guess the event and give the
name of the disciple.

26

Enemies and opponents of Jesus

As Jesus traveled he healed the sick and taught about God's love. Many believed in Jesus and became his followers. Others could not make up their minds about Jesus. But some actually hated Jesus and became his enemies. It was the enemies of Jesus who finally convinced the Roman governor to kill him on a cross.

The good news

- Jesus' enemies were not able to stop Jesus from teaching and healing.
- Jesus' enemies could not hurt him until Jesus was ready to go to the cross and die for our sins.

In Bible times people sold their goods on the street to the people passing by.

Jesus forced merchants from God's Temple
John 2:12-19

When Jesus came to Jerusalem he saw men selling animals and changing money in the Temple courtyard. Jesus made a whip of cords and chased these men out of the Temple. He turned over their tables and scattered their money.

Why was Jesus so angry? The Temple was a place to worship God. It was not a place to buy and sell. But even more, the merchants in the Temple were robbing God's people (Mark 11:17)!

Animals offered as sacrifices to God had to be perfect. Priests were supposed to examine each animal to see if it could be sacrificed. Some priests would not accept animals that the worshipers brought with them. The priest would make them buy other, expensive animals from merchants at the Temple. And the merchants gave the priests some of the money! This was not honest.

Also, people had to pay a Temple tax in special Temple money. The money changers in the Temple cheated people who came to pay the tax by charging them too much for Temple money.

The priests and merchants who robbed the Jewish people in God's Temple became Jesus' enemies. They were some of the people who hated Jesus.

Wheat is one of the main crops in the East. Often the roads went between two wheat fields.

Pharisees hated Jesus

Matthew 12:1-14

The Pharisees were men who tried to please God by keeping every rule in God's law. The people of Jesus' day respected the Pharisees because they were dedicated to God.

Many Bible students believe that only some of the Pharisees were Jesus' enemies. But the Pharisees we read about in the Gospels did not like Jesus at all.

One Sabbath day Jesus' followers picked grain to eat as they walked with Jesus. The Pharisees complained to Jesus that this was against Jewish Law. [It was not. See What was "Jewish Law"? on page 156.] When Jesus went into their synagogue to worship, he found a man with a crippled hand. It really was against God's law to work on the Sabbath. So the Pharisees asked Jesus, "Is it right to heal on the Sabbath?" If Jesus did heal, the Pharisees planned to accuse him of doing wrong!

But Jesus told them that God's law allows people to do good things on the Sabbath. Doing good to others is not "work." Then Jesus healed the crippled man.

The Pharisees became very angry. They left

155

There were various kinds of priests that served in the Temple.

and began to plan how to kill Jesus!

The Pharisees did not understand God's rules. They did not realize that helping people in need is a way to please God. They were angry about Jesus' helping a crippled man. And it showed how stubborn and unlike God the Pharisees really were.

What was "Jewish Law"?

Matthew 7:1-23

The Pharisees believed that God gave a written law (the Old Testament) and an oral, or spoken law. The oral law was made up of rules passed on from teacher to teacher.

What were some of these rules? The Old Testament said God's people were not to work on the Sabbath day. The Pharisees' rules explained what "work" means. They said it was all right to spit on a rock on the Sabbath. But if you spit on soft ground, the spit might move the dirt. And this was work. The Old Testament said you could only travel a short distance away from home on the Sabbath. But the Pharisees said you could travel farther. All you had to do was leave a little food or clothing one "day's journey" away. The food made that place "home." So you could go on another "day's journey" farther!

These and many other made up rules were as important to the Pharisees as the Old Testament itself. Jesus told the Pharisees, "You have stopped following the commands of God. Now

you only follow the teachings of men" (Mark 7:8).

The Pharisees hated Jesus. They wanted all the Jewish people to think they were especially holy because they kept so many rules. Jesus showed everyone they were not holy but were foolish and wrong.

What were the Pharisees' faults?

Matthew 23

Just before he was killed on the cross, Jesus told the Pharisees their faults. We want to avoid these faults. Even today they keep people from trusting in Jesus.

- Pride   Matthew 23:1-12
- Hypocrisy   Matthew 23:13-15
- Spiritual blindness   Matthew 23:16-22
- Unmercifulness   Matthew 23:23-24
- Evilness   Matthew 23:25-36

There were several different types of Pharisees. Usually a Pharisee could be identified by the kind of clothing he wore.

Who were the Sadducees?

Matthew 22:23-33; Luke 20:20-26

The Sadducees were a group of important priests and rich families. They controlled the Sanhedrin, the Jewish ruling council. They were also in favor of working with the Romans who had conquered their land.

But the Sadducees hated and feared Jesus as much as the Pharisees did. One time Jesus was teaching in the Temple. They sent Temple guards to arrest him. The Temple guards listened to Jesus' words, and refused to arrest him (John 7:45-53).

One time the Sadducees tried to trap Jesus with a trick question. Jesus told them, "You don't understand because you don't know what the Scriptures say. And you don't know about the power of God" (Matthew 22:29).

Usually the Sadducees and Pharisees were enemies. But the two groups each hated Jesus so much they worked together to try to stop him.

Jesus' enemies try to stop him

Matthew 12:22-27; John 8:12-59

The Pharisees wanted the people who came to see Jesus to think that Jesus broke God's law. So the Pharisees argued that healing on the Sabbath was "work" (Matthew 12:1-14). Jesus proved they were wrong. In fact, nothing they or the Sadducees did to stop Jesus succeeded.

Jesus' enemies even claimed that Jesus drove out demons by Satan's power, not God's power. Jesus told them Satan would not fight against his own demons (Matthew 12:22-27).

Jesus said even more. If his enemies were really God's people, they would have believed in Jesus. Jesus did come from God. Jesus' enemies hated him because they did not follow God. But they followed Satan's sinful, evil path (John 8:12-59).

Anyone who is really one of God's children will love Jesus. This is because Jesus is the Son of God.

This second-century synagogue near Capernaum was built over the ruins of a first-century synagogue in which Jesus may have taught.

Jesus may have walked up these steps to Caiaphas' house the night before he was crucified.

How could the Jews kill Jesus?
John 18-19

In John's Gospel, "the Jews" does not mean the Jewish people. "The Jews" are the leaders and rulers who hated Jesus.

These leaders wanted to kill Jesus. But the Roman government did not permit them to put anyone to death. Only the Roman governor could order a person to be put to death. So the Jewish leaders took Jesus to Pilate, the Roman governor. They asked him to order Jesus put to death because he claimed to be "king of the Jews." Pilate was afraid the Jews would write to the emperor if he did not have this "king" killed. Pilate knew Jesus had not done anything wrong. But Pilate gave in when the Jews threatened him (John 19:13-16).

Pilate ordered that Jesus be killed on a cross. Then Jesus' enemies thought they had finally won.

But Jesus' enemies were wrong! Jesus is the Son of God. Jesus died, but in three days Jesus was raised from the dead!

Jesus is alive today. And Jesus is the friend of everyone who believes in him.

Stories about Jesus and his enemies

Jesus clears the Temple	Mark 11:15-19	Jesus tells a story about his enemies	Matthew 21:33-43
Jesus heals on the Sabbath	Matthew 12:9-14	Jesus avoids the Pharisees' trap	Matthew 22:15-22
Jesus rejects human rules for living	Mark 7:1-23	Jesus avoids the Sadducees' trap	Matthew 22:23-33
Jesus is accused of being Satan's friend	Matthew 12:22-27; Mark 3:20-30; Luke 11:14-28; John 8:12-59	Jesus judges his enemies' sins	Matthew 23:1-36

This pictures what Jesus' death on the cross might have looked like.

To Think about and Do

1. Did Jesus' enemies really know who he was? Read these passages, and see what you think: John 3:1-2; John 9:13-33.

2. How angry do you think Jesus' enemies got at Jesus? Read John 8:12-59. Write down words you think were spoken in an angry voice.

3. The Pharisees thought keeping rules was important to please God. What are some rules that people today think are important? Which do you think are in the Bible, and which are just made up by people?

4. Read one of the stories about Jesus and his enemies listed in this unit. Draw a picture of what happened, or act it out with some friends. What can we learn from the story you chose?

5. Look up any words you do not understand. They are in the dictionary at the back of this book. Then talk to someone about what they mean.

27

The death and resurrection of Jesus

*F*or about three years Jesus traveled up and down his little land. He healed the sick and taught about God. Many loved Jesus and believed in him. But the enemies of Jesus grew more and more determined to kill him.

Finally their chance came. One of Jesus' own disciples betrayed the Lord. And the ruling council of the Jews persuaded the Roman governor to order Jesus killed. Jesus was killed on a cross. And his body was put in a garden tomb. But this was not the end! After three days, Jesus was raised from death.

The good news

• Jesus let himself be killed on a cross. He chose to die to pay for our sins.

• Jesus was raised from the dead. Jesus is the Son of God and is alive today.

Jesus' last week

It was a Sunday, around A.D. 30, when Jesus entered Jerusalem on a donkey. He was cheered by crowds carrying palm branches. Each Gospel takes many chapters to tell about Christ's last week (see chart).

This cemetery is in the Kidron Valley outside of the city of Jerusalem. Jesus was crucified on Passover about A.D. 30, died, was buried and then rose to life again after three days. He spent some time preparing his disciples and other followers for the coming of the Holy Spirit, and then he ascended into heaven. He had won the battle against sin and death.

		Matthew	Mark	Luke	John
Jesus' last week on earth					
Jesus enters Jerusalem on donkey	Sunday	21:1-17	11:1-11	19:29-44	
Jesus drives sellers from the Temple	Monday	21:12-13	11:15-18	19:45-46	
Jesus teaches in the Temple	Tuesday	22:23–24:14	11:27–12:12	20:41-44	
Judas agrees to betray Jesus	Wednesday	26:14-16	14:10-11	22:3-6	
Jesus shares last supper with his disciples	Thursday	26:17-25	14:12-26	22:7-30	13:1-30
Jesus gives last teaching to his disciples	Thursday night				14—16
Jesus prays in Gethsemane garden	Thursday night	26:30-46	14:26-42	22:39-46	18:1
Jesus arrested and tried by Sanhedrin	Friday (before dawn)	26:47–27:1	14:43–15:1	22:47-71	18:2-27
Jesus judged to die by Pilate	Friday (morning)	27:11-26	15:1-5	23:1-25	18:28–19:16
Jesus is killed on a cross	Friday	27:31-56	15:20-46	23:26-49	19:17-30
Jesus is buried	Friday to Sunday	27:57-66	15:42-47	23:50-56	19:31-42
Jesus' tomb found empty	Sunday	28:1-10	16:1-8	24:1-12	20:1-10
Jesus seen by Mary	Sunday		16:9-11		20:11-18
Jesus seen on Emmaus Road by two believers	Sunday		16:12-13	24:13-35	
Jesus comes to his disciples	Sunday		16:14	24:36-43	20:19-25
Jesus seen by many in the next 40 days!					

We can follow what happened that last week and on the day of Jesus' death. See the chart above.

Jesus enters Jerusalem
Matthew 21:1-10

On Sunday of the week Jesus was killed, Christ entered Jerusalem riding on a young donkey. Five hundred years before, the prophet Zechariah said that the king God promised his people would enter Zion just this way (Zech. 9:9)! [Zion is another name for Jerusalem.]

The people laid palm tree branches on the road and shouted out joyful praise to God. When the people shouted, "Praise to the Son of David" (Matthew 21:9), they were using a special name. "Son of David," was the name given to the promised Messiah/King.

How did Judas betray Jesus?
Matthew 26:14-16

The Jewish leaders who were Jesus' enemies were angry and afraid when the whole city shouted praises to Jesus. The leaders were

People often put palm branches in the path of someone they wanted to honor.

sure now. They would have to kill Jesus! But how could they arrest Jesus when he was so popular?

Then Judas went to the leading priests and offered to betray Jesus for money. The priests gave Judas 30 silver coins (worth only about $4.80)! For that little bit of money, Judas promised to give Jesus to his enemies.

What did Judas promise? Under Roman law a person had to be charged with a crime by witnesses who would sign papers and come to court to testify. Judas would not only tell the priests when to arrest Jesus. But he promised to speak against Jesus in court! Judas was now on the side of Jesus' enemies.

What happened to Judas? When it was too late, Judas began to feel guilty. He was sorry for what he had done. He tried to give back the money, but the priests would not take it. Judas went out and hanged himself, but the rope broke. He fell down a cliff to his death (Matthew 27:1-5; Acts 1:18).

The "Last Supper" and "Lord's Supper"
Matthew 26:17-37; John 13–16

On Thursday evening Jesus and his disciples ate a Passover supper in Jerusalem. They were in an upstairs room not far from the home of the Jewish high priest (see map, page 164). Passover was a special meal. It reminded the

At the Last Supper Jesus shared the wine and the unleavened bread with his disciples.

Jews of how God spared the Israelites in Egypt when the oldest son in each Egyptian family was killed. At that time the blood of a lamb was sprinkled on each Israelite's door. And God passed over them.

Judas slipped away after the meal was eaten. He knew where Jesus would go after supper. And he was ready to turn Christ over to his enemies.

At the Passover supper Jesus told his followers that soon his own blood would be poured out for all people. It would forgive their sins. This would be the last supper Jesus ate with his friends. The next day Jesus must die on the cross.

Today Christians remember Jesus' death for us by celebrating Communion. It is also called the Lord's Supper. The cup of grape juice reminds us of the blood Jesus shed on the cross for us. The bread reminds us of how much Jesus suffered as his body was broken there.

Jesus taught his disciples many things that night. Jesus commanded his followers to love each other, just as he loved them (John 13:33,34). And Jesus told the disciples how they could stay close to God after Jesus died (John 13–16).

Jesus' prayer in Gethsemane
Matthew 26:30-46

It was night when Jesus and his disciples left the upstairs room. They went down into the Kidron Valley. They walked across it to a garden filled with olive trees. The garden's name was Gethsemane (*Geth sem' a nē*).

Jesus was sad and troubled and went off by himself to pray. He asked God if it were possible for him not to have this time of suffering. And Jesus added, "Do what you want, not what I want" (Mark 14:36).

Jesus' prayer was answered. What God wanted to happen did happen. It was God's plan for Jesus to suffer on the cross. This was so Jesus could take the punishment for our sins.

Jesus finished praying. Then he and his disciples could see the torches of a crowd of people coming up the hill to arrest him.

Jesus was arrested by Roman soldiers in the Garden of Gethsemane. Some olive trees that were in the garden then are still alive there today.

Why was Jesus' trial illegal?
Matthew 26:47–27:1

Judas led the crowd to Jesus. When the crowd grabbed him, all Jesus' followers ran away.

The crowd took Jesus back through the Kidron Valley. Then they went up some steps to the house of the high priest. The Sanhedrin, the Jewish council, was gathered to put Jesus on trial.

Jesus' trial was illegal according to Jewish law. The Sanhedrin could not meet at night. A person could not be tried, judged guilty and sentenced to die all in the same day.

But the high priest asked Jesus, "Are you the Son of God?" Jesus answered, "Yes, I am." Then all the members of the Sanhedrin decided Jesus was guilty of speaking against God and must die.

The Jewish leaders broke their own law when they judged Jesus. But they did not care. They hated Jesus and were afraid of him. They decided that Jesus must die.

JESUS' LAST WEEK IN JERUSALEM

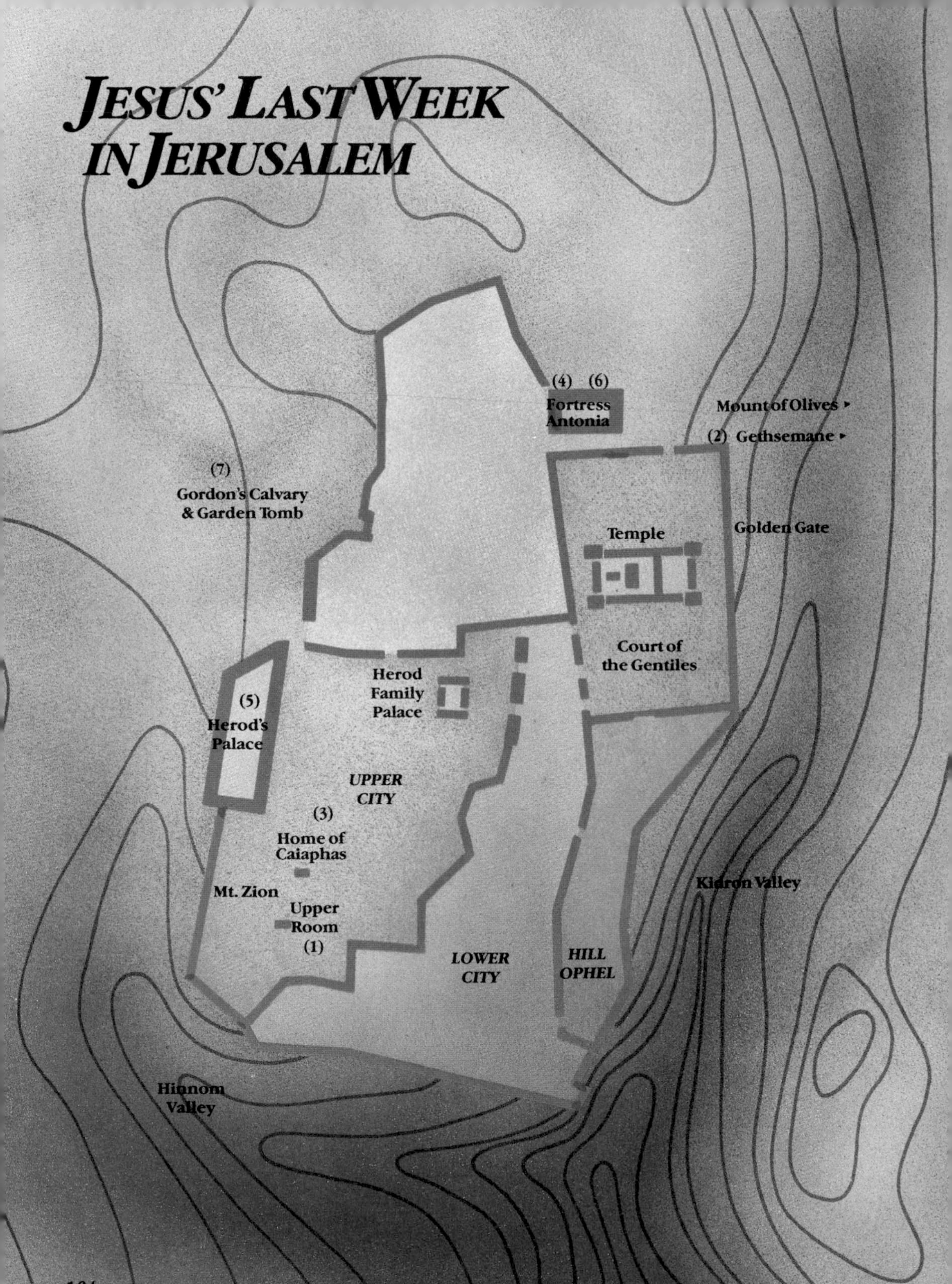

(4) (6)
Fortress
Antonia

Mount of Olives ▸

(2) Gethsemane ▸

(7)
Gordon's Calvary
& Garden Tomb

Temple

Golden Gate

Court of
the Gentiles

Herod
Family
Palace

(5)
Herod's
Palace

UPPER
CITY

(3)
Home of
Caiaphas

Mt. Zion

Upper
Room
(1)

LOWER
CITY

HILL
OPHEL

Kidron Valley

Hinnom
Valley

[Note: Three religious groups questioned Jesus that night. One was at the house of Annas. He was the high priest's father-in-law (John 18:12-14). Another was at the house of Caiaphas, the high priest (Matthew 26:57-68). And finally the Sanhedrin questioned Jesus (Matthew 27:1-2).]

Who was Governor Pilate?

Matthew 27:2-26

Pontius Pilate was the Roman governor who was in charge of Judea. Pilate was the only person who could order that Jesus be put to death.

Early in the morning, the Jewish leaders brought Jesus to Pilate. He was in the Roman fortress next to the Temple (see map, 4).

Pilate did not want to judge Jesus. So Pilate sent Jesus to Herod Antipas (see map, 5). This son of Herod the Great ruled Galilee, and Jesus was from Galilee. Herod sent Jesus back to Pilate (map, 6).

Pilate still did not want to have Jesus killed. But the Jewish leaders threatened to tell the Roman emperor that Jesus was a king. And that might lead to a riot. So Pilate gave in.

Pilate ordered his soldiers to beat Jesus. Then he told them to take him out of the city to be killed on a cross.

What is crucifixion?

Crucifixion is so cruel that only slaves and criminals were crucified by the Romans. The person's arms were nailed to a crossbar near the top of a tall pole. Crucifixion is very painful. And a person hanging on a cross may live for several days.

The soldiers led Jesus outside the city of Jerusalem to a hill called Golgotha (which means Place of the Skull). Jesus was crucified there between two thieves. On page 166 there is a list of things that happened when Jesus was crucified.

Where was Jesus buried?

Matthew 27:57-66

The Bible says that a rich man had cut a new tomb. It was in a rocky hillside near where Jesus was crucified. Before evening Jesus' body was laid in this new tomb by his friends.

The tomb was sealed by a great stone. And the Jewish leaders had soldiers guard Jesus' grave. The leaders were afraid that the disciples would steal Jesus' body and pretend he had come to life again.

But Jesus' disciples were very sad about his death. They were sure their friend was gone. They did not even remember Jesus' promise that he would come to life again.

Stone pavement from Jesus' time, near where the soldiers beat and mocked him.

Jesus on the Cross

Jesus was offered drugged drink	Matthew 27:34
Jesus is crucified	Matthew 27:35
Jesus cries, "Father, forgive them"	Luke 23:34
Soldiers gamble for Jesus' clothes	Matthew 27:35
Jesus is insulted by his enemies	Matthew 27:39-44
Jesus is told cruel things by the thieves	Matthew 27:44
Jesus is believed in by one of the thieves	Luke 23:39-43
Jesus says, "Today you will be with me in paradise"	Luke 23:43
Jesus says to Mary, "Behold your son"	John 19:26-27
Darkness falls over the whole land Matthew 27:45; Mark 15:33; Luke 23:44	
Jesus says, "My God, my God, why have you left me alone?"	Matthew 27:46-47 Mark 15:33
Jesus says, "I am thirsty"	John 19:28
Jesus says, "It is finished"	John 19:30
Jesus cries, "Father, I give you my spirit"	Luke 23:46
Jesus dies	Matthew 27:50 Mark 15:37

How do we know Jesus is alive?

The New Testament was written by men who saw Jesus after he was raised from the dead. They were eyewitnesses. They believed in Jesus so much that they shared his message throughout the world. They were willing to be beaten and jailed and even to die to serve Jesus.

How many people saw Jesus after he was raised from the dead? Here is a list.

Mary Magdalene	John 20:11-18
Two other Marys	Matthew 28:8-10
Peter, the same day	Luke 24:34
Two disciples on Emmaus Road	Luke 24:13-31
Ten apostles together	Luke 24:36-45; John 20:19-24
Eleven apostles together	John 20:24-29
Seven by Lake of Tiberius	John 21:1-23
500 people in Galilee	1 Corinthians 15:6
James in Jerusalem	1 Corinthians 15:7
Many, when he returned to heaven	Acts 1:3-12
Paul, near Damascus	Acts 9:3-6
Stephen, when he was killed	Acts 7:55
Paul, in the Temple	Acts 22:17-19
John, on island of Patmos	Revelation 1:10-19

These witnesses would soon begin to tell others that Jesus is alive. By this time the New Testament had begun. In just a few years, thousands all over the world would believe in Jesus as their Savior.

We can read about the eyewitnesses who saw Jesus after he was raised. But there were some other people who lived after the eyewitnesses. They were not Christians. But they wrote about Jewish history. And they also believed that Jesus was raised. One non-Christian writer was named Josephus. He lived several years after Jesus was raised from death. He wrote that Jesus really did live again. And he believed it. Even non-Christians believed that Jesus is alive because of the historical facts. All these things were written down. So, we can know and believe that Jesus is alive today.

But God remembered! On Sunday morning there was an earthquake. And an angel came to Jesus' tomb to roll the stone away. The soldiers were so frightened by the bright angel that they fainted!

When Jesus' friends and followers came to visit the tomb, they were amazed. The grave was empty. The cloths Jesus' body had been wrapped in were there. But Jesus was gone.

Jesus himself came and talked with his disciples. Only then did his followers remember what Jesus had said. And then they believed that he had risen from the dead.

Jesus was buried in this tomb or another one just like it. A heavy stone was rolled up to close the entrance.

To Think about and Do

1. Make a sandbox model of Jerusalem. Make buildings of Legos. Invite in another class. Show them on your model what happened the week Jesus died on a cross.

2. Many of the times Christians celebrate are associated with the last week of Jesus' life. Ask a teacher to tell you about how you remember the death and resurrection of Jesus in your church.

3. Jesus prayed two different prayers the night before he was crucified. One prayer is the Gethsemane prayer. The other prayer is found in John 17. Read the John 17 prayer. Make a list of what Jesus prayed about for you and other followers of his.

4. The crowd that Judas led took Jesus away. Then the disciples all ran, but Peter did something even worse. What did Peter do? What did Jesus do next? Read about this in Matthew 26:31-35, 69-75; John 21:15-19.

5. Why was Jesus crucified? Find the Bible answer in these passages: Romans 5:6-11; Ephesians 1:5-7; Colossians 1:21-22; Hebrews 9:11-14. Tell someone how you feel about what these verses say.

The church begins

*F*orty days after Jesus was raised from the dead, he returned to heaven. The disciples of Jesus were told to wait for a special gift. The Holy Spirit would come to give them power, and to begin the New Testament church. After the Holy Spirit came, Peter preached the first Christian sermon. And many who heard Peter put their trust in Jesus.

The good news

- Jesus is in heaven today, alive, and taking care of his people.
- Jesus has given the Holy Spirit to his people to strengthen us.
- Jesus' church is a family of people who love each other. And they love and obey Jesus.

The book of Acts

Acts was written by a doctor named Luke. He also wrote the Gospel of Luke. Acts tells how the exciting good news about Jesus was told throughout the world. Acts also tells of the apostle Peter and the apostle Paul. These two men preached and taught about Jesus. Acts is

Arches frame the Mount of Olives. At the highest point on the horizon is the place where Jesus returned to heaven.

filled with adventures about danger from enemies and wild storms. But God's Holy Spirit gave the early Christians the strength they needed to win over their enemies. And they were able to help others come to know the love of Jesus.

Who are the apostles?
Acts 1

The Bible calls the twelve special disciples of Jesus *apostles*. The word apostle means "a person sent on a mission." The Gospels tell how the disciples of Jesus were taught by Jesus. The book of Acts tells how the apostles were sent out by Jesus to tell everyone about him.
tell everyone about him.

Acts tells us about Peter and another apostle named Paul. The Bible does not tell us of the other apostles of Jesus. We do know that John lived many years. Then he was sent to the Island of Patmos by a Roman emperor. Early Christian reports tell us that Thomas went to India and preached there. And Simon and Judas (not Iscariot) were killed preaching about Jesus in Persia.

Were there other apostles?

Other Bible people are called apostles. These were people, like Paul's companion Silas, who also traveled and told about Jesus. Today missionaries travel to foreign countries. They tell others that Jesus died for their sins and is alive today. Missionaries are like modern apostles. They are sent out by our churches to share the good news about Jesus. We Christians want everyone to know and love Jesus and to have their sins forgiven.

Where is Jesus now?
Acts 1

Forty days after Jesus was raised from the dead he took all his apostles to the Mount of Olives. It is a high hill about half a mile from Jerusalem (see map, page 164).

There Jesus rose up higher and higher into the sky until the clouds hid him. The Bible tells us that Jesus returned to heaven. There he is waiting until it is time for him to come again.

What is Jesus doing in heaven? The Bible tells us several things. Jesus is preparing a place for us (John 14:1-3). Jesus defends us when we make mistakes and sin (1 John 2:1,2). Jesus always listens when we pray and helps us when we need his aid (Hebrews 4:14-16). Jesus is Lord (Romans 14:9) and teaches us to do what pleases him. Everything is under Jesus' power, and he is in charge of the church (Ephesians 1:22,23).

Jesus is in heaven today. But he watches over us. He knows our troubles and our problems. Jesus can and will help us when we pray to God in his name.

How will Jesus return?
Acts 1

When Jesus went up into heaven, two angels came and spoke to Jesus' followers. They told the apostles that Jesus "will come back in the same way you saw him go" (Acts 1:11).

The New Testament letters tell us more about Jesus' return. When Jesus comes back, Christians will rise into the sky as Jesus did. They will meet the Lord in the clouds. After that we will be with Jesus forever (1 Thessalonians 4:13-18).

Who is the Holy Spirit?
Acts 1

The day Jesus returned to heaven he gave his followers a special promise. "The Holy Spirit will come to you. Then you will receive power" (Acts 1:8).

Who is the Holy Spirit? The Holy Spirit is God, just as God the Father and Jesus are God. Other names for the Holy Spirit are the Spirit of God, the Spirit of Christ and the Comforter. God the Holy Spirit is Jesus' gift to his people.

What does the Bible tell us about the Holy Spirit? Jesus promised that the Holy Spirit will be with his followers forever (John 14:15-17). The Holy Spirit helps Christians understand about God (John 16:3). And he helps us to make hard decisions (Romans 8:14). The Holy Spirit also gives Christians the strength we need to do

This stained glass window reminds us of how Jesus went back to heaven after he was raised from the dead.

what is right (Romans 8:2-11). The Holy Spirit is a very important and wonderful person. Like Jesus, the Holy Spirit will be our friend and companion forever.

What made Pentecost special?

Acts 2

The Day of Pentecost was a special day of celebration for the Jewish people. It came 50 days after Passover, with the wheat harvest. The Day of Pentecost we read about in Acts came just 50 days after Jesus had died and was alive again.

That Day of Pentecost was very special. God sent the Holy Spirit that Jesus had promised.

God did three things in Jerusalem that day. These things showed Jesus' followers that the Holy Spirit really had come to them. (1) When the disciples were gathered together in one place, God filled the house with the sound of a great wind. (2) Then they saw something that looked like bright flames that stood over each person. (3) Then the followers of Jesus were given power by the Holy Spirit to speak in different languages.

Foreigners were in Jerusalem for the Pentecost celebration. But they all heard the disciples of Jesus speak in the language of their homeland.

The people who lived in Jerusalem did not know the foreign languages. They thought the disciples were drunk and talking nonsense. But people from other parts of the world recognized their own languages.

Peter got up and explained to the crowd. He told them that God had promised long ago to put his Spirit into all people. He promised it through the prophet Joel (Joel 2:28). The sound of wind, what looked like flames of fire and the speaking in different languages were signs from God. They proved that the Holy Spirit had really come at last.

The Day of Pentecost was the birthday of the New Testament church. The Holy Spirit came that day to add everyone who believes in Jesus to the body of Christ (1 Corinthians 12:13). The Holy Spirit joins Christians to each other. And he makes all believers members of God's family.

What is the church?

The word church comes from a Greek word that means "called out assembly." The church is made up of people who believe in Jesus and follow him obediently.

The Bible uses special word pictures to help us understand what Jesus' church is like. The Bible says the church is a *body* (1 Corinthians 12:1-8; Romans 12:12-31). People who believe in Jesus are linked together, as parts of a body are linked together. Each person has a special job in the body. This is just like arms and legs and other parts of our body. Each has a special job of its own. The picture of the church as a body helps us realize that each of us is important.

Christians in New Testament times were like a family. They shared what they had with each other.

And each of us has a way to serve God and other people.

The Bible says that the church is a *family* (Ephesians 3:14-20). Christians in New Testament times called each other brothers and sisters. This was because they were family and loved each other (1 Timothy 5:1,2). The church then is made up of people who are family. We never need to be alone if we take time to become friends with other Christians. They will love us and care for us as family.

The Bible also says that the church is God's *holy temple* (Ephesians 2:20-22). Christians are people who bring praise to God by doing only what is right and good. Christians come together as Jesus' church to worship the Lord. The Jewish people worshiped God in the Temple in Old Testament times.

That first Pentecost Sunday after Jesus was raised from the dead the Holy Spirit came. And the church began. Since that first Sunday we Christians have been God's special people — Jesus' body, God's family and God's holy temple.

The first sermon
Acts 2

Christians are people who believe that Jesus Christ is God's Son and our Savior. That Pentecost Sunday when the church began the apostle Peter preached the first Christian sermon.

171

In that sermon Peter said:

• God did miracles through Jesus to show you how special Jesus is.

• You killed Jesus on the cross, but God planned his death long ago.

• Jesus was raised from the dead, as the Bible said he would be long before it happened.

• Jesus has been lifted up to heaven and now is at God's right side.

• Jesus has been shown by God to be Christ (the one the Bible promised would come) and Lord (God himself).

What did Peter's listeners do?

The people who heard Peter's sermon knew who Jesus was. And they knew he had been killed on a cross. They knew his body was not in its grave. Many of them finally believed that Jesus truly was God.

The people who believed shouted out. They asked Peter what they should do.

Peter told them, "Repent and be baptized, every one of you, in the name of Jesus Christ for the forgiveness of your sins. And you will re-

ceive the gift of the Holy Spirit" (Acts 2:38 *NIV*). Now Moses' wish had come true. All God's people have his Spirit living in them (Numbers 11:29).

About 3,000 people believed the message about Jesus that Peter preached. They were baptized and became members of the church at Jerusalem.

How did the church show love?
Acts 2

The book of Acts tells ways the early Christians showed their love for each other. They studied to learn the apostles' teaching, and they prayed together. They stayed together. They shared money with those who needed help. They met together for worship. They ate meals together, and they praised God together.

Living and meeting together has always been important for Jesus' followers. Today Christians study and pray with each other. Christians become close friends with each other and help each other. And they meet together to worship and praise God.

To Think about and Do

1. The apostles were sent out to tell others about Jesus. Learn the names of missionaries sent out by your church to tell others about Jesus. Locate them on a map. Find out what each country is like. What special job does each missionary do?

2. What are some things that will happen when Jesus returns? Make a list from these Bible passages.

   • 1 Thessalonians 4:12-16
   • 1 Corinthians 15:20-28
   • 1 John 3:1-2
   • Romans 11:25-27
   • 2 Peter 3:10-13

3. Read the verses listed on page 169 that tell what Jesus is doing in heaven. Which are you most glad about? Why?

4. On the Day of Pentecost the disciples spoke languages that foreign visitors understood. Find out: How many languages are there today? How many languages has the Bible been translated into?

5. Read Peter's first sermon in Acts 2. Find each point outlined in this chapter. Listen carefully to a sermon in your church. Then write down its main points.

The church grows

Many in Jerusalem now believed in Jesus. The leaders who had crucified Christ tried to stop the apostles from preaching about Jesus. But the apostles did preach and, like Jesus, performed miracles to prove their new message was from God. Soon the good news about Jesus began to spread.

The good news

- God protects and answers the prayers of his people.
- Everyone who turns to Jesus as Savior will be saved.

Why were the apostles persecuted?

Acts 4,5

The apostles said openly in Jerusalem that Jesus was God's promised Messiah. They said that the leaders had nailed Jesus to a cross. But God had raised Jesus from death. The apostles preached that "Jesus is the only one who can save people" (Acts 4:12).

When about 5,000 people in Jerusalem had become Christians, the Jewish leaders were afraid. They did not want others to believe in Jesus. And they did not want to be blamed for killing God's Son.

The leaders put Peter and John in jail and threatened them. But the apostles were determined to obey God and kept on preaching.

Jesus' followers were often put in jail for preaching about Jesus.

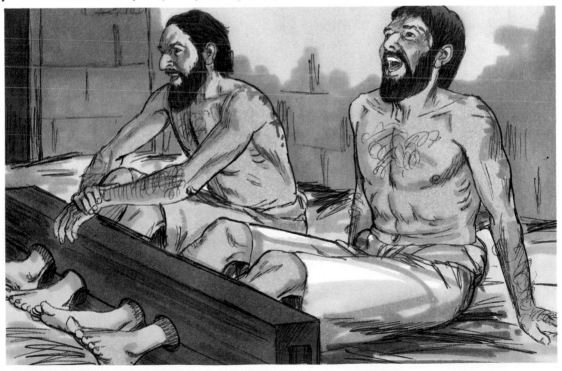

What miracles did Peter perform?

Acts 3,5,9

Peter and the apostles performed many miracles of healing in Jerusalem. Why were these miracles important?

One man Peter healed had been crippled all his life. Peter announced that he was made well "because of the power of Jesus" (Acts 3:6). The miracle showed everyone that what Peter said about Jesus' being raised to life was not just an imaginary story. Jesus was able to save people. And he could also make even the sickest people well.

The priests and rulers of the Jewish people who had killed Jesus arrested Peter and John. But they did not dare hurt the apostles because all the people were praising God for healing the crippled man. The miracles made the apostles popular. And they helped to protect them from their enemies (Acts 4:18-22).

Soon the people were saying good things about the apostles. And the leaders could not touch them. Also, more and more people believed in Jesus as they saw Jesus' power to heal (Acts 5:12-16).

Later Peter healed a man who was paralyzed for eight years. And he brought a good woman back to life after she had died (Acts 9:32-43). All the people in the towns where this happened heard about the miracles. And many of them believed in the Lord Jesus.

So the miracles the apostles performed were important. The miracles proved that the apostles' message about Jesus was true. They made the apostles popular. And they helped protect them from the leaders who killed Jesus. And the miracles helped many people to change their hearts and minds about Jesus. They turned to him as their Savior.

The believers' prayer

Acts 4:23-31

The Jewish leaders threatened Peter and John. They told them to stop talking about Jesus. Then the Christians prayed. What did they pray?

- They remembered that God is the all-powerful creator and praised him.
- They remembered that what happens is part of God's plan and praised him.
- They asked God to help them speak God's word without fear.
- They asked God to help them be brave by showing the power of Jesus.

When the apostles and believers had prayed, God's Holy Spirit filled them with courage. And they fearlessly told others about Jesus.

How does this help us when we are in trouble or are afraid? When we pray we need to praise God first. Praise him for being so great and for being in control of all things. Then we can ask God for the help we need to be brave. Praising God is an important part of praying. Thinking about God's greatness helps us trust him to answer our requests.

Who are deacons?

Acts 6

The word deacon means "service" or "ministry." Deacons are leaders who serve other people in Jesus' church.

Because of the apostles' preaching, there were soon thousands of Christians in Jerusalem. Some of them were widows who were given food daily by other Christians. But some widows weren't given a fair share of the food. So an argument started.

The apostles told the church to choose seven good, wise men who were filled with God's Spirit. The seven were put in charge of the work of giving out the food. They were to see that everyone got a fair share.

Today Christians choose good people who love Jesus to be deacons. The deacons do work that serves the other members of the church.

Who is a martyr?

Acts 7

This Greek word means a "witness." A witness is a person who tells what he or she has seen and heard. A Christian martyr is a person who faithfully tells others about Jesus. But he may be persecuted or killed for his faith.

Stephen was the first Christian to be killed for preaching about Jesus.

The first Christian martyr was Stephen, one of the deacons in the Jerusalem church. He preached boldly about Jesus. And he showed from the Old Testament that Jesus is the Son of God. One day Stephen was arrested. That day he bravely told the Jewish leaders that they had not given their hearts to God. But they were against what the Holy Spirit tried to tell them.

The leaders were so angry that they dragged Stephen outside Jerusalem. And they threw stones at him until he died.

As the stones hit Stephen, he asked Jesus to welcome his spirit into heaven. And he asked Jesus not to hold his murder against the people who killed him.

After Stephen was killed, the leaders of the Jews tried to destroy the church. They put men and women in jail and made many suffer. Many Christians fled from Jerusalem. But everywhere the Christians went they told people the good news about Jesus.

What is personal evangelism?

Acts 8

The word evangelism means "to tell good news." When Peter preached his sermons in Jerusalem (Acts 2,3) he was telling the good news about Jesus to great crowds.

Acts 8 tells of Philip, one of the seven deacons of the Jerusalem church. Philip was preaching the good news about the power of Jesus and the forgiveness of sins to many people. Then an angel from God sent Philip to wait beside an empty road. Soon an important official from another country came along the road. He was reading about Jesus' death from an Old Testament prophecy in Isaiah. Philip explained the Bible passage to this one man and told him the good news about Jesus.

The man Philip talked to believed in Jesus. And when they came to some water, he asked to be baptized right away.

Personal evangelism is telling people about Jesus.

The story of Philip illustrates one of the secrets of Christianity. Christian faith is spread not just by preaching to crowds. But believers share the good news about Jesus with one or two friends at a time. Acts 8:4 tells us that when the Christians were forced out of Jerusalem because of persecution that "everywhere they were scattered, they told people the good news."

What do "clean" and "unclean" mean?

Acts 10,11

The Old Testament law told the Jews not to eat certain animals that were "unclean." "Clean" and "unclean" did not mean that something was washed or dirty. These are religious terms. A "clean" animal or thing could be used by God's people. An "unclean" animal or thing should not be touched.

The Jewish people thought of all non-Jews as "unclean." They did not even go into the house of a non-Jew, called a Gentile. But God told Peter in a dream to kill and eat unclean animals. God now said all animals were good! This taught Peter and the Jews who became Christians that Gentiles were not "unclean" in God's sight. They should also be told the good news about Jesus.

Acts 10,11 tell how Peter came to visit an officer in the Roman army named Cornelius. This non-Jewish soldier and his relatives and friends believed in Jesus, too. Then the Holy Spirit made the Gentiles able to speak different languages. This was as the Jewish Christians did at Pentecost. This sign proved to the Jewish Christians that the message of Jesus was for non-Jews as well as for the Jewish people.

This is the house of Simon the Tanner in Joppa where Peter stayed for some time.

An interview with Peter

What would the apostle Peter say if he were interviewed on TV today? Here is part of an imaginary interview.

TV: "Peter, were you always a leader?"

Peter: "Yes. But I wasn't always a good leader."

TV: "Didn't your friends think of you as the leader?"

Peter: "Well, I was usually first. I jumped out of the boat into the sea to come to Jesus (Matthew 14:25-29). I was first to say that Jesus is the Christ, the Son of God (Matthew 16:16). But I also told Jesus he shouldn't die on the cross (Matthew 16:22). I even promised I would never desert Jesus — and then I did (Matthew 26:33). It took bravery to be first. But I was often wrong and acted or spoke without thinking."

TV: "After Jesus was raised from the dead and returned to heaven, you were still first, weren't you?"

Peter: "Yes. I preached the first Christian sermon (Acts 2). I performed the first of the apostles' miracles (Acts 3). I preached to the first Gentile, Cornelius (Acts 10,11). I was the first apostle to be put in jail, though Herod Agrippa killed the apostle James before that (Acts 12). So I did keep on being a leader."

TV: "Did you stop making mistakes after Jesus was raised and the Holy Spirit came to give you power?"

Peter: No, I still made mistakes sometimes. Once Paul had to stop me from doing something that was really wrong (Galatians 2:11-21). But God did strengthen me. After Jesus was raised and the Holy Spirit was given, there was a real change in my life.

TV: "Peter, we don't read much about you after Acts 13. What happened to you?"

Peter: "I traveled and preached the good news about Jesus. Jewish groups had settled in all the great cities of the Roman Empire. I went to many cities and worked with my fellow Jews.

"All this time my friend, the apostle Paul,

was preaching and teaching mostly Gentiles.

"I also wrote two letters that are now books in the New Testament.

"In the end I was killed in Rome. I was crucified, as Jesus was, but upside down. My legs were at the top of the cross."

TV: "Peter, if you were to give advice to our TV audience, what would you tell them?"

Peter: "Well, how about these words from my letters, called 1 and 2 Peter?"

Advice from the apostle Peter

"Love each other deeply—with all your heart" (1 Peter 1:22).

"When you do good, you stop foolish people from saying stupid things about you" (1 Peter 2:15).

"If you are always trying to do good, no one can really hurt you" (1 Peter 3:13).

"Strengthen yourselves so that you will live your lives here on earth doing what God wants, not doing the evil things that people want" (1 Peter 4:2).

"If you suffer because you are a Christian, then do not be ashamed. You should praise God because you wear that name [Christian]" (1 Peter 4:16).

"Give all your worries to him [God], because he cares for you" (1 Peter 5:7).

"His [Jesus'] power has given us everything we need to live and to serve God" (2 Peter 1:3).

"God is being patient with you. He does not want anyone to be lost. He wants everyone to change his heart and life" (2 Peter 3:9).

"Try as hard as you can to be without sin and without fault" (2 Peter 3:14).

"Be careful. Do not let those evil people lead you away by the wrong they do" (2 Peter 3:17).

To Think about and Do

1. What can you learn from prayers in the Bible? Here are some to read: Genesis 18:16-33; Ezra 9:5-15; Ephesians 1:16-20 and Ephesians 3:14-19.

2. How do the deacons in your church minister to its members? Talk with a deacon and ask how deacons serve other Christians.

3. Hebrews 11:32-40 tells about martyrs who suffered because of their faith in God. What can you find out about other Christian martyrs? (See if your library has *Fox's Book of Martyrs.*)

4. Personal evangelism is telling someone the good news about Jesus. Even children can share this good news with others. So plan a class project.

   • Decide how to tell other people about Jesus. Write out what you might say.

   • Pray together for people you will speak to.

   • Tell each other what happens when you talk to friends about Jesus.

   • Or, invite friends to a party at church where a grownup can share the good news.

5. Have a class "TV interviewer" contest. Let each team make up three questions you would like to ask Peter. (Be sure the answers are in one of the Gospels or in Acts!) Exchange questions with another team. Write out how you think Peter would answer each question. The team with the best interview wins.

Paul's missionary adventures

A young Pharisee named Saul was glad as he watched Stephen stoned to death for believing in Jesus. Later Saul became a Christian. After that his name was changed to Paul. He led the missionary movement that carried the good news about Jesus through the whole Roman Empire!

The good news

- People throughout the world believed in Jesus when they heard the good news.
- God loves all the people of the world. He wants everyone to hear about our Savior.
- People who are God's enemies can become his friends when they believe in Jesus.

Can enemies become friends?

Acts 9

The Pharisee Saul hated Christians. He believed Christians worshiped a man rather than God. Saul was going to the city of Damascus to put Jewish Christians in prison. On the way Jesus appeared to him.

The first person Paul taught the Good News to on his missionary trip to Europe was a woman named Lydia. Lydia made her living by selling cloth that had been dyed purple.

Saul saw a bright light and fell to the ground. He heard a voice ask, "Why are you doing things against me?" Then the voice told Saul, "I am Jesus, the One you are trying to hurt" (Acts 9:4-5).

Saul was blinded by the light. So his men had to lead him to Damascus. But Jesus sent a Christian named Ananias to Saul. Ananias didn't want to go. He knew Saul was an enemy. But Jesus told Ananias, "Go! I have chosen Saul for an important work" (Acts 9:15).

Ananias told Saul that Jesus had sent him. And he gave back his sight. Saul believed in Jesus now and was baptized right away.

Saul, who had been Jesus' enemy, was now Jesus' friend and follower.

Saul was Jesus' friend

Soon Saul was preaching in the Jewish synagogues of Damascus. He was saying that "Jesus is the Son of God!" (Acts 9:20). His proofs from the Bible were so strong that no one could argue with him. So Saul's enemies decided to kill him!

Saul escaped and went to Jerusalem. But Saul had been such a fierce enemy of Christians that the believers in Jerusalem were afraid of him. Finally a Christian named Barnabas became Saul's friend. And he helped him meet the apostles. Saul began to preach in Jerusalem, too. But again Saul made enemies who wanted to kill him.

Saul's Christian friends finally sent him safely to his home city of Tarsus. It was years later that Saul was invited to be a leader of the church in the Greek city of Antioch. From Antioch Saul, soon to be called Paul, set out with Barnabas and other Christian friends. They were going on missionary journeys to tell people everywhere the good news of Jesus.

The man who had been the greatest enemy of Christianity became the greatest missionary of all. Even God's enemies can become his friends when they come to know Jesus as Savior.

The early missionaries

Paul and his missionary team traveled from city to city in the great Roman Empire. They usually went to cities that were important centers of trade and government.

When they came to a new city the missionaries usually went first to the Jews. There were large groups of Jews in most major Roman cities. The missionaries went to the synagogues and preached there about Jesus. Then the missionaries preached to the Gentiles, the non-Jews.

When a group of people in the city had become Christians, the missionaries taught them. There was now a young Christian church established in that city. After a time Paul's missionary team traveled on to a new city. The Christians in the city they left would keep on telling others about Jesus. And the church would grow.

Later on the missionary team would return to a city they had visited earlier. They would officially appoint leaders for the young church. And they gave the Christians more teaching. Paul also wrote letters to churches he began. These letters, addressed to Christians in cities of the Roman Empire, make up many of the books of our New Testament.

How did the missionaries travel?

People in the Roman Empire could travel safely from one place to another. They traveled on highways made of stone. Or they went on the ships that sailed along the coasts of the Mediterranean Sea.

The ships in Paul's days were trading vessels that carried freight from city to city. Some were as much as 180 feet long. They could carry several hundred passengers as well as over 1,000 tons of cargo. But the ships were not safe in storms. Many ships were wrecked as they traveled between sea ports.

Who were the missionaries' enemies?

In the Roman Empire certain religions were legal. Judaism was a legal religion. For

Paul's Missionary Journeys
Acts and New Testament Letters

Crucifixion of Jesus	A.D. 30
Pentecost (Acts 2)	A.D. 30
Stephen martyred (Acts 7)	early A.D. 35
Paul converted	summer A.D. 35
Paul in Damascus (Acts 9)	A.D. 35-37
Paul to Jerusalem (Acts 9)	summer A.D. 37
Paul in Tarsus	A.D. 37-43
Paul in Antioch	A.D. 43-48
Paul's first missionary journey	A.D. 48-49
Galatians written	A.D. 49
Jerusalem Council (Acts 15)	A.D. 49
Paul's second missionary journey	A.D. 50-52
1 Thessalonians written	A.D. 51
2 Thessalonians written	A.D. 51
Paul's third missionary journey	A.D. 53-57
1 Corinthians written	A.D. 56
2 Corinthians written	A.D. 56
Romans written	A.D. 57
Paul's visit to Jerusalem (Acts 21)	A.D. 57
Paul's arrest (Acts 21-24)	A.D. 57
Paul in prison	A.D. 57-59
Paul's sea voyage to Rome	A.D. 59-60
Paul's first Roman imprisonment	A.D. 60-62
Ephesians written	A.D. 60
Colossians written	A.D. 61
Philemon written	A.D. 61
Philippians written	A.D. 62
Paul released and traveling	A.D. 62-64
1 Timothy written	A.D. 62
Paul travels to Spain	A.D. 64-66
Titus written	A.D. 66
Paul in Greece	A.D. 67
Paul arrested and taken to Rome	A.D. 67
2 Timothy written	A.D. 67
Paul put to death in Rome	A.D. 68
City of Jerusalem destroyed	A.D. 70

years Christianity was thought of as a branch of the Jewish faith.

But Jews from Jerusalem were among the missionaries' most dangerous enemies. They followed the missionaries from city to city and tried to stir up trouble for them. Sometimes there were riots. The missionaries were blamed and even thrown in jail.

In Ephesus many people became Christians. The people who worshiped idols were afraid no one would be left to worship their goddess, Artemis. Workmen who made silver charms and sold them lost business. So they started a riot against the missionaries, too.

It was exciting and dangerous to travel with the apostle Paul and his friends. But everywhere they traveled God helped them find people who would listen to the good news about Jesus.

Because of Paul and missionaries like him, thousands of people in the Roman Empire became Christians!

Some missionary adventures

Acts 13-20 tells about many exciting adventures the missionaries had as they traveled from city to city. They went to tell people about Jesus. Here are some of the adventures they had, with the Bible passage where you can read about them.

• Paul blinds a false prophet on Cyprus (Acts 13:4-12).

• Jealous Jews drive Paul out of Antioch [near Pisidia] (Acts 13:13-52).

• Paul is mistaken for a false god in Lystra (Acts 14:8-20).

• Paul is released from jail by an earthquake in Philippi (Acts 16:16-40).

• Paul is driven out of Thessalonica (Acts 17:1-9).

PAUL'S MISSIONARY JOURNEYS

The Roman people were well known for the excellent roads they built.
The roads were expensive, but they lasted many years.

- Paul preaches to philosophers in Athens (Acts 17:16-34).

- Paul is arrested and cleared in Corinth (Acts 18:1-17).

- Paul performs miracles and lives through a riot in Ephesus (Acts 19:1-41).

- Paul is warned of danger as he heads toward Jerusalem (Acts 20:17-38).

To Think about and Do

1. Read of Paul becoming a Christian in Acts 9:1-22. Then talk with two adults you know about how they became Christians.

2. Why was Paul glad he had become a Christian? Read what he says in Philippians 3:4-11 and 1 Timothy 1:12-17.

3. Was Paul a friend to the people he helped to become Christians? Read 1 Thessalonians 2:7-12. Do you think you would have liked Paul? Why, or why not?

4. Read two of the missionary adventures reported in Acts 13 through 20. Then write a letter to a missionary from your church. Ask about his or her adventures. What do you think you would like about being a missionary?

5. Find all the cities mentioned in Acts 13–20 on the large missionary journey map (page 181).

Under arrest!

*A*fter about 10 years of missionary travel, the apostle Paul decided to go to Jerusalem again. Paul was almost killed in a riot outside the Jerusalem Temple. But he was rescued by Roman soldiers. Paul was arrested then and was finally sent to Rome for trial.

The good news

- God uses troubles his people have to help spread the good news of Jesus.
- God protects his people in their times of trouble.

Why was Jerusalem dangerous?
Acts 21

As Paul traveled to Jerusalem he was warned of danger. He was told that he would be arrested. Paul knew that he was in danger in Jerusalem. But Paul was ready to die for Jesus if that was what God wanted.

It was dangerous for Paul because many Jewish leaders knew of Paul. They thought he taught against the Law of Moses and was against the Jewish people (Acts 21:28). How did Paul really feel about the Jewish people? Paul wrote, "I have much sorrow and always feel much sadness for the Jewish people. They are my brothers, my earthly family. I wish I could help them. I would even wish that I were cursed

A Jewish synagogue was an important meeting place.
They used it as a school, a place of worship and a place to sit and visit with friends.

and cut off from Christ if that would help them" (Romans 9:2,3).

Paul did not teach against the Jews. Paul loved his fellow Jews. And he wanted them to come to know Jesus as Savior.

Was the law for non-Jews?
Acts 15,21

In Jerusalem the Christian leaders told Paul that Jewish Christians felt it was still important to follow the Law of Moses. The leaders asked Paul to go through a special purification ceremony at the Temple. This was to show the Jewish Christians that he was not against the Law of Moses. But the leaders agreed with Paul that the Law was not intended for non-Jewish believers.

The Law of Moses does explain right and wrong actions. But it also contains rules for worship at the Temple and things to eat. And it also gives many other rules that were just for the Jewish people. Right and wrong did not change when Jesus came. But the other rules in the Law of Moses were no longer important.

When Paul traveled in Gentile cities, he lived as the Gentiles did. Paul did not want to trouble the Jewish Christians in Jerusalem. So he chose to follow Jewish customs.

Where did the soldiers come from?
Acts 21

When Paul was worshiping, some men recognized him. They thought he had brought non-Jews into the Temple. The Temple doors were shut, and the crowd was about to kill Paul. Then Roman soldiers came running up.

In Jerusalem the Roman fortress of Antonia was right next to the Temple. During special holidays, visitors from all over the world came to Jerusalem to worship. Extra soldiers were on duty in case there were riots. It was Pentecost time when Paul was in Jerusalem. The soldiers who rescued Paul simply ran out of the fortress of Antonia. When the soldiers came, the crowd stopped beating Paul. Then the officer arrested him.

This is a model of the Fortress of Antonio.

These are the ruins of the famous city of Caesarea, which was named for the ruler Caesar.

Rights of a Roman citizen
Acts 22,25

The Roman soldiers put Paul in chains. They were about to whip him to make him talk. Then Paul told them he was a Roman citizen. When the army commander learned that Paul was a citizen, the commander was very frightened.

Why was the commander afraid? In the Roman Empire very few people were citizens. Many were slaves. Many more were citizens of one of the Roman provinces. Those who were citizens had many special privileges.

A Roman citizen had the right to travel anywhere in the Empire. And he had the right to be protected by the army. A citizen could not be put on trial for breaking local laws unless he agreed. And a citizen could go to Roman courts for help. Non-citizens could be whipped to make them confess to crimes. But it was against the law even to tie up a Roman citizen. This could not be done until he was convicted by a Roman court! Even if a citizen were convicted, he could ask the emperor to hear his case. The citizen would be sent to Rome. He would be tried by the emperor and his officers there. So Paul asked to see Caesar and was sent to Rome.

Paul was from Tarsus, an important city in Cilicia (modern Turkey). Paul's father was a Roman citizen. So Paul was born a citizen. Paul was arrested in Jerusalem. But the Roman army had to protect Paul until he could be tried in a Roman court. The army commander in Jerusalem heard that some men were plotting to murder Paul. So he ordered 470 soldiers to guard Paul and take him to the Roman governor.

Being a Roman citizen helped Paul very much as he traveled and told others about Jesus.

Where was Caesarea?
Acts 23

The city of Caesarea (*Ses a re' uh*) was on the coast, 65 miles north of Jerusalem. Herod the Great took twelve years to build this city. He also built a harbor. He did it by sinking blocks of rock as large as 50 feet by 10 feet by 9 feet in the Mediterranean Sea. Three thousand Roman troops were kept in Caesarea. And the Roman governor lived there.

What rulers did Paul teach?
Acts 24–26

Paul was safely in Caesarea. Then the Jewish leaders sent men there to accuse Paul of crimes. Governor Felix listened to both sides but

People brought their gifts of money and valuable things to the Temple. They placed the gifts in the trumpet-shaped containers there.

office. Festus asked Paul if he were willing to be tried by the Jewish leaders in Jerusalem. But Paul asked that he be sent to Rome to be judged by the emperor.

King Agrippa was a great-grandson of Herod the Great. He ruled territories under the Romans. The king controlled the Temple treasury. And he appointed the Jewish high priests. The Romans often asked Agrippa's opinion on Jewish religious questions. Paul said that Agrippa believed what the Old Testament prophets wrote (Acts 26:25-27). But there is no record that Agrippa became a Christian before his death about A.D.100.

Bernice was the sister of King Agrippa. She lived with him in his palace.

Paul was kept under guard in Caesarea. But being arrested gave him the chance to tell many important people about Jesus.

Where was Paul shipwrecked?
Acts 28

Paul and some friends left for Rome. They were under the guard of a Roman officer and some soldiers. They traveled by ship, but travel was very slow. Before they could reach Rome, the season for storms came. Paul warned the officer not to take them on another ship until the winter passed. But the officer was in a hurry. He would not listen to Paul.

A great storm struck the ship. And it tossed out of control for 14 days. But all 276 people on the ship were saved when it was wrecked on the Island of Malta.

Malta is a small island, 18 miles long and 8 miles wide. It is about 90 miles from Sicily. It was three months before another ship took them away. Tradition says that the church was started there. People who lived on Malta believed the good news about Jesus.

What happened to Paul?

Christians who lived within a hundred years of Paul's life wrote down what they were told of his later adventures.

Paul was kept in Rome for about three

would not make a decision. Finally Paul appealed to Caesar. By asking to see Caesar, Paul was using his right as a Roman citizen. He was asking to go to trial in Rome itself.

While Paul was in Caesarea, he told several important people about Jesus. Who were these people?

M. Antonius Felix was Roman procurator (governor) of Judea between A.D. 52 and 59. Tacitus was an important Roman who knew him. Tacitus wrote that Felix was "a master of cruelty and lust." Felix kept Paul in Caesarea even though he knew Paul was innocent. Felix hoped Paul would offer him a bribe of money to let him go (Acts 24:26). But when Felix and Paul met, all Paul did was talk with him about Jesus.

Porcius Festus was procurator (governor) in Judea between A.D. 59 and 61 or 62. Festus was a good ruler. But he died shortly after taking

years. But finally he was judged "not guilty" and released. Paul then traveled to Spain to continue his missionary work. He had never been to Spain. He spent about three more years there before going back to Greece. In Greece Paul was arrested again and taken to Rome. There the Roman government judged Paul guilty and put him to death. This was about 11 years after Paul had been first arrested in Jerusalem.

Paul had been a Christian for 33 years. He was a missionary traveling the world to share Jesus for about 20 years. He worked to spread Christianity. He wrote 13 of the 27 books in our New Testament. All this made Paul one of the most important men ever to be born.

Paul as a missionary

Here is what Paul wrote in one letter.

"I have been in prison more often [than others]. I have been hurt more in beatings. I have been near death many times. Five times the Jews have given me their punishment of 39 lashes with a whip. Three different times I was beaten with rods. One time they tried to kill me with rocks. Three times I was in ships that were wrecked, and one of those times I spent a night and the next day in the sea. I have gone on many travels. And I have been in danger from rivers, from thieves, from my own people [the Jews], and from those who are not Jews. I have been in danger in cities, in places where no one lives, and on the sea. And I have been in danger from false brothers. I have done hard and tiring work, and many times I did not sleep. I have been hungry and thirsty. Many times I have been without food. I have been cold and without clothes. Besides all this, there is on me every day the load of my concern for all the churches" (2 Corinthians 11:23-28).

What did Paul look like?

The Bible doesn't say, except to note that some people thought "he is weak" (2 Corinthians 10:10). But one early writer from the second century in Asia describes Paul this way. He was "a short man, with a bald head and crooked legs, in a healthy body, with eyebrows meeting and nose somewhat hooked, full of friendliness."

Paul may not have looked important. But Paul was one of the most important men who ever lived.

To Think about and Do

1. Some of the Jewish people were enemies of Paul and Christianity. But many, many Jews, like Paul, became Christians. How does God feel about the Jewish people? Read Romans 1:16 and Romans 11:28-29.

2. From the description of Paul, draw a picture of him talking with King Agrippa or Festus. Which person in your picture looks more important? Who was really more important? What do you think makes a person important?

3. Why was Paul willing to suffer so many hardships as a missionary? Read what Paul says in these passages. Then tell why you think Paul was glad to be a missionary (1 Thessalonians 2:17-20; 1 Timothy 1:12-17).

4. Paul traveled with others on his missionary trips. What can you find out about Barnabas, Silas, John Mark and Luke? Look in a concordance and Bible dictionary.

5. Find the places Paul mentioned in Acts 21–28 on the map on page 181. Do this project with two or three friends.

Paul's letters to troubled churches

A s the apostle Paul traveled he wrote letters. He sent them to the people in the churches he had started on his missionary trips. These letters of Paul were copied and passed on to other churches. Churches throughout the Roman Empire collected Paul's letters. With the four Gospels, these letters taught about Jesus. And they taught about how to live the Christian life. They became our New Testament.

The good news

• Jesus brings us to God and gives us power to please him.

• Jesus will return to punish sin.

• Jesus will return to take those of us who trust him to be with him.

Why did Paul write letters?

Paul and his missionary friends did not stay long in any city. Some visits lasted only a few weeks. Others lasted over a year. In that time

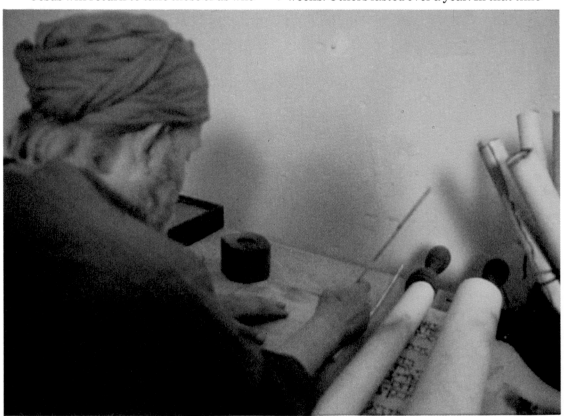

Paul dictated his letters to an assistant and then signed them.

Paul could not teach new Christians everything they needed to understand about God and Jesus.

Often as Paul traveled he received letters from Christian friends. Sometimes they would tell him about troubles in the young churches. Some had misunderstandings about Christian teaching. At times Paul sent co-workers like Titus and Timothy to visit and teach for a while.

Often Paul wrote letters to the churches. Paul's teaching letters were kept and copied. Then they were sent on to other Christians everywhere. Thirteen of Paul's teaching letters are now part of our New Testament.

Paul wrote to the Galatians

On Paul's first missionary journey he traveled to cities in the southern part of the Roman province of Galatia (Acts 13,14). He was followed by Jewish believers. They taught that a Christian must keep the Old Testament law and that they must live as the Jewish people did (Acts 15:1,5). They said that Paul was not a real apostle. And they said that God gave the Old Testament law so it should be kept by everyone.

Paul's letter to the Galatians warns the new Christians. People are not saved because they keep the Law but because they trust in Jesus. Christians are to keep on trusting in Jesus. We count on Jesus to help us live in ways that will please God. The Holy Spirit will fill our lives with love, joy, peace and many other good things.

In the book of Galatians

Paul greets the Galatians	1:1-5
Paul proves he is an apostle	1:6–2:21
Paul shows Jesus is better than the Law	3:1–4:31
Paul shows the Holy Spirit will make Christians truly good	5:1–6:10
Paul says good-bye	6:11-18

The city of Thessalonica

Thessalonica (*Thes e le ni' ka*) was an important city in Greece. It was the largest business center in its part of Europe. The city had a seaport. And it was on a main highway called the Via Egnatia.

In Paul's day many Jewish people had settled in Thessalonica. When Paul came to the city he first went to the Jewish synagogue. He went there three times. But the Jews did not listen to the good news. Paul stayed in Thessalonica long enough to get a job as a tentmaker (1 Thessalonians 2:9). And he received two gifts of money from Philippian Christians (Philippians 4:16). Paul started a strong church in Thessalonica. The Christians there began spreading the good news to neighboring towns (1 Thessalonians 1:8).

The church grew. The Jewish people who did not want to hear Paul's message became jealous. They stirred up a riot, and the missionaries had to leave the city.

Tentmakers used knives to scrape the animal skins they used for tents. They used bone or metal needles and sharp pointed tools to help sew skins together. Why did Paul work so hard to support himself by tentmaking? Most religious teachers in that day were paid money by their students. Paul said, "We worked to take care of ourselves so that we would be an example for you to follow" (2 Thessalonians 3:9). Christians are to work and take care of themselves. And they are to help people in need.

Paul's two letters to the Thessalonians

When Paul was in Thessalonica he taught the new Christians. He told them that Jesus would come back again. After Paul left, the members of the church became confused about what Paul had said. In each letter Paul helps Christians understand more about what will happen when Jesus returns. Paul also gladly remembers how eagerly the Christians in Thessalonica heard God's word. And he remembers how much they wanted to please the Lord.

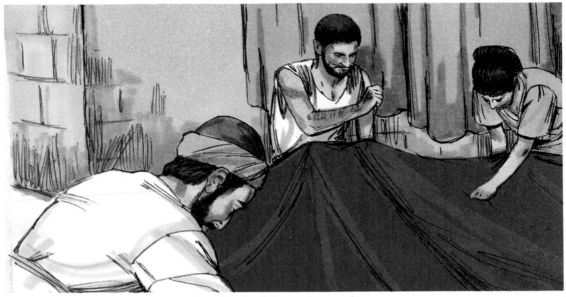

Paul worked as a tentmaker to support himself and to help people in need.

In the book of 1 Thessalonians

In the book of 2 Thessalonians

The city of Corinth

Corinth is another city in Greece. Corinth was a very important trade city, with ports on two seas (see map, page 181). In Paul's day the city had about 600,000 people. It was bigger than Denver, Colorado or Miami, Florida!

The city of Corinth had a very bad reputation. People who study old things have found one short street that had 33 drinking places! The city was so sinful that to call a person a "Corinthian" in Paul's day was a terrible insult.

Paul stayed in Corinth for at least a year and a half. He taught first in the Jewish synagogue. The Jews forced him out of the synagogue. So Paul taught in the house of a Roman Christian that was right next door (Acts 18:7).

Paul later wrote the book of Romans from this city. In the last chapter, he mentioned a man named Erastus (Romans 16:23). Today you can see a paving block on one of the roads in ancient Corinth. It has an inscription about this same Christian man. He was also an important city official (city treasurer).

The city of Corinth was wicked and sinful. The Christians there had to learn how to live a good and holy life. The Corinthian church had many problems. And Paul's letters to Corinth were written to help the church solve its problems in a Christian way.

In the book of 1 Corinthians

Many people in Corinth were upset at Paul's letter. They did not like what he told them they must do. But many others did listen to the apostle and did what he taught them. Paul wrote another letter to Corinth. He praised the people who had done what he said. And he warned the people who would not obey his instructions.

In the book of 2 Corinthians

Dungeon at St. Peter Gallicantu

Promises for Christians from Paul's letters

"You are God's child, and God will give you what he promised you because you are his child" (Galatians 4:7).

"The Spirit gives love, joy, peace, patience, kindness, goodness, faithfulness, gentleness, self-control" (Galatians 5:22,23).

"We will be taken up in the clouds and meet the Lord in the air. And we will be with the Lord forever" (1 Thessalonians 4:17).

"[God] will give you strength and protect you from the Evil One" (2 Thessalonians 3:3).

"He [Jesus] will keep you strong, so that there will be no wrong in you on the day our Lord Jesus Christ comes again" (1 Corinthians 1:8).

"You can trust God. He will not let you be tempted more than you can bear. But when you are tempted, God will also give you a way to escape that temptation. Then you will be able to bear it" (1 Corinthians 10:13).

"When Christ comes again, those who belong to him will be raised to life" (1 Corinthians 15:23).

"[God] comforts us every time we have trouble, so that we can comfort others when they have trouble" (2 Corinthians 1:4).

"We all show the Lord's glory, and we are being changed to be like him. This change in us brings us more and more glory. And it comes from the Lord, who is the Spirit" (2 Corinthians 3:18).

"God can give you more blessings than you need. Then you will always have plenty of everything. You will have enough to give to every good work" (2 Corinthians 9:8).

"Try to be perfect. Do what I have asked you to do. Agree with each other, and live in peace. Then the God of love and peace will be with you" (2 Corinthians 13:11).

To Think about and Do

1. Read one of these five letters of Paul in a Bible that is easy to understand like the *International Children's Bible, New Century Version*. Draw a line under one important thing that you read. Then tell someone why you think it is important.

2. Make a list of some bad things that people do that they seem to get away with. Read 2 Thessalonians chapter 1. What does it say will happen to them?

3. The Bible says that Christians are like parts of a body. Each part has something special to do to help others. Draw a picture of a person. Choose what part of the body you would like to be, and tell why. Then read 1 Corinthians 12. See what you learn about living like a part of Christ's body. What will you do to help others?

4. Love is very important to God. Together with your class make a list of as many "Love is…" statements as you can. Then read 1 Corinthians 13. Which of your "Love is…" ideas are most like things in this Bible passage?

5. 2 Corinthians 8 and 9 tell about Christian giving. Write down five things you learn about giving. Tell your parents what you learned. Ask them how and why they give money to your church and for Christian work.

Paul's letters to strengthen Christians

Paul's travels took him to some of the most exciting and important cities in Europe and Asia. Everywhere he went he started churches. And when Paul's missions team traveled on, the great apostle often sent letters back. They helped to instruct and guide the churches.

The good news

- Jesus makes people who are not righteous truly good.
- Jesus is the one who makes every good thing possible for people who trust in him.
- Jesus brings us joy.

Rome in Paul's time
Romans

Rome was the busiest and most exciting city on earth. Paul wrote his letter to Christians in Rome five or six years before he was taken there as a prisoner.

A Roman villa. During the time of the Roman Empire, most citizens were either very rich or very poor. Rich people had large homes with beautiful gardens, and poor people lived in tiny apartments.

Water was brought into Rome through brick waterways called *aqueducts*. This is the famous Aqueduct of Caesar.

Rome was 12 miles wide. It was built on seven low, flat hills just east of the Tiber River. The city was 800 years old when Paul went there. It had a population of about one million people. Over half the people in Rome were slaves.

Most people in Rome were either very rich or very poor. Prices were very high. Most people lived in tiny rooms in apartment houses. One person wrote about a man whose room was 200 steps up! The rich people, however, had large houses with swimming pools and gardens.

The middle of the city was very crowded. The apartment houses were there for people who had to walk to work. The city had sewers. But it had no street lights at night.

Water was carried to Rome by 14 high brick and stone waterways called aqueducts. They ran for 1300 miles and carried 300,000,000 gallons of water to Rome each day!

Rome had libraries. And it had bookstores where you could buy a hand copied book for as little as $1.50.

About 20,000 Jews lived in Rome. But Roman emperors often drove them out of the city because they were disliked. Later Christians in Rome were persecuted, too. Jews, and then Christians, dug out long tunnels and rooms in the soft rock under the city. They used them to bury their dead or hide. These underground passages and the rooms where Christians met to worship are called catacombs. There are about 600 miles of catacombs under the city of Rome!

The Roman emperors tried to make their capital city beautiful. They used marble and gold to cover their temples and public buildings.

In Paul's day sports events were held in the Circus Maximus. These games often meant that men called gladiators fought and killed each other. Or they fought wild animals. Later Christians were killed by animals or gladiators for sport. And the Roman crowds looked on and cheered.

Rome was a big, busy city. But Rome was a cruel city, too. Individual people were not important to the Romans.

But Paul wrote a letter to the Romans. In it the great apostle shows how much God loves each person. And he shows how trust in God's Son Jesus can lead a person to a truly good life.

In the book of Romans

The city of Ephesus
Ephesians

Ephesus was the largest Asian city in the Roman Empire. Ships from every country docked in its port.

But Ephesus was most famous for the Temple of Diana. Diana was also called Artemis.

This temple was one of the Seven Wonders of the ancient world. There were 100 columns 55 feet tall outside the building. The building was 164 feet wide and 342 feet long. This giant temple was 42 feet longer than a football field.

Each year over half a million people came to Ephesus for a month-long festival to Diana.

The temple treasury was very rich. The priests used the temple money like one of our modern banks. They loaned it out at interest. Probably the world's first "traveler's checks" were issued by the Temple of Diana at Ephesus.

The people of Ephesus were proud because so many people came to visit their beautiful temple. Also, many silversmiths made a good living. They made idols of their goddess and symbols of their religion. The religion in Ephesus was very superstitious. And the people there practiced evil magic.

Many people became Christians when Paul and the other missionaries stayed in Ephesus. In fact, so many became Christians that the silversmiths lost much business. And thousands of dollars' worth of books about magic were publicly burned.

The people of Ephesus were proud of their

Christians were often forced to fight wild animals or Roman fighters called *gladiators* in the Roman Coliseum. Often the Christians were killed.

temple and their false goddess. But Paul knew that only Jesus is Lord. Christians are to be proud of Jesus. And they should be thankful to be Jesus' people. So Paul's letter to the Ephesians reminded them all about Jesus. This letter is called a Christological letter. It is all about Jesus Christ. And it is about how important it is for us to know and worship Jesus.

In the book of Ephesians

Jesus has brought us forgiveness and salvation.	1:1-14
Jesus brings us strength and power.	1:15-23
Jesus brings us new life	2:1-10
Jesus unites enemies and makes all Christians one.	2:11–3:13
Jesus' love is something we can experience with other believers.	3:14-21
Jesus' one body is made up of all Christians.	4:1-16
Jesus makes us holy— and we are to live good lives for him.	4:17–6:20

Slaves in Bible times
Philemon

About half the people in the Roman Empire were slaves. Most slaves were laborers. They worked on farms or built roads or did other hard work. Some slaves were well educated. They copied books, ran businesses and taught their masters' children. Several of the letters in our New Testament urged Christian slaves to work hard to please their masters.

One book in the Bible, Philemon, was written about a runaway slave. This slave, named Onesimus (*On e' se mus*), was put in prison with Paul and became a Christian. Philemon, a leader in the church in Colossae, was the slave's Christian master. Paul sent the slave back to him. Paul asked Philemon to welcome his runaway slave. He was not just a servant but a Christian brother now.

How did people become slaves? Some were captured in war. Some were born of slave mothers. Some were sold by their parents. And some sold themselves to pay debts.

Many slaves were better fed and housed than poor free men. But slaves had to obey their masters. They had to do what was good for their owners, not what was good for themselves.

A person who was a slave could become free. He might be freed by his master. Or he might be bought by another person. Or he might save enough money to buy his own freedom.

God's word urged people who were slaves in New Testament times to serve their masters well. It also told them to take any opportunity to win freedom.

Paul also used slavery as a Christian illustration. Jesus died to free us from slavery to sin. We do not have to do what sin urges us to do. Jesus' death bought us for God. We who are Christians are free now to choose to serve God. Jesus has freed us to love others and to do good.

The Philippian jail
Acts 16; Philippians

Prisons in the Roman Empire were dark and awful places. There was no fresh air, no bathrooms and terrible food. Paul and his fellow-missionary Silas were beaten in Philippi. They did not have a trial and were thrown in jail. They were put in the worst cell. The jailer even put their feet in stocks. These were probably holes in the stone floor. Paul and Silas would not be able to sleep or lie down with their feet locked in stocks.

Paul and Silas could have been discouraged. Instead they sang songs and praised God. Then God sent an earthquake that opened the doors of the jail and freed the prisoners! Find out how the Philippian jailer became a Christian. You can read about it in Acts 16:16-40.

Paul and Silas were filled with joy even in the worst of their troubles. Paul wrote a letter to

Paul and Silas were once in prison in the city of Philippi. These are the ruins of a prison there.

the Philippians. In it he talks about how all Christians can find joy.

In the book of Philippians

Christians find joy by telling other people about Christ.	1:1-30
Christians find joy by caring for each other.	2:1-30
Christians find joy by trying to please Jesus.	3:1-21
Christians find joy by trusting Jesus in everything.	4:1-23

The book of Colossians

Colossians is another Christological letter—a letter all about Jesus. Paul reminded the Colossians that Jesus really is God. And he came and lived on earth as a real, living person. Jesus

pleased God by doing what is right every day. Christians can please God by doing what is right each day, too. You can read about all this in Colossians.

In the book of Colossians

Paul greets and prays for the Colossian Christians.	1:1-14
Paul shows that Jesus really is God.	1:15 – 2:4
Paul shows how not to live in the Christian life.	2:5-23
Paul shows how we can live a Christian life and please Jesus.	3:1 – 4:6
Paul tells news about Christian friends.	4:7-18

Words about Jesus in Paul's letters

"Jesus was given to die for our sins. And he was raised from death to make us right with God" (Romans 4:25).

"[Nothing] in the whole world will ever be able to separate us from the love of God that is in Christ Jesus our Lord" (Romans 8:39).

"God made Christ more important than all rulers, authorities, powers and kings. Christ is more important than anything in this world or in the next world" (Ephesians 1:21).

"Christ's love is greater than any person can ever know" (Ephesians 3:19).

"Christ himself was like God in everything. He was equal with God" (Philippians 2:6).

"God raised Christ to the highest place. God made the name of Christ greater than every other name. God wants every knee to bow at the name of Jesus — everyone in heaven, on earth and under the earth" (Philippians 2:9,10).

"No one has seen God, but Jesus is exactly like him" (Colossians 1:15).

"Through his [Jesus'] power all things were made — things in heaven and on earth, things seen and unseen, all powers, authorities, lords and rulers. All things were made through Christ and for Christ. Christ was there before anything was made. And all things continue because of him" (Colossians 1:16,17).

"Christ has made you God's friends again. He did this by his death while he was in the body, that he might bring you into God's presence. He brings you before God as people who are holy" (Colossians 1:22).

"All of God lives in Christ fully (even when Christ was on earth). And in him you have a full and true life" (Colossians 2:9,10).

"Christ is sitting at the right hand of God" (Colossians 3:1).

To Think about and Do

1. Read about these things in an encyclopedia or Bible dictionary.

• Catacombs   • Slavery (in Roman times)   • Rome

Tell someone what you learn.

2. Read chapters 1 – 3 of Romans. How many proofs can you find that people are not righteous (good)? Make a list. Then find articles in the newspaper that show people still do these kinds of things.

3. Read chapters 1 and 2 of Ephesians. Make a list of things that Jesus has done for you and for other Christians.

4. Count the number of times that "joy" and "rejoice" (or "happy") are used in the book of Philippians. Read the "happy" verses carefully. What do you think can make you happy in life?

5. Make a "Life in Christ" booklet. First read Colossians 3:1 – 4:6. Then make a list of things that people with new life from Jesus will do. For instance, Christian people will be patient (3:12). Write each of these things on a separate sheet of paper. You may want to draw a picture showing how a child can do what you have written. Then for two weeks write a sentence or two to tell what happened when you did one of these things. Write your report on the correct page of your "Life in Christ" booklet.

Letters to young leaders

*T*imothy and Titus were younger members of Paul's missionary team. In time, each of them became an important leader. Paul sent them to visit churches that needed special help or teaching. Three letters in our New Testament were written by Paul to these young leaders.

The good news

• Even young people can become leaders and help others grow as Christians.

• Older leaders like Paul will help young people become good leaders.

Who was Timothy?

Timothy is mentioned often in Acts. He is also mentioned in some of Paul's letters to churches. Paul probably met Timothy on his first missionary journey.

Timothy was a young preacher who often traveled with the apostle Paul.

Timothy's father was a Greek and his mother was a Jewish Christian. His mother, Eunice, and his grandmother, Lois, taught Timothy the Old Testament when he was just a child (2 Timothy 1:5).

Timothy may have been just a teenager when he joined the missionaries. As Timothy grew older, Paul trusted him with special missions. Paul sent him to Thessalonica to see how the church there was doing. Later Paul sent Timothy to Corinth to help them solve their problems.

Paul and Timothy were very close friends. Paul had no children of his own. But he thought of the younger Timothy as "a dear son" (2 Timothy 1:2).

Paul's first letter to Timothy was written while Timothy was working with the church at Ephesus. He was helping the church choose good leaders. And he was teaching those leaders. Paul's second letter to Timothy was written while Paul was in prison in Rome. This was just before Paul was killed.

Timothy was not a very bold person. In fact, he was shy. And Paul had to urge him not to be frightened of people. But Paul was sure that God would help this young man. He would be one of the church's leaders when Paul and the other apostles died.

Who was Titus?

No one knows just when Titus joined Paul's missionary team. Titus was a Greek Christian. He was a good leader. And he was able to work even with the troublesome Corinthian church (2 Corinthians 7:6-14).

When Paul wrote to Titus he was in Crete. This was a hard place to be. Paul says "there are many people [there] who refuse to obey" (Titus 1:10).

Paul felt very close to Titus, too, and also called him "a true son in the faith we share" (Titus 1:4).

Titus was another of the men who would lead the church after Paul and the other apostles died.

Wise words to young leaders

"Continue to have faith and do what you know is right" (1 Timothy 1:19).

"Pray for all people. Ask God for the things people need, and be thankful to him" (1 Timothy 2:1).

"You are young, but do not let anyone treat you as if you were not important. Be an example to show the believers how they should live. Show them with your words, with the way you live, with your love, with your faith and with your pure life" (1 Timothy 4:12).

"Do not speak angrily to an older man, but talk to him as if he were your father" (1 Timothy 5:1).

"Treat older women like mothers and younger women like sisters" (1 Timothy 5:2).

"Tell those who keep on sinning that they are wrong" (1 Timothy 5:20).

"Try to live in the right way, serve God, have faith, love, patience and gentleness" (1 Timothy 6:11).

"Do not be ashamed to tell people about our Lord Jesus" (2 Timothy 1:8).

"Stay away from the evil things young people love to do. Try hard to live right" (2 Timothy 2:22).

"You should do good deeds to be an example in every way for young men" (Titus 2:7).

"Be under the authority of rulers and government leaders, to obey them and be ready to do good, to speak no evil about anyone, to live in peace with all, to be gentle and polite to all men" (Titus 3:1,2).

"Those who believe in God will be careful to use their lives for doing good. These things are good and will help all people" (Titus 3:8).

"If someone causes arguments, then give him a warning. If he continues to cause arguments, warn him again. If he still continues causing arguments, then do not associate with him" (Titus 3:10).

What makes a Christian leader?

A person does not become a Christian leader quickly. Timothy and Titus traveled with

SPREAD OF CHRISTIANITY

ISLAND OF BRITAIN

SPAIN

ITALY

• Rome

Mediterranean Sea

AFRICA

Black Sea

BITHYNIA
AND PONTUS

CAPPADOCIA

PHRYGIA

GALATIA

Tigris River

Antioch (Pisidia)

• Antioch

• Philippi

Thessalonica

Pergamum

Colossae

LYCIA AND
PAMPHYLIA

CILICIA

• Ephesus

• Athens

CYPRUS

• Corinth

CRETE

JUDEA

• Jerusalem

• Alexandria

Memphis

EGYPT

Nile River

Red Sea

The apostle Paul wrote many letters to the churches in different cities. The letters were probably written on scrolls, and they were probably read aloud to the church.

Paul for many years. They learned first how to be good Christians. Then they became leaders.

In Paul's letters to these young leaders he tells them what makes a person a Christian leader. First, a Christian leader is a good example. The leader shows people how they should please Jesus with "the way you live, with your love, with your faith and with your pure life" (1 Timothy 4:12). Second, a Christian leader is a good teacher. Paul says young leaders are to "continue to read the Scriptures to the people, strengthen them and teach them" (1 Timothy 4:13).

Leaders in every local church are to live Christian lives. And they must be able to teach others what the Bible says.

Even children can learn to be leaders. We get ready to be leaders by making right choices. And we get ready by learning to live the way the Bible teaches.

Read the New Testament's letters to the young leaders, Timothy and Titus. They can help any Christian prepare to be a leader. You can find out how by reading some verses in Paul's letters. They answer the following questions.

In the book of 1 Timothy

- How can we help people have love?   1:1-11

- How can we be sure our faith is not destroyed?   1:12-20

- How are we to pray and worship God?   2:1-15

- How are we to choose new leaders for our church?   3:1-16

- How can we recognize false teachers?   4:1-5

- How can we recognize good teachers and leaders?   4:6-16

- How are we to treat other people?   5:1–6:2

- How are we to feel about money and riches?   6:2-21

In the book of 2 Timothy

- What gifts does God give us, and how can we use them?   1:1-18

- What can we do to be good soldiers of Jesus?   2:1-13

- What can we do to be good workers for Jesus?   2:14-26

• What troubles will Christian workers have?	3:1-9
• What can we learn from older Christians?	3:10-17
• What commands should young leaders be sure to obey?	4:1-18

In the book of Titus

• What kind of people are to be leaders in the church?	1:1-9
• What can we do about false teachers?	1:10-16
• What will people who follow true teaching be like?	2:1-15
• What difference does knowing Jesus make in a person's life?	3:1-11

Christianity after Paul and the apostles

Everywhere the apostles had traveled they started churches. Each of these churches had elders and deacons who were leaders. The elders and the deacons taught the people and helped them live Christian lives.

Also people like Timothy and Titus traveled from city to city. They helped the leaders and taught the people.

Paul and his missionaries had started churches in important cities. People traveling through these cities also heard about Jesus. And Christians from the cities also traveled to nearby towns. Soon there were many Christians in the Roman Empire.

The leaders who were trained by the apostles trained other leaders. And the New Testament church grew and grew.

To Think about and Do

1. Paul, Lois and Eunice all helped young Timothy grow as a Christian and become a leader. Who helps you grow as a Christian? Write the person or persons a "thank you" letter for helping you grow.

2. The apostle Paul wrote some wise words for young leaders. Imagine he wrote you a letter. Choose advice he would be most likely to give you. Try for one week to follow that advice.

3. Who helped the leaders in your church become leaders? Talk to one or two elders in your church. And talk to your preacher. Who was most important in helping each one become a leader?

4. Choose one question that is answered in Paul's letters to young leaders. Read the Bible passage. Underline the sentences that tell you the answer to the question.

5. The map on page 201 shows centers of Christianity in the Roman Empire. This was about 100 years after the death of the last apostle (John). What can you find out about the growth of Christianity during that time? Who were the leaders? Where did missionaries travel? How many people became Christians? You can find answers in a church history book or a good encyclopedia. Ask your teacher or parents to help you.

Letters to encourage Christians

Paul was not the only missionary and teacher in the early church. There were many others. Five of them wrote books in our New Testament. They encourage and teach Christians. These books are called the General Epistles. They were addressed to all Christians rather than certain cities or individuals. Who wrote these books? Peter and John were apostles and early disciples of Jesus. James was Jesus' brother, another son of Mary and Joseph. Jude may have been his brother, too. No one knows who wrote the letter we call Hebrews. It was written to Jewish Christians.

The good news

- Jesus keeps every promise the Old Testament makes.
- Jesus strengthens us in our hard times.
- Jesus makes us able to love others and obey God.

Keeping Old Testament promises
Hebrews

The Old and New Testaments are two parts of our one Bible. The Old Testament was written

How Jesus Keeps God's Promises

The picture		The promise	How Jesus keeps the promise	Verses in Hebrews
LAW		God will make his people good.	Jesus puts God's law in our hearts, not just on stone tablets.	8:7-13
SACRIFICE		God accepts the death of a sacrifice. This is in payment for sin, and God gives forgiveness.	Jesus' one sacrifice on the cross paid for all our sins. Now we can be forgiven forever.	9:23–10:18
HIGH PRIEST		God will listen when the priest offers sacrifices and prays for a person.	Jesus is our high priest who is alive today. He loves us and always prays for us.	4:14–5:10 7:1–8:6

before Jesus came. The New Testament was written after Jesus came.

There are other differences between the two testaments. The Old Testament is about the Jewish people. They were from the family of Abraham. The New Testament is about the church. It is made up of people from every nation and family.

Some people have wondered how this can be. Has God changed his mind? Why are there these differences in the two testaments?

Actually, both the Old and New Testaments talk about the same things. Both testaments talk about listening to God's word. Both talk about keeping God's law. Both talk about sacrifice for sin, and forgiveness. Jesus came. He showed us new and better ways to keep God's law and find his forgiveness.

Many Jewish people became Christians. But they wondered if they should go back and live in the Old Testament ways.

The book of Hebrews was written to these Jewish Christians. Hebrews shows that the Old Testament rules and practices were really promises — pictures of what God intended to do in the future. When Jesus came, God kept the promises he had made in the Old Testament. People who have Jesus do not need the picture-promises anymore.

What were some of the picture-promises made in the Old Testament? And how did Jesus keep those promises? You can find out in the chart on page 204.

There are many more wonderful things about Jesus in Hebrews. In every way Jesus fulfills the picture-promises of the Old Testament. The Jewish Christians read the book of Hebrews. Then they realized they did not have to go back to Old Testament ways to please God. The Old Testament gives us pictures of Jesus. Christians have the real Jesus.

How does a person with faith act?

James

James was a common name in Jesus' day. There are several people named James in the New Testament. Which one of them wrote the book of James?

The most important James was a younger brother of Jesus. James was a leader of the church in Jerusalem. At first James did not believe that his older brother was the Savior (John 7:2-5). After Jesus was raised from the dead, James did believe, along with Jude. He could have been Jesus' brother also.

Early Christian writings tell us that James' nickname was "camel knees." James got the nickname because he prayed so much. His knees became rough and hard, like the knees of a camel.

You can read about this James in these passages of the New Testament: Acts 12:17; Acts 15:13; Acts 21:18; 1 Corinthians 15:7; Galatians 1:19; Galatians 2:9.

The letter James wrote tells what makes Christian faith special. Some people think they have faith because they believe God really does exist. James wants us to understand that faith in Jesus is more than just thinking God exists. It is more than just thinking that Jesus died for us. Faith in Jesus is giving ourselves to Jesus so fully that we live for him and do good.

What can you find out by reading the book of James? You can find out about the kind of life you will live if you have faith in Jesus.

In the book of James

You can ask God for wisdom.	1:2-8
You can know God does not send temptations.	1:9-18
You can be sure to obey God.	1:19-27
You can love all people.	2:1-13
You can do good works.	2:14-26
You can control the things you say.	3:1-12
You can become truly wise.	3:13-18

Roman coins often had an imprint of the ruler on them.

You can give yourself to God.	4:1-12
You can let God plan your life.	4:13-17
You can be sure wicked people will be punished.	5:1-6
You can be patient till Jesus comes.	5:7-11
You can pray and God will help.	5:13-18
You can help save others.	5:19-20

What did Peter write?

1,2 Peter

Many people in the Roman Empire did not like Christians. Yet for many years Christians were protected by law.

The Christians would not always have that protection. The Roman emperor Nero (A.D. 54-68) blamed Christians for a great fire in Rome. He killed many Christians who lived in Rome. The apostles Paul and Peter were probably killed at this time.

Later the Roman emperor Domitian (*Dō mish'i an*) (A.D. 81-96) ordered the persecution of Christians everywhere. This emperor wanted to be called "lord and God." Christians knew that only Jesus is really Lord and God. And they would not worship the emperor. Many were killed or driven from their homes and businesses by this evil emperor.

The apostle Peter wrote two letters to encourage Christians who would soon be persecuted. The first letter tells Christians how to face suffering. The second letter reminds Christians what will happen when Jesus comes.

In the book of 1 Peter

God protects us.	1:1-12
God calls us to a holy life.	1:13–2:17
Jesus gives us an example.	2:18–3:7
God brings good if we do good but still suffer.	3:8–4:6
God calls us to help others.	4:7-11
God wants us to trust him if we suffer as Christians.	4:12-19
God will make everything right after our suffering is past.	5:1-11

In the book of 2 Peter

God has given us all we need to live and serve him.   1:1-21

God warns us against false teachers who try to deceive us.   2:1-22

God promises that Jesus will come and set all things right.   3:1-18

What did John write?

1,2,3 John

John lived to be a very old man. In John's letters he wrote about God's love for us. And he wrote about how we Christians can love God and others. John's first letter is to encourage Christians. And it is one of the most beautiful letters in our Bible.

In the book of 1 John

We show we love God when we tell others about him.   1:1-4

We show we love God when we confess our sins to him.   1:5–2:12

We show we love God when we love other people.   2:7-29

We know God loves us because he has made us his children.   3:1-10

We know we are God's children when we love other people.   3:11-24

We know God loves us because he sent his Son to die for us.   4:1-21

We know God loves us because we have eternal life now.   5:1-21

What did Jude write?

Jude

Jude could also have been a brother of Jesus (Matthew 13:55; Mark 6:3). Jude warned against the danger of false teachers in the church. Real Christian leaders will be loving

The apostle John is said to be the only apostle who was not killed for being a Christian. But he was forced to live the rest of his life here on the Isle of Patmos.

people who want to please God. And what they teach will be found in God's word, the Bible.

Encouraging words

"He [Jesus] can help those who are tempted. He is able to help because he himself suffered and was tempted" (Hebrews 2:18).

"Everything good comes from God, and every perfect gift is from him" (James 1:17).

"When a good man prays, great things happen" (James 5:16).

"God's power protects you through your faith, and it keeps you safe until your salvation comes" (1 Peter 1:5).

"You are a people who belong to God. God chose you to tell about the wonderful things he has done" (1 Peter 2:9).

"If you are always trying to do good, no one can really hurt you" (1 Peter 3:13).

"Yes, you will suffer for a short time. But after that, God will make everything right. He will make you strong. He will support you and keep you from falling" (1 Peter 5:10).

"[Jesus'] power has given us everything we need to live and to serve God. We have all these things because we know him" (2 Peter 1:3).

"God has made a promise to us. And we are waiting for what he promised — a new heaven and a new earth where goodness lives" (2 Peter 3:13).

"If we confess our sins, he will forgive our sins. We can trust God. He does what is right. He will make us clean from all the wrongs we have done" (1 John 1:9).

"The Father has loved us so much! He loved us so much that we are called children of God. And we really are his children" (1 John 3:1).

"When God makes someone his child, that person does not go on sinning. The new life God gave that person stays in him" (1 John 3:9).

"God gives us the things we ask for. We receive these things because we obey God's commands and we do what pleases him" (1 John 3:22).

To Think about and Do

1. Draw a picture of the last time your parents punished you. Then explain the picture. How did you feel when you were punished? Sometimes people feel God punishes them. Read Hebrews 12. Decide what you would tell someone who thinks God is punishing him.

2. Work with one or two friends to find and write down 10 encouraging verses in the book of Hebrews. Use an easy-to-understand Bible like the *International Children's Bible, New Century Version.*

3. Talk to a member of your church missionary committee. Ask him to tell you about a country where Christians are persecuted or suffering today. Find something in 1 Peter that might help these Christians. Then write a letter to someone in that country who is your age. Tell what you found in 1 Peter that might help.

4. Look in James for five things that you do because you have faith. Be sure to do these things this week.

5. Read 1 John, and underline the word "love" every time it occurs. Look at all these places. Then draw three cartoons showing Christian love.

Things to come

*T*he last book in the New Testament is not a letter. It describes a vision of the future given to John. He was the last living apostle of Jesus. The book of Revelation is very hard to understand. The parts we do understand tell us that God has a plan. God's plan will be completed. Then he will bring people who believe in Jesus to heaven. They will enjoy eternal life with him.

The good news

- God will judge sin and destroy evil.
- Jesus will come again to defeat Satan.
- God will welcome us into a glorious and wonderful heaven.

Where was Revelation written?

As a very old man, the apostle John was sent to the island of Patmos. This barren, rocky island lies off the coast of Asia Minor. It is just 37 miles from Miletus (see map).

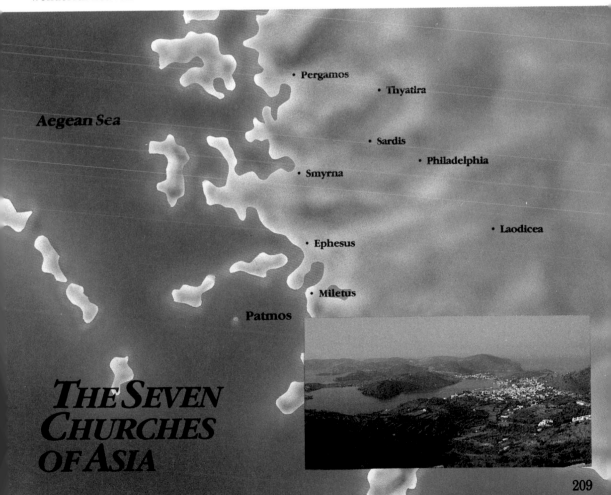

- Pergamos
- Thyatira

Aegean Sea

- Sardis
- Philadelphia
- Smyrna
- Laodicea
- Ephesus
- Miletus

Patmos

THE SEVEN CHURCHES OF ASIA

God gave John a vision. John wrote down what he saw, and this became the book of Revelation.

While John was on Patmos, God gave him a vision. John saw Jesus in heaven. And then John saw things that would happen in the future.

Some Christians believe that these visions are about the history of the church. Some Christians are sure that the visions describe what will happen when history ends. But all Christians agree that the visions remind us of an important truth. God is in control of the future. Whatever happens will lead to the wonderful life with God that Jesus had promised his followers.

What are symbols?

Revelation 1:12-16

Symbols are words or images that stand for something else. For instance, a dove is used in the Bible as a symbol for the Holy Spirit. Usually you can tell when the Bible uses something as a symbol. Then the Bible will say that something is *like* the thing named.

Some Bible symbols are easy to understand. Other symbols are harder.

When John describes Jesus, he uses many symbols. Here is John's description. "He [Jesus] was dressed in a long robe. He had a gold band

around his chest. His head and hair were white like wool — wool that is white as snow. His eyes were like flames of fire. His feet were like brass that glows hot in a furnace. His voice was like the noise of flooding water. He held seven stars in his right hand. A sharp two-edged sword came out of his mouth. He looked like the sun shining at its brightest time" (Revelation 1:13-16).

We know what some of these symbols mean, but not all of them. Brass was used in the altar where sacrifices were offered. Some people think the brass stands for judgment on sin. The white wool-like hair is also a symbol of judgment.

We might not know the meaning of the symbols. But this description of Jesus would tell us how great and powerful he really is. All of Revelation tells this message. Jesus is all-powerful. One day Jesus will come in power and punish sin and sinners.

What does John's vision mean?

John's vision has three parts. The first part is a vision of Jesus. He has a message to be delivered to seven churches (Revelation 2,3). The second part is a vision of judgment on the earth (Revelation 4–19). The third part is a vision of heaven and victory (Revelation 20–22).

Each part of Revelation helps us to realize how great and powerful our God is.

Where were the seven churches?
Revelation 2,3

In his old age John had settled in Ephesus. the churches mentioned in Revelation are in cities near Ephesus (see map, page 209).

Jesus had a message for each of the churches in these cities. Some churches were praised for things that pleased Jesus. Most were also warned and given commands to obey.

Christians today study the letters to the seven churches. We study them to learn the things that win Jesus' praise. And we learn how to obey his commands.

Does Revelation describe an atomic war?
Revelation 4–19

The middle part of Revelation is filled with awful pictures of judgment. Trumpets blare. And angels pour out smoking bowls filled with terrible judgments on our earth.

We read in Revelation about hail and fire falling on the earth. It burns up a third of all the plants (8:6-7). Revelation describes fire falling into the ocean. It kills a third of all sea life (8:8-9). Revelation tells about star material falling on earth. It poisons a third of the fresh water (8:10-11). Some people believe that these terrible things must be caused by an atomic war. Others are sure John's vision is about

punishments that God himself sends on earth. They are not something that people do.

We are not sure just what all the symbols in the book of Revelation mean. But we are sure that God will bring terrible punishments on people who do not love and obey Jesus. How good to know that Jesus is our Savior. He will keep us safe whatever happens here on earth.

Who will win history's last war?
Revelation 19

Revelation 19 begins with a song of praise. Jesus is about to come again. Then we see Jesus riding a white horse. He is followed by the armies of heaven. The enemies of Jesus are gathered together with their armies.

Jesus wins this final battle. His enemies are killed, and their leaders are punished forever.

Then even people who will not believe God will learn that he is all-powerful.

Is there a real hell?
Revelation 20

The Bible tells us that there is a real hell. Jesus warned people about hell many times (Matthew 5:22,29,30; Matthew 7:19; Matthew 23:15; Matthew 25:30,41; Mark 9:43,45; Mark 12:40; Luke 12:47,48; Luke 16:19-31).

People who die do not just stop living. Every human being will exist forever. Those who have obeyed Jesus as Savior will live forever with God. Those who will not trust or obey God will be forever in a place of punishment called "hell."

What will hell be like? The Bible says it is

The book of Revelation tells how the earth will be completely destroyed someday.

like a "lake of burning sulfur" or a "lake of fire" (Revelation 20:10,14). This is the place where wicked people will be punished "day and night forever and forever" (Revelation 20:10).

Hell sounds like such a terrible place. Many people have wondered how God could send people there. Jesus gives us a wonderful answer. Jesus said that hell was prepared for "the devil and his helpers" (Matthew 25:41). Hell was not prepared for people. In fact, Jesus died on the cross so that people could be forgiven.

If Jesus is your Savior and you are living for him, you do not have to be afraid of hell. Jesus died for you. And you could be with him forever in heaven.

What will heaven be like?
Revelation 21,22

The Bible tells us that our universe will not last forever. One day it will disappear (2 Peter 3:10-13). Then God will create a new heaven and earth that will be perfect and holy.

What will heaven be like? Revelation tells us about a beautiful city. It is called the holy city, or the New Jerusalem. It shines like a very expensive jewel. It is over 135 miles long, 135 miles wide and 135 miles high! The streets of this city are of pure gold as clear as glass. The city is always bright and beautiful. This is be-

cause the presence of God and Jesus are its light. And people are spread out all over the beautiful new world it governs.

Life will be very wonderful then for those who love Jesus. John tells of a voice he heard in his vision that makes us this promise. "Now God's home [will be] with men. He will live with them and they will be his people. God himself will be with them and will be their God. He will wipe every tear from their eyes. There will be no more death, sadness, crying or pain. All the old ways [will be] gone" (Revelation 21:3,4).

Come, Lord Jesus!
Revelation 22

John's vision ends with a promise from Jesus. "Listen! I am coming soon. I will bring rewards with me. I will repay each one for what he has done" (Revelation 22:12).

John has described the terrible things that will happen on earth (Revelation 4–19). But John has also seen and told us about the wonderful new world. Jesus will create it for his people. John can hardly wait for Jesus to come back.

No wonder that John, like Christians through the ages, cries out as he hears Jesus' promise to come soon.

"Yes!" John says.

"Come, Lord Jesus!"

To Think about and Do

1. Be a reporter for an imaginary newspaper. Ask three children or adults how they think the world will end. Do they think a lot about the end of the world? Are they worried or afraid?

2. Imagine Jesus is sending a message to you like the message he sent to the seven churches. How would he praise you? What would he say is wrong? What commands might he give you?

3. How will people act when God finally sends his terrible judgments on the earth? Find out what others in your class think. Then read Revelation 6:15-17 and 9:20-21.

4. Revelation 15 and 16 describe some of the terrible things that will happen before Jesus comes back. Make a class mural showing the judgments described in these chapters. Then add panels showing what the new heaven and earth will be like after God has punished all sin.

5. If you were planning heaven, what would you include? List the things you think would be important. Compare your list to the good things promised us in Revelation 21 and 22.

Dictionary and Index

*T*his dictionary/index helps you explain Bible terms and concepts to children in words they can understand. It also tells you the pages in the *International Children's Bible Handbook* where you can find more information on each topic.

A

Aaron (*A -run*) was the older brother of Moses. Aaron was the first high priest of Israel. Only men from the family of Aaron were allowed to be priests under Old Testament law (Exodus 4 – 40). See pages 49, 52.

Abraham (*A -brah-ham*) was the most respected man in the Jewish nation. He is called the father of the Jewish people. He was a man of great faith in God (Romans 4). See pages 13, 30.

Acts (*AX*) is the Bible book that tells how the church began. It also tells how the good news of Jesus was carried to the world by the apostles. See pages 18, 168-170.

Adam (*AD-um*) means "out of the earth." He was the first man. God made him from the dust of the ground. You can read about Adam in Genesis 2:7. See page 24.

Ahab (*A -hab*) was Israel's most evil king. He tried to make God's people worship the false god Baal. Ahab and his wife, wicked Queen Jezebel, worshiped Baal. You can read about them beginning in 1 Kings 16:29. See pages 92, 95.

Ai (*A -i*) was a city near Jericho. When one of the people of Israel sinned, the Israelite army was defeated at Ai. When the sin was punished, the Israelites won (Joshua 7). See pages 61, 62.

altar (*ALL-ter*) was a place where sacrifices, gifts, or prayers were offered to God. God's law commanded the Israelites to offer their sacrifices only at an altar served by priests. This altar was at the Tabernacle (Meeting Tent) or Temple, where God was to be worshiped. See page 28.

Amos (*A -mus*) was a prophet whom God sent to warn the rich cities of Israel. Amos told the people they would be punished for their useless worship and because they did not care about the poor. But the people of Israel did not listen to Amos. The Bible book of Amos reports what he said about doing right and worshiping God. See pages 16, 89, 92-94.

angel (*AIN-jel*) is a Greek word that means "messenger." Angels are heavenly beings who can sometimes look like people. God used angels to help his people. Angels announced important events, like the birth of Jesus. Some angels turned against God and now help the devil (Matthew 25:41; Luke 2:8-15; Hebrews 1:14; 13:2; 2 Peter 2:4). See pages 126, 169.

apostle (*uh-POS-'l*) is a Greek word that means "someone who is sent." Jesus gave this name to his twelve disciples. He sent them to tell the good news about him. Paul and others who were missionaries are also called apostles in the New Testament (Matthew 10:1-4; 1 Corinthians 15:9). See pages 169, 173.

Arameans (*ar-a-ME-ans*) were Israel's enemy during the years of the divided kingdom. The Arameans are also called Syrians. They lived in what is now the modern land of Syria. Ben-Hadad and Hazael were kings of Aram in those days. See pages 92, 97.

ark of Noah was a large boat built by Noah and his sons. God punished sinful people by sending a great flood. But God saved Noah's family and the animals in this large boat (Genesis 6 – 9). See page 73.

ark of the covenant (Box of the Agreement) was a wooden box, covered with gold. Once a year Israel's high priest sprinkled the blood of a sacrifice on the top of the Holy Box. The blood of this sacrifice was a picture of the blood of Jesus shed on Calvary for our sins (Exodus 25:10-22). See pages 52, 73, 77, 78.

Ashtoreth (*ASH-to-reth*) was the name of a Canaanite goddess thought to be the wife of the god Baal. See page 66. See Baal.

Assyria (*a-SIR-i-a*) was a powerful nation in Old Testament times. In 722 B.C. the Assyrians defeated the kingdom of Israel and took its people away as captives. The capital city of Assyria was Nineveh. See pages 92, 103.

B

Baal (*BALE*) is the Canaanite name for "god." These pagan people worshiped many baals, in the form of idols. The worship of Baal was wrong because it did not recognize the one true God. See pages 66, 92, 100.

Babylonia (*bab-i-LONE-i-a*) is the name of a powerful empire of Bible times. Its capital city was Babylon. About 600 years before Jesus, the Babylonians defeated Judah and took captive the Jewish people who lived there. After about 70 years the Jewish people were able to return to the promised land. See pages 101, 105-113.

Balaam (*BAY-lam*) was a man thought to have magical powers at the time the Israelites left Egypt. The king of an enemy nation hired Balaam to curse Israel, but God would not let him (Numbers 22–24). See page 56.

baptize (*BAP-tize*) is a Greek word that in New Testament times meant to dip or immerse. Christians are baptized in water. They practice baptism as a reminder of Jesus' death, burial and rising to life again (Acts 2:38,41; Acts 8:36-39; Romans 6:3,4). See pages 130-133.

beatitude (*bee-A-tih-tood*) means "blessed" or "happy." Part of a sermon Jesus gave is called The Beatitudes. It is written in Matthew 5:3-12. It tells us how to please God and live a blessed and happy life. See page 135.

Ben-Hadad (*ben-HAY-dad*) was a king who led the Arameans (Syrians), who were Israel's enemy in the days of Elijah and Elisha. Read about him in 1 Kings 20. See pages 92, 97.

Bethel (*BETH-el*) was a city in Israel where kings of that divided nation set up a worship center. This act was against God's law. See page 90.

Bethlehem (*BETH-le-hem*) is a name that means "house of bread." It is a small town about five miles from Jerusalem. Bethlehem was the home of Ruth and the hometown of David in the Old Testament. It is the town where Jesus was born (1 Samuel 16:4; Matthew 2:1). See pages 120, 127.

Bible (*BY-bul*) means "the book." The Bible is a group of books and letters which Christians accept as the word of God. The Old Testament of the Bible has 39 books and was written before Jesus was born. The New Testament of the Bible has 27 books and was written after Jesus was born. See pages 8-19.

C

Canaan (*KAY-nan*) is one name of the land God promised to Abraham's descendants. Other names for the same land are Palestine and Israel. The people who lived there before the Israelites were called Canaanites. They were wicked people who worshiped idols (Genesis 12:6,7). See pages 40, 45, 60, 63.

Christ (*KRYST*) means "anointed one" in Greek. In Hebrew the word is Messiah. See *Jesus*. See page 131.

church means "called out assembly." In the New Testament it refers to a group of Christians. In those times the church often met in someone's home (Matthew

16:18; Acts 2:47; 14:27; Romans 16:5). See pages 168-175.

Colosse (*kuh-LAH-see*) was a city in what is now the country of Turkey. Paul wrote a letter to Christians in Colosse that became our Bible book of Colossians (Colossians 1:1,2). See page 197.

commandments (*kum-MAND-ments*). See *laws* and *Ten Commandments*.

confess (*kun-FESS*) means to admit that something is true. The New Testament teaches a believer to confess that Jesus is the Son of God. Also, when believers sin, they are to confess their sins to God and admit they have done wrong (Romans 10:9,10; 1 John 1:9). See page 207.

Corinth (*CORE-inth*) was a port city in the country of Greece. It was known as a very wicked city. The apostle Paul went there and started a church. Later he wrote two letters to the Corinthians. We have these letters as our Bible books 1 and 2 Corinthians (Acts 18:1-11). See page 190.

covenant (*KUV-e-nant*) is a promise, contract or special agreement. God made such agreements with his people in the Old Testament. God made a special promise / agreement with Abraham. He made another agreement, called the "law of Moses," with Abraham's descendants. God made a special agreement / promise with David, too. And he made a new covenant with his people through Christ in the New Testament. Hebrews 8–10 explains the difference between the old agreement through Moses and the new agreement through Jesus. See pages 32, 36, 49, 78, 204, 205.

create (*kree-ATE*) or **Creation** (*kree-A-shun*) means "to make." The Bible teaches that God made our universe. He made the world we live in and all living creatures (Genesis 1,2). See pages 21-25.

cross refers to a cruel way of killing criminals in New Testament times. That way of killing was called crucifixion. The person was nailed to wooden posts put together to make a "t" or an "x." Then he was left hanging in a public place to die. Jesus was killed this way. But Jesus did not die as a criminal. He died to save us from our sins. In the New Testament the word "cross" is often used to remind us that Jesus' death was God's way to save us from our sins (1 Corinthians 1:18-25). See pages 154, 160, 165, 176.

crucifixion (*CREW-ci-FIX-shun*). See *cross*.

curse in the Bible often means punishments that God has announced for doing wrong. People may try to put a curse on other people. But there is no evil magic that anyone can work against people who belong to God (Numbers 22,23). See pages 56, 99.

Cyrus (*SY-rus*) was the Persian leader who defeated Babylon. Cyrus said that any of the Jews there who wanted to return to their homeland could. Cyrus also ordered them to rebuild God's Temple. And he promised to pay the costs! See pages 111, 113, 115.

D

Dan was a city in Israel where kings of that divided nation set up a worship center against God's law. See pages 90, 103.

Daniel (*DAN-yell*) was taken captive to Babylon as a teenager. He was trained to be in the government of the Babylonian Empire. And he became an important leader. God used Daniel to give his message to Nebuchadnezzar, the king of Babylon, and to the kings who followed him. The Bible book of Daniel tells about him. It also contains what God told Daniel would happen in the future. See pages 17, 110-113, 118.

David (*DAY-vid*) was Israel's greatest king. He is also known for killing Goliath. You can read about David in the Old Testament books of 1 Samuel and 1 Chronicles. David made Israel a powerful nation. David also loved God, and he wrote many of the poems in the book of Psalms. Jesus is called a "son of David" in the New Testament because he was born to members of David's family (Luke 1:69; Acts 2:29-31). See pages 16, 69, 74-80.

deacon (*DEE-kun*) is a Greek word meaning "servant." Deacons were chosen to serve other Christians in the church in special ways (Acts 6:1-6; 1 Timothy 3:8-13). See pages 174, 175.

Dead Sea Scrolls are ancient copies of parts of Old Testament books. See pages 8, 9.

death has several meanings in the Bible. There is physical death, which means our bodies die. There is spiritual death, which means that a person is separated from and does not respond to God. There is also "the second death." This means that after a person dies physically he or she can be separated from God forever, in a place of punishment for sins. Jesus died to save us from this "second death." We can have eternal life instead. Because of Jesus, we can be alive to God again and live with God forever after our bodies die (Genesis 2:17; Ephesians 2:1-2; Revelation 20:11-15). See pages 140, 141, 212.

Deborah (*DEB-o-rah*) was a leader in Israel in the time of the judges (Judges 4, 5). See pages 15, 66.

demons (*DEE-muns*) were evil spirits. Some think demons were bad angels who followed the devil. Demons made people sick and harmed them in other ways. But Jesus has more power than demons, and he could send them away (Matthew 12:22; Luke 8:26-39). See pages 137, 140, 157.

Deuteronomy (*do-ter-ON-omy*) is the fifth book in the Old Testament. It means "second law." It is a book of sermons by Moses about God's law. Moses gave them just before the people of Israel entered Canaan. See pages 51, 57.

disciple (*dih-SY-p'l*) is a person who is learning from someone. Jesus' disciples are those who believe and obey his teaching. During his ministry Jesus chose 12 special followers (disciples) and made them his apostles (Matthew 15:32-39; Acts 6:1-7). See pages 125, 148-153.

dreams in Old Testament times were believed to carry messages from the gods. Sometimes the true God did speak in dreams. Often one of God's people would be sent to explain what the dream meant (Exodus 40; Daniel 2). See pages 39, 112.

E

Ecclesiastes (*e-klez-e-AS-teez*) is a Bible book written by Solomon. King Solomon tried to find out if life is worth living without God. He learned that life without God is empty and unhappy. See pages 87, 88.

Eden is the name of the special garden God prepared for the first man and woman, Adam and Eve (Genesis 2:8). See pages 24, 25.

Egypt (*E-jipt*) is in the northeast part of the continent of Africa. It was an important and powerful country in Bible times. God's people, the Israelites, were slaves there for hundreds of years. God sent Moses to lead them out. God saved the Israelites by punishing the Egyptians with ten miracle plagues. You can read about this in Exodus 1-11. Later, Mary and Joseph took the baby Jesus to Egypt to keep Herod from killing him (Matthew 2:13-15). See pages 14, 35, 37-47.

Elijah (*ee-LIE-juh*) was a prophet in the northern kingdom of Israel during the days of King Ahab, who brought Baal worship into Israel (1 Kings 17-21). See pages 16, 92, 95.

Elisha (*ee-LIE-sha*) was a prophet in the northern kingdom who followed Elijah and continued his fight against evil (2 Kings 2). See pages 16, 92, 95.

Ephesus (*EF-eh-sus*) was the largest city in the Roman state of Asia in New Testament times. It also had a famous temple of the goddess Diana. But the New Testament church was very strong in Ephesus. Paul wrote a letter to the Christians in Ephesus that is in our Bible as the book of Ephesians (Acts 18:19-21). See pages 180, 195, 196.

eternal life (*ee-TER-nal LYFE*) is the new kind of life promised to those who follow Jesus. It is living now with new help from God. It is also a life that will never end (John 3:16; Galatians 2:20; 1 John 5:11-15). See pages 145, 207.

Esau (*E-saw*) was the older twin brother of Jacob. They were sons of Isaac. Esau did not care about God or God's covenant (agreement) with his grandfather Abraham. You can read about Esau in Genesis 25. See page 35.

Esther (*ES-ter*) was a Jewish girl who became queen of the Persian Empire. It came after the Babylonian Empire. God used Esther to save the Jewish people when an enemy planned to have all the Jews killed. You can read about this in the Bible book of Esther. See pages 17, 113.

evangelism (*ee-VAN-jell-ism*) means to "tell the good news." The Christian good news is that Jesus died to save us from our sins. And he gives people who follow him eternal life. All Christians can tell others the good news about Jesus. See page 175.

Eve (*EEV*) means "mother of all living." She was the first woman. God made her from a rib which he took from Adam, the first man. You can read about Adam and Eve beginning in Genesis 2. See pages 24-26.

evil spirits. See *demon*.

Exodus (*EX-o-dus*) means "going out." It is the name of the second Bible book. It tells how God saved the Israelites from slavery in Egypt about 1450 years before Jesus was born. This is found in the book of Exodus in the Old Testament. See pages 41-52.

Ezekiel (*ee-ZEEK-yell*) was a prophet who was taken to Babylon as a captive. He acted out messages from God, warning that Jerusalem would be destroyed. The Bible book of Ezekiel tells about this interesting man and the visions he saw. It also tells God's promises to bring the people of Judah back to their land after a time as captives in Babylon. See pages 111, 112.

Ezra (*EZ-rah*) was the leader of a group of Jewish people who went back to Judah from Babylon. He studied and taught the Scriptures to those who returned. The Bible book of Ezra tells about the exciting return of the people to the promised land. This was after their many years as captives. See pages 17, 116.

F

faith (*FAYTH*) is belief and trust. Faith in Jesus means believing that he is the Son of God and trusting him as Savior. People who have faith obey God and his word. This is because they believe God can be trusted to tell people what is truly right and good (Hebrews 11). See page 205.

fear of God means to respect God. People who fear God are not afraid of him. But they love him and choose to live a good life in order to please him. See page 57.

follower. See *disciple*.

forgiveness (*for-GIV-ness*) means to be excused and not punished for a wrong thing done. A sinner who trusts in Jesus and follows him is promised forgiveness of his sins. That person will not be punished by God. Christians are to forgive others for wrong things done to them (Matthew 6:12-15; Acts 8:22; Romans 4:7; Ephesians 4:32). See pages 52, 131, 153.

G

Galatia (*guh-LAY-shuh*) was a district of Asia in what is now the country of Turkey. The Bible book of Galatians was written by Paul to churches that he had started in this area (Acts 18:23). See page 189.

Galilee (*GAL-li-lee*) was an area in Palestine in the days of Jesus. Jesus was from Galilee. The large lake there is called the Sea of Galilee. See the map on page 134 (Matthew 4:23-25). See pages 127, 129, 137.

Genesis (*JEN-i-sis*) is the first book of the Old Testament. See pages 20-40.

Gentile (*JEN-tile*) means "nations." The Jews called anyone who was not a Jew a Gentile. The good news of Jesus is for all people, both Jews and non-Jews (Acts 10:44-48; Romans 11:11-13; Ephesians 3:6-8). See page 176.

Gethsemane (*geth-SEM-uh-nee*) was a grove of olive trees just outside the city of Jerusalem. Jesus went there to pray the night before he was killed. Jesus was there when Judas brought people to take him away (Matthew 26:36; Mark 14:32). See page 163.

Gideon (*GID-e-on*) means "great warrior" in Hebrew. Gideon was one of Israel's judges. God gave Gideon and only 300 men a great victory over an enemy army (Judges 6-8). See pages 15, 67.

God is the One who made the world and everything in it. He is a spirit and does not have a body as people do. But people can know what God is like because he sent Jesus to show them. God hates evil, but he loves people so much that he sent his Son to die for them. God is the wisest and most powerful being in the universe. God has always been alive, and he will always be alive. He is love. Christians are called "children of God" because they have been given a life like his (Genesis 1:1; Matthew 5:9; John 4:24; Romans 1:18; 5:8-11; Hebrews 1:1-14; 1 John 4:7-12). See pages 20-29, 42, 49, 57, 120.

Goliath (*go-LI-ath*) was a giant Philistine, over nine feet tall. He was killed by the young David, who trusted God to help him fight the enemies of the Lord's people. See pages 16, 74.

Gomorrah (*go-MORE-ah*) is the name of a city that God destroyed in the time of Abraham because the people were so wicked (Genesis 19:28). See page 33.

gospel (*GOS-p'l*) means "good news." It refers to what Christ has done for us (Philippians 1:5,7; 2 Thessalonians 1:8). See page 151.

gospels (*GOS-p'ls*) is a name for the first four books of the New Testament: Matthew, Mark, Luke and John. The gospels tell about the birth, life, death and resurrection of Jesus. See pages 125, 169.

Greek (*GREEK*) is the language mainly of the people of the country of Greece. It was spoken by most people in the empire of Jesus' day. It is the language in which the New Testament was written. See page 200.

H

Habakkuk (*ha-BACK-uk*) was a prophet who lived in the time of good King Josiah. The book of Habakkuk asks how God can let people do wrong without punishing them. God explained to Habakkuk that he always punishes sin, and Judah would soon be destroyed by an enemy. But God would give strength to those with faith in him. See pages 17, 105.

Haggai (*HAG-i*) was a prophet in Judah after the people returned from captivity. The Bible book of Haggai tells sermons he preached. He urged the people to get busy and rebuild God's Temple in Jerusalem. The people did what Haggai said. And God promised to bless them because they obeyed. See pages 17, 116.

heal means to recover from sickness or injury. Many of the miracles of Jesus made sick people well. Not everyone who asks God will be made well. But God will always use even our troubles for good. See pages 137-139.

heaven (*HEV-'n*) is the home of God. In the New Testament it is said to be a place where there is no pain, no crying, no sadness, no night and no death. Jesus left heaven to come to earth and die on the cross. People who love Jesus will live with him in heaven forever (John 3:13; 6:38-40; 14:1-6; Revelation 21:4). See pages 132, 169, 212.

Hebrew (*HE-broo*) is the language of the Jewish people. Most of the Old Testament was written in Hebrew. "Hebrew" is also one name given to the Jewish people. See pages 8, 9.

Hebrews (*HE-brooz*) is the name of one of the books of the New Testament. It was written to help Jewish Christians realize how much better Christianity is than the Jewish law. This is because Jesus came and died for our sins. See pages 204, 205.

hell is a place of punishment for those who do wrong and will not come to Jesus for forgiveness. The New Testament describes hell as a place of fire, pain and sorrow (Matthew 23:33; 2 Peter 2:4,9; Revelation 20:14,15; 21:8). See page 212.

Herod (*HEH-rud*) was the family name of different rulers mentioned in the New Testament.

> **Herod I** (Herod the Great) was king from 40 B.C. until about 4 B.C. He tried to kill the baby Jesus because Jesus was to be a king (Matthew 2:1-16; Luke 1:5). See pages 121, 126, 128.

> **Herod Antipas** was the son of Herod I. He had John the Baptist's head cut off. He ruled from about 4 B.C. to A.D. 39 (Matthew 14:1-12; Luke 23:6-12). See page 165.

> **Herod Agrippa I** was king of Palestine for about three years. He had the apostle James killed. And he arrested Peter. Later he died a terrible death because he let people treat him as if he were a god (Acts 12:1-21). See page 176.

> **Herod Agrippa II** was king of Palestine from A.D. 48 to 93. He was the great-grandson of Herod I. He heard the apostle Paul speak (Acts 25:13,26; 26:1-32).

Hezekiah (*HEZ-eh-KI-ah*) was one of Judah's good kings. He prayed to God when Jerusalem was in danger from the Assyrians. And God saved the city. Read about him in 2 Kings 18,19 and Isaiah 36 – 39. See pages 17, 103.

holy (*HO-lee*) means pure, belonging to God. Holy also means good, doing what is right. God is holy, for he does only what is right. God's people are called holy because they belong to him. And they are supposed to do only what is right (1 Corinthians 1:2; Ephesians 1:4; 1 Peter 1:15,16). See pages 25, 156.

Holy Spirit (*HO-lee SPIH-rit*) is one of the three persons of God. The other two are God the Father and God the Son (Jesus). The Holy Spirit gave people power to do important things and to help them be good. The Holy Spirit helped the apostles do miracles. The Holy Spirit led men to write the word of God. The Holy Spirit lives in Christians today. He is called the Spirit of God and the Comforter (John 3:6-8; Acts 2:1-4; Romans 8:9-16; 2 Peter 1:20,21). See pages 132, 168, 169, 210.

Hosea (*ho-SAY-a*) was a prophet whom God sent to Israel. He told the people that they were being unfaithful to God. He warned Israel that God would punish them. But if they returned to God, he would forgive them. The Bible book of Hosea contains his message on faithfulness. See pages 92, 94.

I

---

idol (*EYE-d'l*) is a false god. The non-Jewish people often worshiped statues they made from wood, stone or metal. They worshiped these idols rather than the true God of heaven (Isaiah 44:6-20; Acts 7:40-43; 17:16-23). See pages 100, 114, 136.

image of God is a phrase that tells why human beings are so special. It means that God made people to be like him in some ways. Only human beings were created "in the image of God" (Genesis 1:26,27). See pages 24, 28.

inspiration (*in-spur-AY-shun*) means God worked in the people who wrote the Bible so that what they wrote was his exact message. See page 10.

Isaiah (*eye-ZAY-eh*) was one of the Bible's greatest prophets. Isaiah helped King Hezekiah trust God. Isaiah also warned that God will punish sin. But Isaiah wrote many wonderful prophecies about Jesus long before he was born. Isaiah 53 tells about Jesus' death. And it promises that Jesus will save his people from the punishment they deserve for their sins. The Bible book of Isaiah is one of the longest books written by a prophet. See pages 17, 104.

Israel (*IZ-rah-el*) was first of all a new name given to a man called Jacob, the grandson of Abraham (Genesis 32:28). Members of his family, the Jewish people, are also called by the name of Israel (and Israelites) (1 Samuel 7:6). Israel is also the name given to the land of Canaan that God promised to Abraham. See pages 36, 89, 92-95.

Isaac (*EYE-zak*) means "laughter." He was the son of Abraham and Sarah. You can read about Isaac in Genesis 21. See page 34.

J

Jacob (*JAY-cub*) was the younger twin brother of Esau and a son of Isaac. His name was changed to Israel. He was the father of the 12 tribes, or family groups, of God's chosen people. His story begins in Genesis 25:21. See pages 14, 35.

James was the name of several men in the New Testament.

> **James, the son of Zebedee** was an apostle of Jesus. He was the brother of the apostle John. He was killed by Herod Agrippa I (Matthew 10:2; Acts 12:2). See page 150.

> **James, the son of Alphaeus** was also one of Jesus' apostles (Matthew 10:3). See page 151.

> **James, the brother of Jesus** was a respected leader in the church in the city of Jerusalem. He probably wrote the Bible book of James in the New Testament (Matthew 13:55; John 7:5; Acts 12:17; Galatians 1:19). See page 205.

Jehu (*JAY-hoo*) was a king of Israel. He stopped Baal worship and killed the whole family of wicked King Ahab. But Jehu did not try to keep God's law. You can read about Jehu in 2 Kings 9 – 10. See pages 92, 100.

Jephthah (*JEP-tha*) was one of the judges whom God used to save Israel from their enemies (Judges 10 – 12). See page 67.

Jeremiah (*jer-e-MI-ah*) was a great prophet who lived in the years just before Jerusalem was destroyed by the army of Babylon. The Bible book of Jeremiah was filled with warnings to the people of Judah. It also had wonderful promises. God would bring his people back to Judah from captivity. Jeremiah has a promise for us, too. This book tells us about Jesus and a New Covenant (agreement) that God will make to forgive sins. See pages 17, 106, 107.

Jeroboam (*jer-o-BO-am*) became king of the northern kingdom of Israel when David and Solomon's one nation was divided. Jeroboam was an evil king. He set up a false worship system that was against the law of God. See page 89.

Jericho (*JER-i-coh*) was a walled city in the days when the Israelites were led out of Egypt. God made the walls of Jericho fall down when the people marched around the city as he commanded them. See pages 14, 60.

Jerusalem (*jeh-ROO-suh-lem*) was the greatest city in the country of Israel. King David made it the capital city. And his son Solomon built God's Temple there. Jesus was killed on the cross near Jerusalem. The city was destroyed by the Roman army in the year A.D. 70. The city was rebuilt and today is the capital city of modern Israel. See pages 77, 101, 116, 161.

Jesus (*JEE-zus*) means "savior." Jesus is the Son of God. He was born to Mary, a young Jewish woman. An angel told Mary that she would have a baby boy who would not have a human father. Mary was to name the boy "Jesus," because he would save his people from their sins. Jesus is also called "Christ" and "Messiah." These names mean "anointed one." In Bible times a person appointed for a special task for God had sweet olive oil poured on his head. This was called anointing. Jesus was appointed by God to save people.

Jesus lived a perfect life and did not sin. But Jesus was rejected by the Jewish people. And he was killed by Roman soldiers on a cross near Jerusalem. Jesus then came back to life. And he now lives in heaven with God the Father. One day Jesus will come again.

Jesus is one of the three persons of God: God the Father, God the Son and God the Holy Spirit. See pages 18, 26, 69, 120, 125, 165.

Jew at first meant a person from the land of Judah. It came to mean any person from the family of Abraham, Isaac and Jacob (Israel). Jesus is the most famous Jew who ever lived. So the Jews were the earthly family of Jesus. In the Gospel of John, though, "Jew" is used in a special way to mean the rulers who were the enemies of Jesus. See pages 31, 120-124, 158.

Jezebel (*JEZ-e-bell*) was the wicked wife of evil King Ahab. She tried to make God's people worship her false god, Baal. You can read about her beginning in 1 Kings 16:31. See page 95.

Joash (*JO-ash*) became king of Judah when he was only seven years old. You can read about this good king in 2 Kings 11,12. See page 102.

Job was an honest man who suffered even though he did what was right. The Bible book of Job tells how Job and his friends tried to understand why such bad things were happening to him even though he was good. See page 83.

Joel (*JO-el*) was a prophet who warned Judah about God's coming judgment. The Bible book of Joel also makes the promise that God would come to his people to bring peace. See pages 16, 104.

John was the name of several men in the New Testament.

> *John the Baptist* was Jesus' relative. He preached that people should repent because Jesus, the Savior, was coming soon. John baptized Jesus in the Jordan River. Herod Antipas had John killed by cutting off his head (Matthew 3; 11:11-13; 14:3-12). See page 130.

> *John the apostle* was a son of Zebedee. He and his brother James were fishermen. John was one of Jesus' twelve disciples. He wrote the Gospel of John, the book of Revelation and the letters called 1, 2 and 3 John. See pages 150, 207.

Jonah (*JO-nah*) was a prophet in Israel whom God sent to warn the city of Nineveh. Nineveh was the capital of Israel's enemy, Assyria. And Jonah did not want to go. When Jonah finally did go to Nineveh, the people there listened to his warning and changed. So God did not destroy the city. Jonah wrote the Bible book of Jonah. See pages 89, 92.

Jordan (*JOR-d'n*) is the only large river in Palestine. God dried the Jordan River so the people of Israel under Joshua's command could enter the promised land. Jesus was baptized in the Jordan River near the city of Jericho, by John the Baptist (Joshua 3:14-17; Matthew 3:5,6,13). See pages 59, 131.

Joseph (*JO-sef*) is the name of three important Bible people.

> *Joseph* in the Old Testament was a younger son of Jacob. He was sold by his brothers to be a slave, and he was taken to Egypt. There Joseph became an important ruler. And he saved his family when a terrible time without food brought starvation. You can read about Joseph beginning in Genesis 37. See pages 14, 36-40.

> *Joseph of Nazareth* in the New Testament was the husband of Mary, Jesus' mother. The Bible says he was a "good man" (Matthew 1:18-24; 2:13-23). See pages 126-129.

> *Joseph of Arimathea* buried the body of Jesus in a tomb he had prepared for himself. He was a member of the Sanhedrin, but probably believed in Jesus (Matthew 27:57-60; Mark 15:43-46). See page 165.

Joshua (*JOSH-u-ah*) in Hebrew means "God saves." After Moses died, Joshua led the people of Israel to victory as they conquered the land of Canaan. The Bible book of Joshua tells about how the Israelites captured Canaan under this great leader. Joshua was a man of deep faith. See pages 15, 56, 59-64.

Josiah (*jo-SI-ah*) became king of Judah when he was only eight years old. You can read about this good king in 2 Kings 22,23. See page 102.

Judah (*JU-duh*) is the name of one of the twelve sons of Israel. It is also the name given to the southern kingdom when the Jewish nation divided into two countries. The southern kingdom began in 931 B.C. and ended in 586 B.C. See pages 66, 92, 101-107.

Judas Iscariot (*JU-dus is-CARE-ee-ut*) was the disciple who turned against Jesus and handed him over to his enemies to be killed. Later Judas killed himself (Matthew 26:47-50; John 13:26-30). See pages 151, 161.

Jude (*JOOD*) could have been a brother of Jesus and James. Early in Jesus' ministry Jude did not believe Jesus was the Son of God. Later he did believe and became a leader of Christ's church. He wrote the Bible book of Jude (John 7:5). See page 207.

Judea (*ju-DEE-a*) is a district in the country of Palestine. See the map on page 134. See page 127.

Judges (*JUH-ges*) were leaders in Israel for about 400 years. They ruled from the time of Joshua to the time of the first king, Saul. The Bible book of Judges tells what happened in those times. See pages 65-68.

K

kingdom (*KING-d'm*) is anywhere a king rules. Many different kings ruled the Kingdom of Israel (the land where the king of Israel ruled). The Bible speaks of the kingdom of God or the kingdom of heaven. God rules the whole universe. But God rules in a special way the lives of people who believe in and obey Jesus. See page 89.

Kings The Bible books of 1 and 2 Kings tell about kings who ruled Israel and Judah from around 1,000 B.C. to 586 B.C. A list of the kings of Israel is given on page 90. A list of the kings of Judah is given on page 102.

L

Lamentations (*lam-en-TAY-shuns*) are cries of sorrow. The Bible book of Lamentations tells how unhappy the Jewish people were to live in Babylon. They were away from the land of Palestine that God had promised would be their home. See page 111.

Law means "rules." God gave the Jewish people special rules to live by. God's laws teach people how to please him and how to love others. Sometimes the first five books of the Bible are called the "Law of (given by) Moses." Sometimes the whole Old Testament is called "the Law." See pages 48-51, 57, 156.

leprosy (*LEH-prah-see*) is a skin disease. In Bible times there was no cure for it. A person with leprosy was called a leper. He had to live away from other people. Jesus healed many people with leprosy (Matthew 8:1-3; Luke 17:11-19). See page 99.

Levi (*LEE-vi*) was one of the sons of Jacob. He was the head of one of the twelve tribes or families of the Israelites. The Levites were set apart to serve God in the Tabernacle and the Temple.

lord means "master" or one who is in control. In the Old Testament the word LORD in capital letters is the personal name of God, Yahweh. The New Testament calls Jesus Lord because he rules over all the world and the universe. This is also because he is our master as well as God (John 20:28; Romans 10:9; Colossians 3:17-24). See page 42.

Lord's Supper is the special meal Jesus' followers eat to remember how Jesus died for us. The bread reminds us of his body. The fruit of the vine reminds us of Jesus' blood. The Lord's Supper also shows that Jesus came back to life and now lives in heaven with God (Luke 22:14-20; 1 Corinthians 11:23-32). See page 162.

Luke was a non-Jewish doctor who traveled with the apostle Paul on his missionary trips. Luke was a very educated man. He wrote the Bible books of Luke and Acts in the New Testament. See page 168.

M

Malachi (*MAL-a-ki*) wrote the last book of the Old Testament. Malachi's book tells how quickly God's people turned away from God. They did that even though the Lord brought them back to their land from Babylon as he promised. But Malachi also said that people who do love God are his special treasure. See page 117.

manna (*MAN-nah*) was food that God supplied for his people when they left Egypt and traveled for years in the desert. You can read about manna in Exodus 16. See page 48.

martyr (*MAR-ter*) is a Greek word that means "witness." A witness tells people what he or she knows about something. Later martyr came to mean a person who was killed because he or she witnessed for Jesus. Stephen was the first Christian martyr. See page 174.

Mary is the name of several women in the New Testament.

> **Mary, the mother of Jesus,** was a young Jewish woman God chose to give birth to his only Son. This was a great honor and blessing. She married a man named Joseph (Matthew 1:18-25; Luke 1:27-45). See pages 126-129.

> **Mary Magdalene** was a follower of Jesus. She was the first person to see Jesus after he came back to life (Matthew 27:56; Mark 15:40,47; John 20:1-18). See page 166.

> **Mary of Bethany** was the sister of Martha and Lazarus. All three were dear friends of Jesus (Luke 10:39-42; John 11:1-45). See page 141.

Matthew (*MATH-you*), also called Levi, was a tax collector. He became a disciple of Jesus. He wrote the Bible book of Matthew (Luke 6:12-16). See page 151.

memorials (*mem-MOR-i-als*) were objects or festivals, like the Passover, that were reminders of what God had done for his people. Memorials helped the Israelites remember to trust God and to thank him for his help. See page 60.

messiah (*meh-SIGH-a*) means "anointed one." See Jesus. See pages 121, 131.

Micah (*MY-cah*) was a prophet who warned the people of Israel and Judah against worshiping idols and not keeping God's law. The Bible book of Micah also gives us God's word of what to do to please him. See page 104.

miracles (MEER-ih-k'ls) is a word that means "wonderful things." A miracle is a special sign from God to show his power. Miracles showed that people who performed them were true messengers from God. See pages 44, 96, 133, 136.

missionary (*MI-shun-AIR-ee*) is a person who travels to tell people about Jesus and help them become Christians. See pages 169, 178-180.

Moses (*MO-zez*) in Hebrew means "saved from the water." Moses led God's people out of the land of Egypt where they had been slaves for 400 years. The book of Exodus in the Old Testament tells about Moses. Moses wrote the first five books of the Old Testament. On Mount Sinai God gave Moses the law for the Jewish people. So, it is often called the "Law of Moses." See pages 14, 41-43, 48, 49.

N

Nahum (*NAY-hum*) was a prophet who had good news for Judah. The Bible book of Nahum tells his sermons which promised that the enemy city of Nineveh would be destroyed. See page 105.

Nazareth (*NAZ-uh-reth*) was the city in Galilee where Jesus grew up. See the map on page 134. See pages 127, 129.

Nebuchadnezzar (*neb-u-cad-NEZ-er*) was the greatest king of Babylon. He led the army that destroyed Judah and burned down Jerusalem in 586 B.C.. Daniel was later an adviser to this great king. Nebuchadnezzar came to know that God truly is all-powerful. Read about Nebuchadnezzar in Daniel 4. See pages 110, 116.

Nehemiah (*Nee-he-MI-ah*) was a high official in the Persian Empire. He asked to go to Judah to be governor there. The Bible book of Nehemiah tells how he rebuilt the walls of Jerusalem and encouraged the people of Judah to obey God's laws. See pages 17, 116.

Noah (*NO-ah*) was a good man in an evil time. God warned Noah that he was about to destroy all evil things by a great flood. And he told Noah to build a great boat. Noah did as God told him. And Noah's family and the animals were saved when the flood came. See pages 13, 28.

Numbers is one of the first five books of Moses. It tells what happened as the Israelites lived in the wilderness. This was while they were waiting to enter Canaan, the land God promised to Abraham's descendants. See page 53.

Nuzi (*NU-ze*) is an ancient city where records of customs during Abraham's time have been found in the ruins. See page 31.

O

Obadiah (*o-ba-DI-ah*) was a prophet who spoke against the Edomites. They helped enemies of God's people. The Bible book of Obadiah has just one chapter and tells his prophecy. See page 92.

obey (*oh-BAY*) or **obedience** (*oh-BEE-dee-ence*) means doing what we are asked or told to do. God promised to bless the Israelites when they obeyed him. Jesus taught that obeying God is a way that we show we love the Lord (Deuteronomy 28; John 14:21-24). See pages 49, 142, 145.

P

parable (*PARE-eh-b'l*) is a story that teaches a lesson by comparing things. Jesus often used parables to teach the people. All Jesus' parables are listed in Unit 24. See pages 142-144.

Passover Feast (*PASS-oh-ver FEEST*) was an important holy day for the Jews each spring. They ate a special meal and remembered that God had freed their people from being slaves in Egypt. You can read about the first passover in Exodus 12. Jesus was killed at Passover time (Matthew 26:2,17-19). See pages 45, 124, 162.

Paul is the Roman name for "Saul." Paul the apostle was a Pharisee. At first he did not believe in Jesus and tried to jail Christians. But Jesus appeared to Paul, and Paul's life changed. He believed in Jesus and traveled everywhere to teach people about Jesus. Paul also wrote many books of the New Testament and sent them as letters to Christians in different cities (Acts 7:58-60; 9:1-31; Philippians 3:5-7). See pages 18, 139, 179-203.

Pentecost (*PEN-tee-kost*) means fifty. Pentecost was a Jewish feast day that took place 50 days after Passover. The apostles began telling the good news about Jesus on the Pentecost after Jesus was raised from death (Acts 2). See page 170.

Perea (*pur-EE-a*) was a district in the country of Palestine in Jesus' day. See the map on page 134. See page 120.

Peter (*PEE-ter*) was a fisherman. He and his brother, Andrew, were the first two disciples Jesus chose. Peter was the first to preach the good news of Jesus to Jewish and non-Jewish people. The Bible books of 1 and 2 Peter were written by the apostle Peter. See pages 149, 168, 173-177.

pharaoh (*FAY-row*) means "king." It was the title given to the ruler of Egypt in Old Testament times. See pages 14, 39.

Pharisees (*FARE-uh-seez*) means "separated people." This was a Jewish religious group that wanted to keep all the religious laws and customs very strictly. But many of the rules of the Pharisees were just human ideas about God's laws. Jesus spoke against the Pharisees often because many of them did not really care about other people or about God (Matthew 23). See page 155.

Philip (*FIL-ip*) was the name of several New Testament men.

> **Philip the apostle** brought Nathanael to Jesus (Matthew 10:2,3; John 1:43-48). See page 150.

> **Philip the evangelist** was one of the seven men chosen to be deacons in the church in Jerusalem (Acts 6:1-6; 8:5-40). See page 175.

> **Philip the Tetrarch** was the son of Herod I. He built the city of Caesarea Philippi (Matthew 16:13; Mark 8:27; Luke 3:1).

Philippi (*Fil-i-pie*) was a city in Greece. It was on the main road from Rome to Asia. And it was one of the most important cities in the Roman Empire. Paul wrote a letter to Christians there. It became our Bible book of Philippians. See page 196.

Philistines (*FIL-i-stines*) were a people who settled along the Mediterranean coast of Palestine. They were a powerful and important enemy of the people of Israel for nearly 200 years. This was from the days of the Judges into the time of King David. See pages 68, 73.

Pontius Pilate (*PON-shus PIE-lut*) was the Roman governor in Judea from A.D. 26 to 36. The Jews who wanted to kill Jesus brought him to Pilate. This was because only the Roman governor could order a person to be put to death. Pilate knew Jesus was not guilty. But Pilate had Jesus killed anyway, because he was afraid of the Jewish leaders (Luke 23:1-53; John 18:28–19:16). See pages 158, 165.

praise (*PRAYZ*) means to say good things about someone or something. God's people can praise him by singing, praying and by living the way he tells us to live (Luke 2:13,14; 19:37; Acts 2:47; 3:8,9; Hebrews 2:12). See page 83.

prayer (*PREHR*) is talking to God. People who love God can talk to him at any time. We can ask God for help and tell him how we feel. We can also thank him for the many good things he does for us. We can tell God about what we have done that is wrong, and we can ask him to forgive us. Jesus prayed often when he was here on earth. Sometimes Jesus even prayed all night (Matthew 26:36-44; Luke 6:12; Acts 4:23-31; 7:57-60; James 5:13-18). See pages 145, 146, 163.

priest (*PREEST*) in the Old Testament was a person appointed to serve God at God's house. Priests helped the people by offering sacrifices for them and by bringing their gifts to God. The New Testament tells us that Jesus is our high priest. He brings people and God together. The sacrifice Jesus offered to God was his own life on the cross. Today all Christians are priests because we can pray to God ourselves. And we help other people come to know Jesus as Savior (Hebrews 7:26-28; 1 Peter 2:5,9; Revelation 1:6). See pages 52, 64.

prophecy (*PRAH-feh-see*) means "message." It is God speaking through chosen people called prophets. Often these prophets told what would happen in the future. See page 90.

prophet (*PRAH-fet*) means "messenger" or one who speaks for someone else. The prophets of the Bible spoke God's message to people. See pages 90, 104-106.

psalms (*SALMS*) are songs or poems used to help people worship and praise God. Many were written by King David. There are 150 psalms in the Bible book of Psalms. See pages 75, 79, 83-85.

R

Red Sea in Hebrew is *yam suph*, which means "Sea of

Reeds." The waters of the *yam suph* opened up to let the Israelites through. Then the waters closed to drown the Egyptian army that was chasing them. You can see where the Red Sea probably was by looking at the map on page 55. See also page 47.

repent (*ree-PENT*) means to change your heart and life. A person who repents stops doing bad things and chooses to do good (Matthew 4:17; Mark 1:15). See pages 130, 172.

resurrection (*REZ-uh-REK-shun*) is when a dead person is raised to a new life. Two people who came back from the dead were Lazarus (John 11:38-45) and a widow's son (Luke 7:11-17). But these people died again. Jesus was raised to live forever. Christians will be resurrected, too, when Jesus returns. Then they will live forever with God in heaven (Matthew 28:1-10; 1 Corinthians 15; 1 Peter 3:21,22). See pages 141, 160.

Revelation (*rev-uh-LAY-shun*) means to show plainly something that had been hidden. The last book in the New Testament is called the Revelation. It was written by John. See pages 209-213.

Roman Empire (*ROAM-an EM-pyre*) means all the land controlled by the government and army of Rome, a city in Italy. In the time of Jesus the Roman Empire included most of Europe. It also included much of the land east of the Mediterranean Sea. The map on page 120 shows the size of the Roman Empire in Jesus' day. Not everyone who lived in the empire was a citizen of Rome. A Roman citizen had many special privileges. The apostle Paul was a Roman citizen. See pages 120-123, 178, 188.

Romans is the name of a Bible book. The apostle Paul wrote the book as a letter to Christians who lived in Rome. Rome was the capital of the Roman Empire. See pages 193-195.

Ruth (*ROOTH*) was a woman who lived in the days of the judges. She was not an Israelite, but chose to follow Israel's God instead of the gods of her homeland, Moab. The Bible book of Ruth tells her story. See pages 65, 69.

S

Sabbath (*SAB-uth*) means "rest." It is the seventh day of the Jewish week. It was a day set aside for rest and worship. Jesus was raised to life again on the first day of the week, Sunday. Christians set aside this day to worship Jesus who died and rose to life again. See pages 48, 49, 155, 156.

sacrifice (*SAK-ri-fice*) in the Old Testament means killing an animal to offer it to God. God commanded sacrifices in order to teach his people that sin must be punished by death. Jesus' death on the cross was a sacrifice. He took the punishment for our sins when he died for us. Because of Jesus' sacrifice, people who trust in and follow Jesus can be forgiven of all their sins (Hebrews 9:28; 10:14). See pages 26, 51, 205.

Sadducees (*SAD-you-seez*) were a Jewish religious group. They were rich and important men. They did not believe in angels or life after death (resurrection). They helped the Romans who had conquered their country. See pages 121, 157.

Samaritan (*suh-MEHR-ih-t'n*) was a person who lived in the area of Palestine called Samaria. See map, page 134. The Jews of Judea and Galilee did not accept them as true Jews. They hated the Samaritans (John 4:9). See page 144.

Samson (*SAM-son*) means "strong" in Hebrew. Samson was the strongest man who ever lived. He killed many soldiers of the Philistines, Israel's enemy. But Samson was not strong in faith. He was one of Israel's judges about a thousand years before Jesus was born (Judges 13–16). See pages 15, 68.

Samuel (*SAM-u-el*) in Hebrew means "asked of God." Samuel was born in answer to prayer. He was Israel's last judge. And he poured sweet olive oil on the head of Saul. Later he did the same thing to David. This showed that God was appointing them to be kings. The Bible books of 1 and 2 Samuel tell about Samuel and Israel's first two kings. See pages 72-75.

Sanhedrin (*san-HEE-drin*) was the highest court of the Jews in the days of Jesus. It is sometimes called "the council" in the Bible. See pages 121, 163.

Sarah (*SAIR-ah*) in Hebrew means "princess." Sarah was the wife of Abraham and the mother of Isaac. See page 33.

Satan (*SAY-t'n*) in Hebrew means "enemy." It is a name for the devil, who is the enemy of God and man (Matthew 4:10; Luke 10:18,19; Acts 5:3). See pages 26, 140, 157.

Saul was the first king of Israel. He failed because he did not obey God fully (1 Samuel 15). Saul was also the name of the great apostle until his name was changed to Paul (Acts 13:9). See pages 73, 178.

Savior (*SAVE-yor*) means someone who saves people from danger. The name "Jesus" means "savior." Jesus is the Savior of the people in this world. His life, death and resurrection make it possible for people to be saved from death and punishment for their sins (Luke 2:11; John 3:16). See pages 121, 131, 174.

scribe is a Hebrew word that means to write or to put in order. The scribes of the Bible were men who studied the Scriptures so they could teach it and obey God's word. They were very respected persons in the Jewish nation. Scribe is also the name for a person who made copies of the Scriptures. See page 9.

Scriptures (*SCRIP-churs*) means "writings." These are special writings of God's word for man. When the word Scriptures is used in the New Testament it means the Old Testament. Later the word came to mean the whole Bible (Luke 24:27; Acts 8:32-35; 2 Timothy 3:16; 2 Peter 1:20).

sin is a word, thought, or act against the law of God. Sin is wrong, and God must punish sin. Jesus died to pay for our sins. He saved us from being punished. He took the punishment we deserve for the wrong things we have done (Romans 3:23; 5:12; 1 Corinthians 15:3; Galatians 1:4; 1 John 1:8-10). See pages 13, 25-28, 78, 172.

Sinai (*SIGH-nigh*) is the name of the mountain where God gave Moses his law for the Israelites. You can find this mountain on the map on page 55. See also pages 14, 49.

slave was a person owned by someone else. The owner could tell the slave to do whatever he wanted. Many slaves and masters became Christians. The New Testament tells masters and slaves how to do good to each other (1 Timothy 6:1-2; 1 Peter 2:18-19).

Christians are to be slaves to Christ, and obey him completely (Romans 6:18; Ephesians 6:5-9). See pages 35, 36, 41.

Sodom (*SOD-'m*) is the name of a city that God destroyed in the time of Abraham. This was because the people of the city were so terribly wicked. See page 33.

Solomon (*SOL-o-mon*) followed his father David as king of Israel in 931 B.C. Solomon was very wise and made his kingdom very wealthy. He wrote many sayings in the Bible book of Proverbs. He also wrote the Bible books of Ecclesiastes and Song of Solomon. See pages 16, 80, 82, 87.

Spirit of God. See Holy Spirit.

synagogue (*SIN-uh-gog*) is a Greek word that means "a meeting." The Jews met in the synagogue to read and study the Scriptures. Both Jesus and Paul often went to the Jewish synagogues to teach and to discuss the Scriptures (Matthew 4:23; Luke 4:16; Acts 15:21; 17:1,10). See pages 123, 155.

T

tabernacle (*TAB-er-NAK-'l*) was a tent used by the people of Israel as a place of worship. Later a Temple made of stone replaced this tent made of animal skins. You can find a description of the tabernacle in Exodus 25–27 and 35–38 in the Old Testament (Hebrews 9:1-10). See pages 51, 64.

temple (*TEM-p'l*) is a building where people worship. God told the Jewish people to worship him in the Temple in Jerusalem. This Temple was built by King Solomon in Old Testament times. It was destroyed later and then rebuilt. Jesus worshiped at a rebuilt Temple.

The New Testament also calls a Christian's body a temple. That is because God's Holy Spirit lives in the Christian (Acts 7:48; 1 Corinthians 6:19). See pages 16, 78, 115, 154.

temptation (*temp-TAY-shun*) is anything that seems attractive or worth having, but is wrong. Jesus was tempted by the devil. But he did not give in. God promises to help so that we do not have to give in to temptations and do wrong, either (Matthew 4:1-11; 1 Corinthians 10:13). See pages 132-135.

Ten Commandments are special rules God gave the Israelites to show them how to love him and to live with other people. Nine of the Ten Commandments are repeated for Christians. Only the command to "keep the Sabbath day holy" is not found in the New Testament. You can read the Ten Commandments in Exodus 20. See pages 49-51.

tent. See tabernacle.

Thessalonica (*thes-eh-lo-NY-kah*) was an important business city in Greece. The apostle Paul started a church there. He later wrote two letters to the Thessalonians. These letters are in our Bible as 1, 2 Thessalonians. See page 182.

Timothy (*TIM-oh-thee*) means "one who honors God." He was a close friend and helper of the apostle Paul. Paul wrote two letters to this young leader. They are in our Bible as the books of 1 and 2 Timothy (Acts 16:1-3; 17:13-16; 1 Thessalonians 3:1-6; 2 Timothy 1:2-5). See pages 139, 199-200.

Titus (*TIE-tus*) was a trusted friend and helper of the apostle Paul. Paul wrote one letter to him which is in our Bible as the book of Titus. See pages 199-200.

U

Ur is the name of the land where Abraham lived when God spoke to him and told him to leave. See page 31.

W

wisdom (*WIZ-dom*) in the Bible means understanding and doing what is right and good. It is much better to be wise than to be rich. The New Testament teaches that if you ask God for wisdom, he will give it to you (James 1:5). See pages 82, 85.

wise men was the name given to the Magi, who were advisers to kings of Persia. Daniel was probably one of these wise men. The Magi who came to Jerusalem to ask about Jesus' birth may have learned about him from the Old Testament. See page 128.

witches (*WICH-es*) were people who claimed spirits helped them find out information no person could know without supernatural help. God told his people not to go to witches. He promised to help his people choose the right way to go (Deuteronomy 18:9-13). See pages 75, 136.

worship is to praise and serve God. When we worship God we show that we honor him as ruler of our lives (Matthew 28:9; Luke 4:8; John 4:20-24; Revelation 19:4,5). See page 155.

X

Xerxes (*ZURK-sees*) was the Persian ruler who married Esther. You can read about this king and his brave Jewish wife in the Bible book of Esther. See page 113.

Y

Yahweh (*YA-way*) is the personal name of God. It means "The One Who Is always Present." When you read the word LORD in capital letters in the Old Testament, the Hebrew word is Yahweh. See page 42.

Z

Zechariah (*zek-a-RY-ah*) was a prophet who lived at the time the captives returned from Babylon to Judah. The Bible book of Zechariah gives his prophecies about what would happen until the Lord came to save his people. See pages 17, 116.

Zephaniah (*zef-an-I-ah*) was a prophet who warned Judah. The Bible book of Zephaniah contains his sermons telling God's people that God will surely punish sins. See page 106.

Zion (*ZY-on*) was a hill outside Jerusalem. Later the name "Zion" was used for all Jerusalem as a special and wonderful city of God. See page 161.